SPIRITUS MUNDI

SPIRITUS MUNDI

Essays on Literature, Myth, and Society

NORTHROP FRYE

Indiana University Press
BLOOMINGTON & LONDON

Published in Canada by Fitzhenry & Whiteside Limited, Don Mills, Ontario

Manufactured in the United States of America

Library of Congress Cataloging in Publication Data
Frye, Northrop.
Spiritus mundi.

CONTENTS: Contexts of literature: The search for acceptable words. The university and personal life. The renaissance of books. The times of the signs.—The mythological universe: Expanding eyes. Charms and riddles. Romance as masque. Spengler revisited.—Four poets: Agon and logos. Blake's reading of the Book of Job. The rising of the moon. Wallace Stevens and the variation form.

1. Literature—Addresses, essays, lectures. I. Title.
PN37.F7 809 76-12364
ISBN 0-253-35432-3 2 3 4 5 80 79 78 77

Contents

Preface

This is a collection of my more recent essays, most of them written since 1970. As with most such collections, there is a certain amount of repetition, much of it unavoidable because the argument is decentralized, and some things need to be stated more than once to fit into their different settings. At the same time, the book as a whole possesses a unity and can be read consecutively, and the repetitions then become like similar repetitions in music, thematic returns to the same subject after a new context has been established for it.

There are twelve essays, divided into three groups of four essays each. The first four deal with general issues related to literary criticism; the next four with general issues within literary criticism itself; the final four with more specific criticism of authors who have turned up constantly in my writing, Milton, Blake, Yeats and Wallace Stevens. Every essay was a response to a specific request and usually, also, was first orally delivered to a meeting or conference on a specific occasion. I have not tried to obliterate the sense of these occasions, and some account of them may be useful if the reader is interested in the question of why certain topics were selected.

The first and second parts both begin with articles that might be described as autobiographical, in the sense in which John

Stuart Mill speaks of a "mental history": that is, they attempt to show how certain ideas and concepts have taken shape genetically in my work. The opening essay, "The Search for Acceptable Words" (the title refers to Ecclesiastes 12:10), was contributed to an issue of *Daedalus* devoted to research in the modern university. I accepted the invitation to contribute with some misgivings, feeling that what I had done was not strictly "research," and certainly did not illustrate how a university fostered and encouraged research. But as I went on I felt that my own experiences were more relevant than I had thought to the question, and that my work did at any rate show how the university functions as a special kind of community for a humanist. The article contains a number of *obiter dicta* about the contemporary university which express my own opinion but have no special knowledge behind them.

The other three papers in the first section deal with the kind of issues that are discussed a good deal in connection with literary criticism, but are still on the periphery of the subject as usually treated. "The University and Personal Life" was a contribution to an educational conference dealing, more or less, with the educational problems connected with what I still think of as the Age of Hysteria, the period between, roughly, 1968 and 1971. I had little sympathy with the kind of activism then going on, however much I had with its antagonism to the Vietnam war and to racism. I felt that the movement was fundamentally sick, so sick that it could really do nothing but die. It did very soon die, but its existence manifested something that seems to me still very much alive. This is the political side of what I describe in "Expanding Eyes" as the crisis of distinguishing the mythological from the empirical consciousness. I had already discussed other aspects of the same crisis in an earlier book, *The Critical Path* (Indiana University Press, 1970).

"The Renaissance of Books" deals with books as a physical element in communication, a theme brought to public awareness through the work of Marshall McLuhan, Walter Ong, George Steiner, and others. The article is designed mainly to make two points: first, that the book is one of the most efficient technological instruments ever devised, and second, that it is the technological instrument that makes democracy a working possibility. The latter is a principle applicable to countries that are so often said to be "not yet ready for democracy," a phrase that seems to me to be either a pretext for tyranny or a racist euphemism. The paper was contributed to a publishers' conference at Williamsburg in Virginia, and its publication in *Visible Language* appears to have brought me some new readers whom I was delighted to acquire. It was written while I was engaged on a series of lectures later delivered at Harvard on the Charles Eliot Norton Professorship of Poetry, and some of its arguments run parallel to those lectures (now published as *The Secular Scripture*).

"The Times of the Signs" was written for a special conference of the Royal Society of Canada to celebrate the five hundredth anniversary of the birth of Copernicus, held in Ottawa in November, 1973. My paper is an attempt to outline one of the chief assumptions of the present book, as well as of my work generally, that all literature is written within what I call a "mythological universe" constructed out of human hopes and desires and anxieties; that this mythological universe is not really a protoscientific one, even though it is often believed to have scientific validity; and that literature is written within this universe because literature continues the mythological habit of mind. The latter, being an imaginative habit, is quite as subtle, profound, and in touch with "reality" among Australian aborigines as among twentieth-century poets. All attempts to deal with mythological thinking as "primitive," based on hazy analogies to biological evolution, are in my view totally mistaken. Copernicus is the great symbol in our culture of the beginning of the separation of the mythological from the scientific universe, a separation which has completed itself and has now to seek new ways of recombining.

This conception of a mythological universe is taken up again in the second autobiographical article, "Expanding Eyes" (the title is from Blake's *Four Zoas*, and the passage is quoted in the body of the essay). This article was contributed to the *Journal of Critical Inquiry*, after an article on me by Angus Fletcher had appeared in the same periodical. My reasons for writing the kind of article I did instead of "replying" to Mr. Fletcher's are given at the beginning. In a sense this article is the keystone of the book, raising most of the assumptions around which my work at present revolves. Two aspects of it, which are barely mentioned, need further development. One is the reference to structuralism, which interests me because it seems to me a movement heading in the direction of what I call interpenetration, the interrelating of different subjects in a way that preserves their own autonomy, instead of subordinating them to some grandiose program of mental imperialism. The other is a political inference from the conception of a mythological universe: the fact that without such a universe we have only the relation of man to his natural environment, and the question of human freedom (as Sartre says in *Being and Nothingness*) cannot be worked out within that relation alone.

"Charms and Riddles" was a paper read to the New England Stylistics Club at Northeastern University in Boston early in 1975. It was read at the invitation of Professor Morton Bloomfield, whose PMLA article on "The Complaint of Deor" as a charm poem entered largely into its argument. The article was written out soon afterwards, but has not been published elsewhere. "Romance as Masque" was read at a conference on Shakespeare's romances held at the University of Alabama in October, 1975. It is preceded by a short discussion of Old and New Comedy, a revised version of an older article of mine with that title, originally a paper read to a group meeting at Stratford, England, some years earlier. As will be seen, both this article and the preceding one on charms and riddles use the same "mandala," as I call it in "Expanding Eyes," of descending and ascending movements of imagery, a contrast which also underlies the more familiar contrast of tragedy and comedy.

The Spengler article, which uses material from some very early writings of mine, was contributed to another *Daedalus* issue on "Twentieth-Century Classics Revisited," to which the opening paragraphs refer. Spengler, as is obvious from other references to him in this book, has always been a formative influence in my own thinking, for reasons which have often puzzled me, he being, as a creative personality, so antipathetic to me. This article is, so to speak, an effort to lay a ghost to rest, along with an attempt to show where Spengler belongs in twentieth-century criticism and poetic imagery.

Of the four essays in more practical criticism, the reading of *Samson Agonistes* was contributed to a conference at the University of Western Ontario in 1971. The title of the book in which the conference essays appeared, *The Prison and the Pinnacle,* referred to the fact that 1971 was the tercentenary of the publication of both *Samson Agonistes* and *Paradise Regained,* and most of the other papers dealt with both. I had already written a long article about *Paradise Regained,* which is why so little is said about it in this one; I have for the present book, however, added a sentence or two which bring the two poems more closely together. *Paradise Regained* in its turn is a poem of testing and ordeal for which the chief model is the Book of Job. The essay on Blake's Job illustrations was contributed to a *Festschrift* in honor of Foster Damon, to whose 1924 book on Blake I have many times recorded my considerable debt. The original article was written quickly, under the pressure of many other commitments, and has been completely rewritten for the present volume.

The article on Yeats's *A Vision* originally appeared in a book of essays on Yeats called *An Honoured Guest,* edited by Denis Donoghue and J. R. Mulryne. Yeats's *Vision* has baffled and exasperated me for many years: this essay is by no means completely successful in laying a second haunting ghost to rest, but it supplies some analogical context for Yeats's schematisms which may be useful. Its relation to the rest of this book, more particularly the second part, is perhaps worth a comment. If the conception of the mythological universe is necessary, as I think it is, to any resolution of the problem of freedom, the critic is involved once again in what Milton calls the "rule of charity" in interpreting the Bible: whatever interpretation rationalizes human slavery and bondage is wrong, however unwarranted the statement that it is wrong may logically sound.

The universe I sketch out in the second part of this book contains a cyclical movement in which tragic actions descend to a low point of death and comic ones rise to a high point of vision. The association of tragic movement with descent is at least as old as the metaphor in the word "catastrophe." In Yeats, on the other hand, comic actions descend through the "primary" gyre to an indistinguishable mass of primitive society, and tragic actions rise out of them, up the "antithetical" gyre, to the height of the heroic act. For reasons that I hope a study of my second part would make clearer, such a reversal of movement encloses the whole mythological universe in a mechanism of fatality, a closed trap. The vision of life that results is admirable for Yeats's more ironic poems, such as "Blood and the Moon," but grotesquely inappropriate for, say, the two Byzantium poems. *A Vision* keeps bringing me back to the passive state of mind in which Yeats produced it, and what seems to be its irresponsible fatalism also seems to me the inevitable result of that state of mind.

Yeats describes his instructors as being, or behaving like, disembodied intelligences, without caring much whether we take this metaphorically or descriptively. Accepting it as at least a metaphor, I should say, if the reader will detach the statement from moral disapproval or superstitious *frisson,* that Yeats's instructors were obviously devils. That is, all they knew was the vision of life as hell, and hence, like other devils, they lacked a certain comprehensiveness of perspective. In Yeats himself their influence, though destructive, was not disastrous; but they were of the same family as those who have produced so much of the terror and hysteria of our time.

The Wallace Stevens essay was read, in a much shorter version, at a conference in Istanbul, and the longer version, the one reprinted here, was contributed to a *Festschrift* for W. K. Wimsatt, for whom my great affection and admiration is now saddened by the fact that he is no longer with us. It is the second of two essays I have written on Stevens, and as compared with the first, it concentrates less on the *Collected Poems* and more on the letters and the *Opus Posthumous.* Stevens seemed to me an appropriate topic for a *Festschrift* for Professor Wimsatt, whose point of view was basically a conservative one, and though Stevens's conservatism was of a very different type, he is a useful counterweight to the sometimes exclusive radicalism of the tradition that is embryonic in Milton, fully developed in Blake, and, perhaps, already decadent in Yeats. Traditionally, God is the creator, man is a creature, and man's creative power is confined to second-hand imitations of the nature which, according to Sir Thomas Browne, is the art of God. For Blake and Yeats, on the other hand, there is nothing creative except what the human imagination produces. Stevens polarizes the imagination against a "reality" which is otherness, what the imagination is not and has to struggle with. Such reality cannot ultimately be the reality of physical nature or of constituted human society, which produce only the "realism" that for Stevens is something quite different. It is rather a spiritual reality, an otherness of a creative power not ourselves; and sooner or later all theories of creative imagination have to take account of it.

The title, *Spiritus Mundi,* from Yeats's "Second Coming," was suggested by my friend Mr. William Goodman, formerly of Harcourt Brace Jovanovich, as a title for the book of essays published with them which was eventually called *Fables of Identity.*

N.F.

Victoria College
Massey College
University of Toronto

JANUARY 1976

Acknowledgments

"The Search for Acceptable Words" reprinted by permission of *Daedalus*, Journal of the American Academy of Arts and Sciences, Boston, Massachusetts. Spring 1973, *The Search for Knowledge.*

"The University and Personal Life" originally appeared in *Higher Education: Demand and Response*, ed. W. R. Niblett, Tavistock Publications Limited. Reprinted by permission of the publishers.

"The Renaissance of Books" originally appeared in *Visible Language*, Vol. VIII, Number 3, Summer 1974. Reprinted by permission.

"The Times of the Signs" originally appeared in *On a Disquieting Earth, 500 Years After Copernicus.* Reprinted by permission of the Royal Society of Canada.

"Expanding Eyes" originally appeared in *Critical Inquiry*, Winter 1975, Vol. 2, Number 2. Reprinted by permission.

"Spengler Revisited" originally appeared as "*The Decline of the West* by Oswald Spengler." Reprinted by permission of *Daedalus*, Journal of the American Academy of Arts and Sciences, Boston, Massachusetts. Winter 1974, *Twentieth-Century Classics Revisited.*

The original version of "Agon and Logos" appeared in *The Prison and the Pinnacle*, University of Toronto Press. Reprinted by permission of the publishers.

The original version of "Blake's Reading of the Book of Job" appeared in *William Blake: Essays for S. Foster Damon*, Brown University Press. Reprinted by permission of the publishers.

"The Rising of the Moon" originally appeared in *An Honoured Guest*, ed. D. Donoghue and J. R. Mulryne, Edward Arnold Publishers Ltd. Reprinted by permission of the publishers.

"Wallace Stevens and the Variation Form" originally appeared in *Literary Theory and Structure: Essays in Honor of William K. Wimsatt*, ed. Frank Brady, John Palmer, and Martin Price, Yale University Press. Reprinted by permission of the publishers.

A portion of "Romance as Masque" originally appeared as "Old and New Comedy" in *Shakespeare Survey*, 22, 1969. Reprinted by permission.

SPIRITUS MUNDI

Part One

CONTEXTS OF LITERATURE

The Search for Acceptable Words

I had grave doubts about my fitness to discuss the question of research in the humanities, because I have been deflected from everything that could conventionally be described as research, in the sense of reading material that other people have not read, or have read for a different purpose. The reason why I take an autobiographical line in what follows, even at the risk of sounding egocentric, is that my experiences as a scholar have seemed to me, for a long time, to be atypical, and that more recently I have begun to think that they may be more typical than I have suspected.

Towards the end of the nineteenth century, the system of Ph.D. training was established in American universities, largely, it is said, on a German model. The idea of the Ph.D. was to define the condition that a practicing scholar was supposed to keep himself in. His thesis was there to demonstrate that he had the capacity to make original contributions to scholarship, and the rest of the training was to prepare him to teach over a wider field than his special scholarship covered, and to be able to make use of research materials in other languages. Scholarship in the humanities was conceived at that time largely in terms of the division of labor, and the model, implicitly or explicitly, was science. The scholar was by definition a specialist, connected with his community through his teaching. The implication was that the highest reward of the scholar would be relief from teaching duties, at least in the undergraduate school, so that he could devote his time to his speciality. Behind this lay a further assumption about the place of the university in the community at large. Because of its innate tendency to build smaller compartments in knowledge, research gives an illusion of withdrawing from social issues, hence a hierarchy of scholarship in which pure research is at the top also assumes a university that constitutes a social counter-environment.

At this time and later a number of learned journals were established, many of them with the word "philology" in their titles, which indicated that the scholarly organization of literature had been derived from the comparative study of languages. And though the Ph.D. took a much longer time to establish itself in the British universities, especially Oxford, where I studied during the thirties, still Oxford had also adopted the philological conception of literature. There were three courses in the English school at Oxford when I was there: course one, which had the highest rating, featured Gothic and Old Norse; course two covered English literature down to 1500; course three, established for the benefit of Rhodes scholars and the like, covered English literature down to 1830. Whatever the course, the emphasis was on philological elements, rather than on literary or critical ones. On both sides of the Atlantic it has been relatively recently that we have had a sustained body of scholarship in the Old and Middle English periods that is not critically infantile.

The excuse offered for this was that, as any cultivated person ought to be reading literature on his own, giving academic credit for doing so was a weak permissiveness. There are colleges in Oxford which to this day refuse to employ a tutor in English for this reason. It is part of the same perverted ethos that what is regarded as serious in the study of the modern languages is the philological aspect of it. It strengthens the moral fibre to learn the classes of Old English strong verbs; it weakens it to study the rhetorical devices in *Ulysses.* Here again is a lurking analogy to science, and when nineteenth-century philology gave place to twentieth-century linguistics, some of the old prejudices against literature as such revived.

A dissatisfaction with this ethos reached its climax around the forties of the century in America, when a movement described as "new criticism," because it was new to the *Wissenschaft* mentality, raised a question that was almost a moral one. Why should people be regarded as scholars in the area of literature who did not know the first thing about literature? For the first thing about literature to know is how to read a poem as a poem and not as a philological document. In endeavoring to develop this, the new criticism lost itself in a labyrinth of explication. Many aspects of the reaction, as usually happens in such cases, were carried to absurd lengths. A strong undergraduate feeling developed that departments of English in universities were under a moral obligation to be as contemporary as possible, and a similar feeling expressed itself recently under the neo-Nazi slogan of "relevance." There were also graduate students who would propound the thesis that literary works could be properly read only when they were deprived of all context in language, history and experience. In the meantime the old philological journals had begun to lose their prestige and were being replaced by new journals, most of them with "review" in their titles, and which printed poetry and fiction as well as criticism. For all the excesses, the reaction itself was inevitable and in its main emphasis healthy. After a long period of specialized scholarship concerned with literature which had no real basis in literature, a great body of information about literature had been built up which very seldom led to any increased insight into it. Hence there had to be a period of drawing things together, of trying to look at literature itself in a broader and more general way.

It seemed to me, entering this situation a generation ago, that the first thing to look for was a basis for critical principles within criticism itself, trying to avoid the kind of externalized determinism in which criticism has to be "based on" something else, carried around in some kind of religious or Marxist or Freudian wheelchair. At that time, scholars who regarded their work as historical assumed that anyone dissatisfied with their methods must be anti-historical. This was the reverse of my own attitude: I was dissatisfied with the methods of historical scholars who did not know any history. That is, who did not know the history of literature. There were many who knew dates and the numbers of the centuries and a certain amount of non-literary history, but who did not know anything about the actual development of the conventions and genres of literature itself. I think that enough theoretical work has been done now to make visible a shift of emphasis, and that we are at the beginning of another phase of scholarship, based more solidly on a properly established critical theory of literature. There may again be some specialization and division of labor, but the old pseudo-scientific analogy has had it. I should be very pleased if I were to become regarded as one of the people who had assisted in the process of transition.

It is true that I have also suggested that criticism may become a scientific activity. But the conception of science involved is different. The older conception rested on a work-and-play antithesis: philology was the one way of working with words, so far as was then known, which seemed to have affinities with scientific procedure. Consequently philology was work, whereas literature, to which only a purely emotional reaction was thought of as appropriate, escaped every form of systematic and progressive study. I have tried to show, or help show, that literature itself is a structure, and can be studied in sequence like anything else; hence for me the entire study of it can assume a scientific shape. I am thinking, of course, of a future development of science in which the social sciences will have rediscovered the fact that they are equidistant from the humanities and the physical sciences, and are as closely related to the former as to the latter.

The transition however leaves many problems unsolved, notably the question of the Ph.D. The humanities resist the division of labor much more actively than the sciences, and the collapse of the scientific analogy in graduate work in the humanities puts this degree in a curiously paradoxical position. In the humanities, things stick together, get involved with one another, and merge into larger configurated patterns. Consequently, the graduate student's Ph.D. thesis is almost always going to be his first book.

So, obviously, he has to get the thesis done, because if he doesn't it will block up everything else he might do. It is possible to pick a thesis topic which is a pure academic exercise, and can be done in a limited time, but such topics are rare, and many of them are exercises in which the student will learn nothing except the technique of the exercise. Much more frequently, he gets discouraged by the terrible waste of time and effort involved in writing first a dissertation and then a book on the same material.

There are many things in the Ph.D. program which are extremely valuable, as I know to my cost. I avoided the Ph.D. myself by sheer accident, but there were elements in the training which I wish I had got in the regular way, and have always felt the lack of. Some efforts have been made to put in additional degrees in place of the Ph.D., with very limited success. To put in a degree that is simply an inferior degree seems to me entirely useless. A few years ago, some graduate departments at Toronto, including English, experimented with an M. Phil. degree, but soon abandoned it. The attempt was part of a move to get qualified teachers into classrooms in a hurry during a period of rapid expansion. But periods of rapid expansion in the university never last: depression is the university's normal state, and second-class degrees merely supply a pretext for cutting staff in harder times.

The same thing is true, I should imagine, of degrees regarded as theoretically equivalent to the Ph.D., but with emphasis on teaching rather than research. In the new conception of the university's place in the community which is now emerging, teaching and research cannot be separated even in emphasis. If research is subordinated to teaching, the instructor soon falls behind in his subject, and his teaching suffers accordingly. If teaching is subordinated to research, the instructor, unless he leaves the university and attaches himself to a research institute, loses touch with the social context of his research. I understand that in the University of London a doctoral degree is awarded on the completion of a certain body of work, but is independent of graduate study as such. This seems to me to make very good sense for the humanities. But in general I really have no solution to the doctoral problem in literature, and can only offer one or two observations about the nature of the academic area which may be of some use.

I notice that whenever I publish an article and get offprints, I may send the offprints to friends, but I seldom get any requests for them. On the other hand, when I gave an address to a convention of psychiatrists that was printed in a psychiatric journal, I got over a hundred requests for offprints. It was no surprise to me to learn that scientists tend to work with offprints and abstracts, but I had not realized before so strongly how much the humanist tends to wait for the book. It is as though the humanist cannot really understand any aspect of his subject unless he studies a large configuration of it.

The book is a by-product of the art of writing, and is the technological instrument that makes democracy a working possibility. The expository treatise, in particular, is a democratic form in which the writer is putting all his cards on the table, avoiding all rhetorical tricks designed to induce hypnosis in an audience, relying on nothing but the inner force and continuity of his argument. The reader cannot directly reply, but he can always turn back in the book to a previous point, and find that the same words are repeated no matter how often they are consulted, a model of patience for the teacher in itself. Behind the book is the larger social context of a body of written documents to which there is public access, the guarantee of the fairness of that internal debate on which democracy rests.

The authority established here goes back to the fateful point in Greek philosophy represented by Socrates. Students of Pythagoras or Heraclitus were expected to be disciples, pondering the dark sayings like "change is a rest," "all things flow," "don't eat beans," and the like, which had the unquestioned authority of a guru or oral teacher. Then we have Socrates approaching the youth of Athens and saying, in effect: "I don't know anything, but I'm looking for something. Come and help me look." Those who responded found themselves pursuing a straight line of dialectic, an argument which had its own authority and autonomy independent of the teacher. Socrates was not a writer, but his linear habit of thought made him an inspiration to writers, beginning with Plato and Xenophon. Socrates was also a philosopher, and philosophy has, up until quite recent times, also been based on the book. The centrifugal drift towards scientific procedures has affected philosophy as well, with, possibly, though I speak with very little authority, the same result. I remember as a student of the subject having to read, for example, Lotze's *Mikrokosmus.* I have totally forgotten what Lotze's philosophical "position" was, or into what ocean of thought the delta of his argument debouched itself. But I do remember feeling that I was reading a wise and humane book, which had got to be that through the relaxed and comprehensive form adopted. The shape of the book, in short, has a great deal to do with the liberality of the discipline that produces it.

I am on a commission in Canada concerned with communications, and when I first joined it I read a policy report which recommended that publications should be issued from time to time. The recommendation began: "Despite the disadvantages inherent in the linear representation of a world that is increasingly simultaneous, print still retains its medieval authority." This sentence is typical of the nit-witted McLuhanism (I am not speaking of McLuhan himself) which is confusing the educational scene. I recently spoke to an audience of university graduates, and was asked, quite seriously, what I thought of the university's building such a huge library when the book would be out of date by the time it was opened. The book *qua* book is not linear: we follow a line while we are reading it, but the book itself is a stationary visual focus of a community. It is the electronic media that increase the amount of linear experience, of things seen and heard that are as quickly forgotten. One sees the effects on students: a superficial alertness combined with increased difficulty in preserving the intellectual continuity that is the chief characteristic of education.

I mentioned the fact that scholarship tends to become pluralistic and increasingly specialized, increasingly unintelligible even to its nearest neighbors. The core of truth in the older conception of the scholarly life, which placed pure research at the top of a hierarchy, is that scholarship always holds a potential power of veto over everything else. That is, the tiniest alteration of established fact may have repercussions that will totally change the generally held view of the whole subject. But the scholar remains connected with his community as a teacher, as a public figure, and as a popularizer (in the best sense, naturally) of his own subject. This is the level for which the book is the inevitable form of presentation. Perhaps, as remarked above, we may expect in the humanities a new crop of research articles and special studies which can be produced after new theoretical principles have been established. I gather from talking to scientists that they feel that they are at the other end of the cycle, and that all the sciences, even the physical ones, are feeling a greater need for books and for larger and more comprehensive patterns of thought.

The book raises the question of the nature of influence in literature. This is one aspect of literary study that has received a good deal of attention, because its basis appears to be historical. But scholars trained in extra-literary perception, interested in the history of ideas and the like, are apt to think of an influence transmitted from A to B as a large body of consciously held ideas. This is hardly the way that influence exerts itself among poets. One may assume, for example, that Blake, Shelley, Keats and Wordsworth would all have made an intensive study of Milton. But what they got from Milton they got as poets, and consequently the derivation is a mainly unconscious derivation of phrases, even words, that flow from a single source into four very different contexts. Probably the best way to document the influence of Milton on these poets is to run their texts through a computer: the result would not, in general, tell us much that we could not already guess, but the documentation would be useful.

The computer has made, or can make, other changes in the structure of literary study. A hundred years ago, even fifty years ago, there was a strong existential reason for emphasizing values in the study of literature. It was one thing to decide to commit a large part of your life to making a concordance to Shakespeare or to collating manuscript variants of Chaucer, but would you want to do that kind of work for medieval homilies, or for the kind of poetic achievement represented by Googe or Churchyard? The computer has not only altered the answer to the question, but has helped to erode the fallacy of hierarchical values behind it. When Professor Douglas Bush produced his book on Classical mythology in the Renaissance a generation ago, he tells us that he had made an immense number of observations about the treatment of some Ovidian myths in minor Elizabethan poets. He regarded this work as largely a waste of time, and remarked that even though he knew more than anyone else about such subjects he should keep his information to himself. I suspect that this information was not really too trivial to be passed on, but I think it may indicate an area where some kind of mechanical aid might be of assistance. Whatever was highly regarded in its day, such as the Pyramus and Thisbe legend, is of great importance merely for that reason, whatever a contemporary scholar may think of it.

But there is another type of influence that it is impossible to trace except by an occasional accident. Every creative person has an interconnected body of images and ideas underneath his consciousness which it is his creative work to fish up in bits and pieces. Sometimes a phrase or a word comes to him as a kind of hook or bait with which to catch something that he knows is down there. Reading Yeats, one would think that he owed a large-scale debt to the writings of Villiers de l'Isle Adam, and to *Axël* in particular, which would be a ready-made subject for the scholar to explicate. On examination, we find that Yeats had been fascinated by a single phrase, "As for living, our servants will do that for us," extracted, totally out of its context, from a play he could hardly understand in the original French, and applied in contexts even more remote. Poets are full of influences of this kind, vagrant seeds blown toward a responsive soil, and not only poets.

When one reads the studies of influence made on creative people by their teachers, by factors in their early environment, by their reading, one is usually struck by the great plausibility of these constructs: one does, in fact, become what one is through influences. At the same time we should remember that it almost certainly did not happen like this at all. Anyone reading *Finnegans Wake* thinks he can see at a glance that *Alice Through the Looking-Glass* was a major formative influence on it, especially the figure of Humpty Dumpty and his portmanteau words. Yet we learn that Joyce had not in fact known what was in that book until it was called to his attention by others. Again, one can see that of all writers in the past, the one closest to Joyce in both temperament and technique is Rabelais, and one could study the parallels between them exhaustively. Yet Joyce says that he had not read Rabelais, though he expects nobody to believe him.

Even in my own work I can occasionally trace the same process of transmission by seed. When I began teaching, the University of Toronto possessed an honor course in English Language and Literature (now destroyed, in a fit of hysterical exuberance, because it was said to be "elitist"), which was spread over four colleges, each of which had its own department. This meant that I not only had to teach Milton, but teach Milton opposite Professors A. S. P. Woodhouse and A. E. Barker, two of the best Milton scholars anywhere, who were teaching it in the other colleges. One result of this was that for several years I confined my reading to primary sources, there being no time to read secondary ones. Later on, when the pressure slackened a bit, I attempted to adopt the normal routine of checking through learned journals. I soon cut down on that activity, not because I regarded the articles as useless, but for the opposite reason: I was interested in everything, everything seemed to have some relevance to my interests, and yet the pursuit of knowledge in all directions at once was impracticable. Ever since then, I have realized that scholarship is as much a matter of knowing what not to read as of knowing what to read. While writing *Anatomy of Criticism* in particular, endless tantalizing vistas opened up on all sides, yet I had to close my eyes to them, as Ulysses closed his ears to the sirens, because exploring them would get my main thesis out of proportion.

Fortunately, one of my colleagues when I began teaching was Professor Wilson Knight, later of Leeds. I think Wilson Knight influenced me more than I realized at the time. At that time he was completely possessed by Shakespeare, and gave the impression of not knowing a Quarto from a Folio text, certainly of caring even less. He showed me once his main instrument of scholarship—a Globe Shakespeare with a mass of pencilled annotations. Like most students of my generation, Knight's books had much the effect on me that Chapman's Homer had on Keats, and the method indicated, of concentrating on the author's text but recreating it by studying the structure of imagery and metaphor, seemed to me then, and seems to me still, the sort of thing that criticism is centrally about.

Nevertheless, I went through a long period in which every publication of mine was followed by neurotic fears of being confronted with proof of having plagiarized it from some source I had not read—or, worse still, had forgotten having read. I gradually became more fatalistic about this, besides realizing that the more obvious what I said seemed to me, the less likely it was that anyone had said it before. I can also trace one or two examples of influence so trivial that I hesitate to record them, except as evidence that the kind of influence I postulate for Joyce and Yeats works on all levels of intellectual activity. Once, when an undergraduate, I was discussing the keyboard music of Bach with a friend interested in the same subject, and spoke of my great interest in the fugues Bach had made on themes by Albinoni. My friend made some such comment as "very scholarly," and the word "scholarly" as applied to Bach's music stuck in my mind. I had always known that it was scholarly, of course, but to know a thing is not to realize it: one may know many things that are still not attached to that submarine body of ideas one is trying to fish up. Forty-odd years later, I wrote an essay on Shakespearean comedy trying to show that Shakespeare is as scholarly a writer as Ben Jonson, except that his scholarship, being connected with the oral tradition, is harder to recognize as such. The analogies with Bach's music are there also, so that here is one example of a seed that I have accidentally caught in the act of germinating.

To carry this point a step further: my first big project was a book on the interpretation of William Blake's longer and more didactic poems, generally called "Prophecies." There were many reasons for getting interested in Blake: perhaps one may be of general interest. I am, in cultural background, what is known as a WASP, and thus belong to the only group in society which it is entirely safe to ridicule. I expected that a good deal of contemporary literature would be devoted to attacking the alleged complacency of the values and standards I had been brought up in, and was not greatly disturbed when it did. But with the rise of Hitler in Germany, the agony of the Spanish Civil War, and the massacres and deportations of Stalinism, things began to get more serious. For Eliot to announce that he was Classical in literature, royalist in politics, and Anglo-Catholic in religion was all part of the game. But the feeling of personal outrage and betrayal that I felt when I opened *After Strange Gods* was something else again. And when Eliot was accompanied by Pound's admiration for Mussolini, Yeats' flirtations with the most irresponsible of the Irish leaders, Wyndham Lewis' interest in Hitler, and the callow Marxism of younger writers, I felt that I could hardly get interested in any poet who was not closer to being the opposite in all respects to what Eliot thought he was. Or, if that was too specific, at least a poet who, even if dead, was still fighting for something that was alive.

When I began work on Blake, around 1933, there was one serious book available on the subject of the symbolism of the Prophecies, Foster Damon's book, which had appeared in 1924. Apart from this there had been hundreds of books, articles, and essays on Blake, to say nothing of thousands of incidental references. There was nothing in any of this material, so far as I know, and I know more about it than most people, which was of the slightest use to me. No device of "information retrieval" would be of any help: the important thing was to get rid of the alleged information, not to get hold of it. And yet, many years later, I was asked to write a bibliographical essay on Blake which was in fact a history of Blake criticism. For it, I had to go over this material again, and I discovered, to my great surprise, that it was a most fascinating and rewarding exercise. The books still told me nothing about Blake, but they told me a great deal about the history of taste in the nineteenth and early twentieth centuries. More generally, they told me a great deal about the human ability to stare at what is straight in front of one's eyes and not be able to focus one's eyes on it. I know now much that I could hardly have learned in any other way about the anxieties and obsessions which prevent a great writer from being properly estimated in his day and for some time after. I note from a reprint catalogue that four of these early books have recently been reissued. As far as telling us anything about Blake is concerned, all these books are trash, and one of them would be a strong contender in the admittedly stiff competition for the title of the world's worst book on Blake. But in a sense, you can't lose in the humanities: if your book is any good, it's a contribution to scholarship; if it's no good, it's a document in the history of taste.

Two morals seem to me to be relevant. First, it is a part of the fallacy of the scientific analogy that, before deciding on a thesis topic, one should look to see whether or not "it's already been done." Of course this did not apply to my Blake project. But in general, in literary criticism, nothing can ever be done in a definitive way, except very specific projects, such as editing texts. I have supervised a good many doctoral theses on Joyce, Yeats, Stevens, and other much-processed writers, and have been well aware that all these theses were saying very similar things. But each represented an individual point of view, and this kind of individuality has to be taken account of in the humanities when we speak of a contribution to knowledge. In this situation the "review of recent scholarship" article emerges as an indispensable scholarly tool.

Second, a principle which follows from the first, the question of personal authority is relevant to the humanities in general, and literary criticism in particular. I think it advisable for every critic proposing to devote his life to literary scholarship to pick a major writer of literature as a kind of spiritual preceptor for himself, whatever the subject of his thesis. I am not speaking, of course, of any sort of moral model, but it seems to me that growing up inside a mind so large that one has no sense of claustrophobia within it is an irreplaceable experience in humane studies. Some kind of transmission by seed goes on here too. I am venturing on an area which so far as I know has been very little discussed, and what I say is bound to be tentative. Keats remarks that the life of a man of genius is a continuous allegory, which I take to mean, among other things, that a creative life has something to do with choosing a life-style. I think the scholarly life has something to do with this too, and one chooses a preceptor among the poets who has something congenial to oneself in this respect. I notice that, at the age of sixty, I have unconsciously arranged my life so that nothing has ever happened to me, and no biographer could possibly take the smallest interest in me. The reason for this unconscious choice is that, for me, an obliteration of incident was necessary to keep the sense of continuity in the memory that fostered the germinating process I have spoken of. And it is clear to me, though not demonstrable to anyone else, that this has been imitated, on a level that consciousness and memory cannot reach, from Blake, who similarly obliterated incident in his own life, and for similar reasons. One who found Byron more congenial as a preceptor would doubtless adopt a different life-style.

Blake, while he is very much a man of his time, tends to pull his critic out of the historical period in which he falls. So while I naturally had to become familiar with Ossian and Gray and Chatterton, I also found myself looking through a great variety of other writers in search of ideas that would give me some clue to Blake. I do not mean that I read very systematically in mystical or occult literature. Most of the misguided critics I mentioned above told me that that was where the real analogues to Blake's thinking were. But I found it hard to understand why Blake interested me so much when most mystical and occult writing interested me not at all. I soon discovered that I had to take seriously Blake's own statement that he belonged with the poets and artists, and read accordingly. But again, reading simply in the 1750–1820 period of Blake's own lifetime was not only insufficient, but in many respects misleading. This fact was important to me, because it dramatized the difficulty of knowing what not to read, which I have already alluded to. The historical period has firmly established itself as the normal area of scholarship because it both limits and directs one's reading, and in nearly every case it is a safe guide to follow. Blake was an exception, and a very significant one.

When I was taking a course in Blake from the late Herbert Davis, I was assigned a paper on Blake's *Milton*, which I sat down to write, as was my regular bad habit in those days, the night before. The foreground of the paper was commentary, which was assuredly difficult enough for that poem, but in the background there was some principle that kept eluding me. On inspection, the principle seemed to be that Milton and Blake were connected by their use of the Bible, which was not merely commonplace but seemed anti-literary as well. If Milton and Blake were alike on this point, that likeness merely concealed what was individual about each of them, so that in pursuing the likeness I was chasing a shadow and avoiding the substance. Around about three in the morning a different kind of intuition hit me, though it took me twenty years to articulate it. The two poets were connected by the *same* thing, and sameness leads to individual variety, just as likeness leads to monotony. I began dimly to see that the principle pulling me away from the historical period was the principle of mythological framework. The Bible had provided a frame of mythology for European poets: an immense number of critical problems began to solve themselves as soon as one realized this.

Further, Biblical mythology had not remained static, but had grown with a catholicity greater than that of the Church itself, annexing the whole of Classical mythology, and the erotic or "Courtly Love" literature as well, as contrapuntal descants on its own theme. The fact that one mythology could absorb another indicated that all mythologies were imaginatively much alike. Christianity had similarly absorbed the older Teutonic mythology, because the latter also had a world tree like that of Eden, a world-girdling serpent like Leviathan, a god hung on a tree as a sacrifice to himself, a last day and a creation. A literature grows out of the primitive verbal culture which contains a mythology; it can grow out of any mythology, but it is a historical fact that our literature is most directly descended from the Biblical myth.

Of course this particular discovery was a natural one for me to make at a time when I was actually a student of theology. This latter fact has proved useful to many people. A "Maoist" pamphlet, for example, describes me as "the High Priest of clerical obscurantism," and its cover depicts a series of black-cloaked monks, with hoods suggesting the Ku Klux Klan. I think the actual effect of my theological training has been rather the opposite of that. It is true that my attitude to teaching, and probably to scholarship as well, has always been an evangelical attitude, and that I was not satisfied with my own theories until I began to see how they could be made the basis for a system of teaching literature in sequence, at all levels from kindergarten to graduate school. But actually the Bible preoccupied me, not because it represented a religious "position" congenial to my own, but for the opposite reason. It illustrated the imaginative assumptions on which Western poets had proceeded; consequently the study of it pointed the way towards a phenomenological criticism which would be as far as possible free of presuppositions. I am not by any means sure that it is possible really to get free of presuppositions, but it is obvious that all genuine advance in knowledge goes along with a continued attempt to objectify and become aware of the assumptions one is starting from. Poets do not write, like Swift's spider, "out of their own bowels, and in a restricted compass." The poet is taken over by a mythical and metaphorical organism, with its historical roots in the Bible, and the integrity of that organism is his Muse, the mother that brings to life a being separate both from herself and from him.

So far from hitching literature to a structure of belief, this principle actually emancipates literature from questions of belief altogether. But, of course, for many centuries the poet was regarded as subordinate in authority to other types of writers, such as theologians. Their method of writing, it was thought, had more direct access to truth; the poet's function was to produce a rhetorical echo of that truth, addressing the emotions and will and trying to persuade them to align themselves on the side of truth. This view assumed that literature was serious in proportion to its allegorical relationship to religion. Later on, as religious anxieties gave place to more secular and political ones, it continued to be believed that the realist, who studied the life around him and reflected it in his writing, had a seriousness that the mere romancer who told stories for fun could not match. The historian of nineteenth century fiction, for example, finds that the backbone of his historical study is constituted by the great realists, George Eliot, Jane Austen, Thackeray, and certain carefully selected aspects of Scott, Dickens and Henry James. Such a book as *Alice in Wonderland* is obviously a masterpiece of its kind, was immensely popular in its day and has never lost its popularity, but somehow it doesn't fit the history. And just as a highbrow in Old English times would probably regard a saint's life as more serious than *Beowulf*, so most modern critics would regard social realism, of the kind that clearly reflects the life around it, as more serious than fantasy or adventure where there is a strong emphasis on the structure of the story, designed primarily to keep the reader turning the pages.

This leads to another far-reaching critical principle. Every primitive verbal culture contains a number of stories, of which some gradually assume a particular importance as "true," or in some way more deeply significant. These are the stories that are most readily describable as myths, and they are the ones that take root in a specific society and provide for that society a network of shared allusion and experience. Such myths differ in social function, but not in structure, from the folk tales and legends that are often told simply for fun by wandering story-tellers. Thus in European literature the Biblical stories have a seriousness not ascribed to folk tales or legends which are closely analogous, if not identical, in structure. As literature develops, some poets, such as Dante and Milton, recreate the central myths; others, such as Shakespeare, have the social role of entertainers, and turn rather to folk tale and legend. But the former group recreate the central myths on the same imaginative basis that the latter are using, and the latter group, if they treat their themes with enough intensity, give them the same kind of significance that the central myths have.

Some time ago I had occasion to read Katherine Anne Porter's *Ship of Fools*. It is not a favorite novel of mine, but it struggles hard to be a serious one, and it seeks seriousness through allegory, like the Sebastian Brant poem from which it derives its name. The setting is a German ship sailing from Mexico to Germany in 1932, and every episode, such as the excluding of a Jew from the captain's table, is part of an allegorical relationship of the story to the rise of Nazism in Germany. Later, when stranded in an airport, I pulled another ship story off the paperback shelves, Paul Gallico's *The Poseidon Adventure.* This was a thriller about a ship that turned upside down in a wreck, leaving the surviving passengers to climb upwards towards the bottom of the ship. This story being designed for entertainment, it concentrated on the shape of the story, and the shape of the story derives from what I call an archetype, a story type that has been used thousands of times before, for which the Biblical model is the Exodus. The author being a professional and intelligent writer, I knew that he would indicate some awareness of this fact before long, and two-thirds of the way through he did so. He explained that the passengers were undertaking this desperate and apparently futile climb because up had always been good and down bad, that damnation went down, the resurrection up, that mythology puts monsters underground and graceful fantasies of light in the upper air. In the same chapter the leader of the expedition, a clergyman, gets fed up with his own notion of God and commits suicide: not a very convincing episode, but an Exodus story needs a Moses figure who doesn't make it all the way.

I am not comparing the two books: I am noting the survival of the distinction between a more serious literature that reflects important truths allegorically, and a less serious literature, designed for entertainment, that follows a certain story-telling formula. I am also suggesting that an *a priori* value distinction between them is critically unsound. The reading of a formulaic book, such as a detective story, may not be in itself a significant experience. But even such a book can take on significance through the resonance of context. A detective story is normally a comedy, and while any individual comedy, from Plautus to modern television, may be silly or trifling, the importance of studying comedy itself, as a whole, is very considerable. For one thing, once a literal belief in a mythology declines, and Biblical stories are no longer generally assumed to be historically factual, it becomes increasingly obvious that the real affinities of a mythology are not with the waking world but with the dream world. A mythology is a construct belonging to art and not to nature: it is not a description of the outer world, a crude form of philosophy or science, but a cultural model, expressing the way in which man wants to shape and reshape the civilization he himself has made. Comedy, which tends toward the victory of desire over reality, indicates this fact more clearly than any other archetypal form.

The same principle is central to the teaching of literature, especially in the most elementary stages. From kindergarten onwards, the teacher is not instilling literature into a mind that doesn't know any, but reshaping the student's total verbal experience. This experience has been built up by television, movies, and the conversation of his parents and classmates as well as by his reading. It already contains a great deal of mythology, much of it phony, derived from advertising or class stereotypes, and literature is or should be the means of leading the student from his present subjective social vision into the total social vision of mankind.

All this may not be very helpful in discussing the question of the university's support of research. The humanities usually get the lion's share of the library budget, but apart from that they are usually regarded by administrators as low-budget departments. In fact there are times when I wonder whether "low-budget departments" would not be the best definition of the humanities. Some branches of the humanities, of course, are inherently expensive, an obvious example being archaeology, on which a good many humane disciplines are heavily dependent. But it is still possible to bring a man into a university at a senior level in the humanities without the great expenditure for equipment and the like which an equivalent appointment in the sciences would necessitate.

Universities however are caught in a paradoxical situation: they have to build up as good a library as they can, and yet they must maintain travel grants to enable scholars in the humanities to go to still better libraries. The immense resources of modern libraries, which can bring so much to the scholar's doorstep, are of course indispensable, but most of them imply that the scholar already knows what he is looking for. If he is doing original research, he may not know. In that case he has still to be turned loose in the British Museum or the Library of Congress with a sense of serendipity built up by his previous experience of the subject.

We have all heard how the Bodleian Library in Oxford got rid of its Shakespeare Folio, which it later had to buy back again at much greater expense. The inference is often that the Oxford librarians of that day were fools. Actually, they were entirely right: in terms of what Oxford then taught and studied, Shakespeare was no more use to them than collections of nineteenth-century sermons would be now to the kind of college that hands out diplomas to young women studying ballet. After the modern languages were established in universities, library buying was largely confined to a select canon of approved writers. The minor writers came in on a preferential list, those that had been dead the longest getting the most attention. The scholarly revolution which I have helped to agitate has resulted in weakening the distinction between classical and popular literature. Some years ago, when I was visiting a university in the United States, a professor responsible for much of the library buying in the Romantic period came in to see me with a catalogue. He had a chance of buying a large amount of the "horrid mysteries" of the 1790's, and was hesitating. I said, "Grab it at once." But he was doubtful whether the inherent value of this work justified the expenditure, because his was a small college with a restricted budget. I imagine that he now regrets his caution, in an age when "Gothic is in" and the best and brightest graduate students are likely to be paying attention to Rider Haggard as well as to George Eliot. For university library purposes, there certainly is such a thing as junk, but junk is no longer definable in terms of a conventional standard of literary values.

The problem of preserving the personal community is crucial to all universities, and to all aspects of it. One should always be aware of the limitations of what is technically possible, because the future that is technically possible is not necessarily the future that society wants or can absorb. One is constantly hearing from gadget-happy technocrats about how it is, or soon will be, no longer necessary to give lectures or attend them, to build libraries or staff them, to write papers or deliver them to audiences. What such fantasies do not take in is the importance of community and personal contact in the scholarly life. Any student faced by a television screen instead of a human countenance could tell them about this.

It is for the same reason that all educational hardware has to be confined to certain specialized uses. Similarly, many libraries acquire a great deal of material that is really archival, and should perhaps be in another institution. This would include the foul papers and other excreta of contemporary poets, for which there was such a vogue a few years ago, and which for some poets made the faking of draft papers quite a profitable business. In my own case, I have had to throw my energy into a more centripetal movement of scholarship, trying to avoid specialization in order to articulate a number of central problems of critical theory. This meant that a specialized research library was only intermittently useful to me, and I have often found myself drifting from the research library into the undergraduate working library, because of the increasing affinity of my work to obvious books. But there is something too of finding one's way back to the focus of the university community. When I mention this tendency of mine to my colleagues, I find that a large number of them share it.

I have always remained in Canada, and perhaps the influences of the Canadian environment have played a significant role in my life, allowing for the indirectness of influence that I have already mentioned. I think in any case that the effect of one's teachers and senior colleagues is derived mainly from the reflections that one is impelled to make as a result of having known them, rather than from what they have directly taught or said. My own teachers in Toronto included Pelham Edgar, whose main academic interest was Henry James and James' treatment of the North Atlantic schizophrenia which is so central to Canadian life also. Then there was E. J. Pratt, Canada's most important English poet, who was a full-time teaching member of the department. His existence helped me to become more detached from the romantic mystique that opposes creative writers to critical ones. In Canada poets are conditioned to utter a good deal of anti-academic patter as a part of their own sales pitch, even when they are struggling for tenure appointments in universities themselves. The mystique tends to assume that creative people are the people who write poems or stories, and feels that such people ought to have a specially protected place in the community, somewhat analogous to that of the people who can speak Irish in Ireland. There is nothing wrong with this except the fallacy of attaching the conception of creativity to the genres of poetry and fiction rather than to the people working in them. This fallacy is world wide, and extends, for instance, to the Nobel Prize Committee in Sweden, who search over the world for poets and novelists but never consider the claims of critical or expository writing. My third teacher, John Robins, was interested in ballads, folk tales, and popular literature, along with Old and Middle English. He had much to do with my understanding of the main features of Canadian literature, including Pratt's poetry, which are so like those of Old English in reflecting a paradoxical tension between the primitive and the over-civilized. He probably had something to do too with my notion of archetypes, which are really an expansion of the themes and motifs of folk tale into the rest of literature.

Later on, I began to understand the extent to which this almost one-dimensional country has been preoccupied with communications of all kinds, from the most physical to the most ethereal. Many Canadians, including Harold Innis and Innis' disciple Marshall McLuhan, have been interested in the totality of communication, and the essential unity of its activity, whether it is building railways or sending messages. Innis developed out of his study of the fur trade in Canada a vast historical communication theory, concerned with the ways in which the control of communication media by a certain class or group in society conditions that society. A similar sense of the unity of communication has affected me, and has had a good deal to do with what I have called my evangelical attitude to the teaching of literature.

The first thing one realizes, of course, is that communication media are formidably efficient, and the effect of this is among other things to make every senior professor a cock-shy of rapid transit. He has his growing body of former students, who send him everything they write as a simple routine act; colleagues who ask his advice about everything from changing jobs or making appointments to rearranging the arguments of their current books; publishers who keep sending new books to him for comment; chairmen of program committees who have found that jet planes make it possible for anyone to visit anywhere, and for conferences to be held in Pakistan or Brazil as easily as closer to home. There is also a continuous cataract of unsolicited material, stacks of song from hopeful poets and theses with notes attached saying in effect: "My supervisor says I'm crazy, but I know *you'll* understand." In this situation, an enlightened university administration should understand that the most important form of assistance they can offer him is that of the non-academic secretary. Such a secretary can make all the difference between a properly functioning scholar and a harried intellectual carpetbagger, and he should not have to undertake an uncongenial administrative job in order to acquire one.

There seem to me to be three main stages in communication. There is the initial stage of separation, where communication is physically difficult and precarious. This developed in Canadian culture what I have elsewhere called a "garrison mentality," and which survives in Canadian separatist movements. The garrison mentality however had its positive, even its heroic, side, as we can see when we think of the sheer physical, to say nothing of the mental, effort that scholars in Saskatchewan or Alberta had to make to maintain their standards before the days of planes and microfilm. The first impact of improved communication is destructive. If one is building a road from point A to point B, the first thing one has to do is bulldoze and cut through underbrush. If a student is being taught at school, the effort to reach him has to cut through the underbrush of the anxieties and prejudices and snobberies by which he attempts to maintain his isolated security. The immediate result of this destructive activity is a sense of uniformity and a loss of individuality. This is the stage that the communication crisis of the sixties is trying to emerge from now.

Similar stages have affected the universities internally. Each department tends to become a garrison in itself; every development of scholarship batters at its barriers. My own conception of mythology is one that attacks the separation of one language department from another, the separation of literature from comparative religion, even the separation of the humanities from the social sciences. One response to this is to introduce interdisciplinary courses, where representatives of departments meet politely but suspiciously, like diplomats arranging for a cease-fire, or courses in general education or general humanities or great books or western civilization. This is the second, or uniform, stage of improved communications, which is less a solution to the problem than a symptom of it. One hopes for rapid emergence to the third stage, when it is clearly realized that knowledge, like St. Augustine's God, has its center everywhere and its circumference nowhere.

The University and Personal Life

The first half of the twentieth century saw two world wars, each of which was started by a reactionary military autocracy operating mainly in Germany and ended in a major Communist revolution, first in Russia, then in China. The second half of the century is seeing the beginning of a new revolutionary development that seems to have more in common with anarchism than with Communism. The anarchist nature of the 'New Left' is often recognized, but usually without much sense of the traditions or context of anarchism.

In my own student days, during the Depression of the thirties, anarchism was a negligible force, at least on North American campuses, and the most influential radical movements were close to Marxism as interpreted by Stalin. The pro-Stalinist radical thought of himself as a 'worker'—that is, he had no quarrel with the work ethic of capitalism as an ethic, only with its economic setting. The metaphors of 'left wing' and 'right wing' were essential to him, because he thought in terms of an eventual separation and struggle for power between proletarian and bourgeois camps. His outlook was intensely international, and his tactics conformed to an internationally directed and organized strategy. His attitude to social issues was rational, every injustice and cruelty under capitalism being only what one would expect of that system. His attitude to the arts was deeply conservative, based mainly on the content of what was said or painted, or, at most, on allegorical reference. I remember a Canadian Communist magazine that condemned practically all twentieth-century Canadian painting as bourgeois formalism, and reproduced Victorian anecdotal pictures, depicting foreclosures of mortgages and the like, as examples of the genuine cultural tradition. The Stalinist's personal ethics, when consistent with his political outlook, tended to be rigorous: self-indulgence or muddling one's mind with liquor and drugs was for him only the kind of thing that capitalism encouraged.

Hardly any of these characteristics are true of the present New Left. Like the nineteenth-century anarchists, contemporary radicals favour direct action, or 'confrontation', and favour also the kind of spontaneous uprising with no context in past or future, which is without precedence and without direction. The word 'existential' is often used approvingly to describe a political action which has no particular point. Unlike the Stalinist with his sacred texts of Marx and Lenin and his libraries of commentary on them, many who call themselves anarchists today have never heard of Kropotkin or Bakunin, or would take the slightest interest in them if they had. The nineteenth-century anarchists lost out to the more disciplined Communists in the struggle for control of the working class, partly because they tended to the extremes of either passivity or violence. There was the Arcadian anarchism of Morris's *News from Nowhere* and the terroristic anarchism of Conrad's *Secret Agent.* Similarly, radicals of today range from 'flower children' to assassins, though their main centre of gravity is of course in an intermediate activism. Their most effective revolutionary tactics are closer to Gandhi than to Lenin, and their great heroes are romantics like Che Guevara, who commands much the same kind of appeal, and for many of the same reasons, that Garibaldi commanded among British liberals a century ago. Even the Mao Tse-Tung of radical folklore seems more the guerrilla leader of thirty years ago than the present ruler of China.

The contemporary anarchist, like his nineteenth-century forebears, tends to localize his protests: he is well aware of the global context of contemporary unrest, but his own movement is likely to be confined to an immediate area of interest. Hence small separatist movements, like those in Quebec or Belgium, are also a part of contemporary radicalism. The conception of 'participatory democracy', which demands a thoroughgoing decentralization, is also anarchist in context. In some respects this fact presents a political picture almost the reverse of that of the previous generation. For today's radical the chief objects of loyalty during the thirties, trade unions and the revolutionary directives of Moscow, have become reactionary social forces, whereas some radical movements like the Black Panthers, which appear to have committed themselves both to violence and to racism, seem to descend from fascism, which also had anarchist affinities. Similarly, anarchism does not seek to create a 'working class': much of its dynamic comes from a bourgeois disillusionment with an overproductive society, and some types of radical protest, like those of the hippies, are essentially protests against the work ethic itself.

Both political movements show many analogies to the religious movements which preceded them. The attitude of the old-line Stalinist to the Soviet Union was very like that of a Roman Catholic to his Church, at least before the Second Vatican Council. There was a tremendous international institution which was the definitive interpreter of the Marxist revelation, and one could work effectively for the world-wide triumph of that revelation only from within the institution. Contemporary anarchists, at least those who can read, are more like the Puritans in the way that they seek a primitive gospel in the early work of Marx, before social and institutional Marxism began to corrupt it. Perhaps the similarity, however, is less with Puritanism than with the Anabaptists (who in the sixteenth century were also anarchists tending to the same polarity of pacifism and terrorism) and the more fervid evangelicals. Among religious bodies, those who are most dramatically increasing their membership today are the most uncritical and fundamentalist sects, and I doubt whether this is simply coincidence. There are some curious parallels between the present and the nineteenth-century American scene, between contemporary turn-on sessions and nineteenth-century ecstatic revivalism, between beatnik and hippy communes and some of the nineteenth-century Utopian projects. Stalinist Marxism had practically nothing in the American tradition to attach itself to, but anarchism is one of the central elements in American culture. Jefferson's states-rights and local autonomy thinking, Thoreau's civil disobedience, Lincoln's view of the Civil War as a revolution against the inner spirit of slavery, many cultural phenomena as diverse as *Huckleberry Finn,* the Chaplin films, and the *Cantos* of Ezra Pound, all show a radical dynamic that has affinities with anarchism. So did the populist movements at the turn of the century, which showed the same revolutionary ambivalence, tending equally to the left or to the right, that I have just noted in the contemporary scene. As for terroristic anarchism, one hardly needs to document that in so violent a country as America. The spirit of the late Joseph McCarthy is still around, but it is much more difficult for it to regard the current type of radical protest as un-American.

Anarchism has another advantage over Communism in its relation to the creative arts. The primary revolutionary categories of today tend to be psychological rather than economic, closer in many respects to Freud than to Marx, as we see in many of the writers who have tried to articulate the present radical mood, such as Herbert Marcuse. When the contemporary radical denounces intervention in Vietnam or Negro segregation, he does not think of these things as merely by-products of the contradictions of capitalism: he sees the emotional and imaginative factors in these situations as primary, and as the main elements to be opposed or supported. This primary place assigned to emotion and imagination means among other things that the anarchist is not hampered, as the orthodox Marxist was (and still is) hampered, by the canons of 'social realism' which judge mainly by content. A ferment in the arts, including a revival of oral poetry, is an integral part of today's radicalism, as, despite a great many spasmodic efforts, it never became in the radicalism of thirty years ago. The drug cults are another aspect of the same psychologically based activity. They are not intended merely to take one's mind off one's troubles: they are part of an attempt to recharge the batteries of the mind after they have been drained by disillusionment: that is, by the withdrawal of libido from consumer goods, or what advertising is still presenting as the good things of life.

The metaphors of left and right wing are still employed, but they have much less relevance to anarchism than to Communism. The Marxist saw a steadily widening split between two parts of society, an eventual struggle for power, and the final victory of the working class. The contemporary radical seems to think rather in terms of a single society, with localized cells and nuclei of radicalism agitating and transforming it from within. Communism was intensely teleological in spirit: every Communist-directed strike or demonstration was one step in the great campaign of class struggle and revolutionary triumph. The anarchism of today seems almost as indifferent to the future as to the past: one protest will be followed by another, because even if one issue is resolved society will still be 'sick', but there appears to be no clear programme of taking control or assuming permanent responsibility in society.

If I am right, then anarchism is committed by the logic of its position to becoming increasingly non-violent. Violence appears to be an inescapable stage in sobering up an unwilling conservatism and in impressing it with the sense that it is not dealing with children. An ascendant class tends to make an indulgent comic strip out of any group from which unrest seems likely: thus we had the Paddy-and-his-pig Irishman in nineteenth-century England, the Rastus-and-Jemima comic or lovable Negro in white America, and so on. But once the pattern of opposition is established, the effectiveness of violence diminishes. Naturally this does not happen easily, violence being the opiate of the revolutionary: even university students are strongly affected by the 'let's do something and not just talk about it' syndrome. But where there is no really serious conception of a climactic struggle for power in which the victor achieves permanent authority, 'talk' is the final mode of radical action, and the form that its ultimate confrontation has to take. I spoke of the affinity between some contemporary anarchism and fascism, with its belief in violence as being in a sense its own end. In Nazi Germany this took the form of a melancholy *Götterdämmerung* nihilism, whose goal appeared to be not so much its professed one of world-rule as annihilation in some heroic last stand, a second Roncesvalles or Thermopylae. This mood is, I think, intelligible to today's anarchist, who has inherited all the heroic gloom of existentialism, as it was utterly unintelligible to the Stalinist radical. I remember when Yeats's *Last Poems* appeared in 1939, and how brusquely their sardonic bleakness was dismissed as 'morbid' by the radicals of that day. But they speak with a peculiar and haunting eloquence now, even to the most self-righteous of student radicals.

I spoke a moment ago of the anarchist strain in American culture: another example of it is the work of Edgar Allan Poe, whose significance as a portent of many aspects of contemporary literature it is hard to do full justice to. Poe wrote an essay called 'The Poetic Principle' in which he asserted that a long poem was a contradiction in terms, that all existing long poems of genuine quality consisted of moments of intense poetic experience stuck together with connective tissues of narrative or argument which were really versified prose. The fact that this doctrine was preposterous so far as it was applied to Homer or Milton did not prevent it from having a tremendous influence on future poetry, including the French *symbolistes* and Pound and Eliot in England. What happens in literature is very likely to happen in life as a whole a century or so later. In Poe's day, and in fact up to about 1945, one of the most solidly rooted assumptions in middle-class Western culture was the sense of continuity in time. That is, life was thought of teleologically, as something that contained a developing purpose and direction. Some gave this feeling a religious reference: for many Christians the essence of Christianity was in the renewed meaning which the Incarnation had given to human history. In Marxist thought the 'historical process', which is an irresistible force on the side of those who accept it, played a similar role. The artist, if faced with hostility or misunderstanding, assumed, with Max Beerbohm's Enoch Soames, that he would be vindicated by posterity, for whom he was really writing. Others, like Spengler in *The Decline of the West*, saw the teleology in history from the opposite point of view, as an organic process that first matured and then declined. For a great number of bourgeois intellectuals, the doctrine of evolution afforded a scientific proof of teleology in human life, and the doctrine of progress in history, though of course much older than Darwin, became increasingly a mythical analogy of evolution. H. G. Wells in his *Outline of History* (1920) concludes a chapter on 'Early Thought' with a picture of human sacrifice at Stonehenge and an appended comment: 'And amidst the throng march the appointed human victims, submissive, helpless, staring towards the distant smoking altar at which they are to die—that the harvests may be good and the tribe increase . . . To that had life progressed 3,000 or 4,000 years ago from its starting-place in the slime of the tidal beaches.' The death-wish in human life, so dramatically emergent in the First World War, could hardly be ignored by anyone writing in 1920: but although the final remark is intended ironically, it echoes with the complacency of the 'long view'.

One of the most striking cultural facts of our time is the disappearance of this teleological sense. We tend now to think of our lives as being, like the long poem as described by Poe, a discontinuous sequence of immediate experiences. What holds them together, besides mere survival, can only be some kind of voluntary and enforced ideology. Thus the artist may keep his life continuous by a belief in creativity, the businessman by a belief in productivity, the religious man by a belief in God, the politician by a belief in policy. But the more intense the immediate experience, the more obviously its context in past and future time drops away from it. The word 'absurd' refers primarily to the disappearance of the sense of continuity in our day. It is not so much that the world around us no longer suggests any meaning or purpose concealed in its design: that in itself, as Robbe-Grillet says, means not that the world is absurd, but merely that it is there. The sense of absurdity comes from time, not space; from the feeling that life is not a continuous absorption of experiences into a steadily growing individuality, but a discontinuous series of encounters between moods and situations which keep bringing us back to the same point.

In this situation there is one positive feature of great importance: the sharpening of moral sensitivity. I spoke of the complacency inherent in the progressive 'long view', and belief in progress can easily become the most morally callous of all beliefs. The thing about Russian Marxism that most sickened its bourgeois supporters was the readiness with which it could (and still can, evidently) embark on a massacre, an invasion of a small independent country, or a deliberately induced famine, for the sake of the greater good that such procedures would bring, from its own point of view, to posterity. In a now neglected book, *Ends and Means,* Aldous Huxley pointed out how means can never lead to ends, because they condition and eventually replace those ends. George Orwell's *1984,* one of the most important books recording the transition in mood from the last to the present generation, shows more vividly how the donkey's carrot of progress can become an indefinite prolonging of misery. It seems to me admirable that contemporary radicals should be concerned with the rights of those who are alive now, and should be protesting against the Vietnam war because it is killing innocent people at this moment, refusing to listen to any long-term rationalizations about the crusade against Communism or the white man's burden.

A less attractive side of the same situation is the general panic, even hysteria, that the loss of reference to temporal context has left us with. The most obvious form of this panic is the flight from the past: the anxiety to be up to date, to be rid of unfashionable ideas and techniques, to condemn everything unsatisfactory with the same formula, that it is too cumbersome and obsolete for the unimpeded movement assumed to be necessary today. A society with a revolutionary basis, like American society, is often inclined to be impatient of history and tradition. 'History is bunk,' said Henry Ford, at one end of the social scale: 'I don't take no stock in dead people,' said Huckleberry Finn, at the other.

The future, in such a view, cannot be the outcome of the past: it is a brand new future, which may be implicit in the present but is to be built out of the materials of the present by an act of will, which cannot operate until it has been released from the past. The strongly negative mood in today's radicalism, the tendency to be against rather than for, is consistent with this: whatever is defined is hampering, and only the undefined is free.

The resulting crisis of spirit is a far-reaching one. That it has caused a political crisis goes without saying. But there is also a crisis in the arts and in the intellect. The creative artist cannot appeal to posterity, as he no longer assumes that the future will be continuous with the present, and, more important, the impetus to produce the 'great' work of art has itself been considerably weakened. For, traditionally, the great work of art became a classic, that is, a work connecting the present with the past. One sometimes wonders if the age of *great* writers or painters or composers is over, and if what is in front of us culturally is not rather a diffused creative energy, much or most of it taking fairly ephemeral forms, a general rather than a specialized social product. Again, there is a crisis in the intellect, for the assumption that science and scholarship are progressively developing, in a semi-autonomous way, is in many quarters questioned or denied. But above all, the crisis is a religious one. The problems connected with the discontinuous and the absurd are problems affecting the way man lives his life, affecting his conceptions of his nature and destiny, affecting his sense of identity. They are, in short, existential problems, and existentialism has been formulated mainly either in the explicitly religious context of Kierkegaard and Unamuno, or in the context of Heidegger and Sartre, which is no less religious for being atheistic. I feel that contemporary radicalism is deeply, even desperately, religious both in its anxieties and in its assertions: that it cannot, for the most part, accept the answers given its questions by the existing religious bodies, and that a great deal of student unrest is based on a feeling that the university ought to be trying to answer such questions, but cannot do so until it has been shaken loose from the 'establishment'. That this is a misunderstanding of what the university is and can do is undoubtedly true. But the questions remain, as urgent as ever, and some people in the universities ought to try to deal with them sympathetically, as questions, before they freeze into immature dogmas.

There are two social conceptions so deeply rooted in our experience that they can be presented only as myths. One is the social contract, the myth which attempts to explain the nature of the conditioning we accept by getting born. The other is the Utopia, the myth of an ideal social contract. Both these myths have religious affiliations: the contract is connected with the alienation myth of the Fall of Man, and the Utopia with the transcendence myth of the City of God. The overtones of the social contract myth are ironic, sometimes tragic. Before we were born, we were predestined to join a social continuum at a certain historical point: we belonged to the twentieth century and the middle class even as embryos in the womb. We belong to something before we are anything, and the first datum of our lives is the set of social conditions and assumptions that we are already committed to. The conservative temperament is strongly attracted by the positive aspects of this contract. He feels that his own development is a matter of growing organically out of the roots of his social context. What is presented to him at birth, he feels, is a set of loyalties given to him before he is capable of choosing them. To try to reject what one is already committed to can only lead to confusion and chaos, both in one's own life and in society. Further, we discover in the permanence and continuity of social institutions, such as Church and State, something that not only civilizes man, but adds a dimension of significance to his otherwise brief and insignificant life.

Such, it seems to me, is the conservative view of the social contract, expounded so lucidly by Burke and still being proclaimed, over a century later, by T. S. Eliot. The radical view of it focuses on the uncritical element in our inherited loyalties, as expressed in such maxims as 'my country right or wrong'. Maturity and development, the radical feels, are a matter of becoming aware of our conditioning, and, in so becoming aware, of making a choice between presented and discovered loyalties. This attitude, developing through Rousseau and Marx, reached a further stage with the existentialism that followed the Second World War. Traditionally, the difference between sanity and hysteria, between reality and hallucination, had always been that sanity and reality lasted longer, and were continuous in a way that their opposites could not be. The rise of Nazi Germany suggested the possibility of a social hysteria indefinitely prolonged by the control of communications. But perhaps what we have been calling sanity and reality is an unconsciously induced hysteria, and the way to deliverance is through and beyond the loyalty of uncritical acceptance. The only real loyalty, then, is the voluntary or self-chosen loyalty.

This is the state of mind which dominates the radical of today: an intensely Utopian state of mind which feels that it owes loyalty only to a social ideal not yet in existence. The Vietnam issue, particularly, raises the question of what was called, in the title of an indifferent book of twenty years ago, the meaning of treason. In Dante's *Inferno,* in Shakespeare's tragedies, the traitor, the man who breaks the social contract assigned him at birth, is the lowest of criminals. In our day the word 'treason', almost without our realizing it, has joined the word 'heresy' as a word that could once intimidate, but is now only a Hallowe'en mask.

We notice that the prose romances called Utopias, from Campanella to Edward Bellamy, have been rather compulsive and anxiety-ridden stories. In literature, at any rate, they have made far less imaginative impact than the Utopian satires, such as *Gulliver's Travels,* which ought perhaps to be thought of rather as satires on the social contract. Some of the nineteenth-century Utopias, like Bellamy's *Looking Backward,* might have looked attractive at the time in contrast to the misery and anarchy of unrestricted *laissez-faire.* But reading them now, we simply cannot believe the author's assertions that the citizens of their ideal states are perfectly happy: if they are, we can only feel, as we feel with all victims of brainwashing, that there is something subhuman about them. The reason for this feeling is not hard to see. The conservative who accepts the loyalties presented to him by his society is, to use two stock words of our time, committed and engaged. Commitment and engagement, in themselves, as just said, contain an uncritical element, and tend also to be somewhat humourless, because, confronted with a genuine absurdity in society, their instinct is to rationalize the absurdity instead of recognizing it. The Utopian attitude begins in detachment, but at that point conceives of an alternative institution and transfers its loyalties to that. This alternative institution will of course also demand commitment, and of a more intense kind: it will tolerate much less dissent and criticism, much less sense of the absurd or ironic, than the conservative outlook, unless frightened by crisis, permits.

It seems to me that the Marxist revolutionary movement is the definitive form of what I have called the Utopian attitude of mind, the transfer of loyalty from one's native society to another society still to be constructed. When Engels contrasted Utopian with 'scientific' socialism he was really completing the Utopian argument. In a world like ours a limited Utopia, confined to one definite place, is an empty fantasy: it must be a world-wide transformation of the whole social order or it is nothing. But for it to be this it must be conceived, not as an *a priori* rational construct, but as the *telos* of history, the end to which history points. The 'scientific' element in Marxist socialism, then, is a religious belief in the teleology of history.

Marxism envisages a social cleavage in which the possibility of argument, discussion, or what is now called 'dialogue' disappears. One does not need to answer an argument: one needs only to identify it as coming from our side or theirs. It is not talk but a planned sequence of actions leading to an ultimate confrontation or showdown that is important. I suggested earlier that the contemporary anarchist radical, though he adopts much of this attitude, is really a post-Marxist revolutionary, forced by the logic of his situation from action into 'dialogue'. He has no real sense of a proletarian society, and his protest is, primarily and essentially, protest, not a mere prelude to taking power himself. Does this mean, then, that the end of contemporary anarchism is compromise with conservatism? To some extent this may be true: I think democracy is in the initial stages of working out a two-party opposition far less cumbersome and hypocritical, and representing a more genuine division of attitudes, than the one now represented in our parliaments and congresses. But it seems to me that the real end at which anarchism is aiming is very different. (We may note in passing that even anarchism cannot avoid all teleology.)

The conservative preference is for commitment and engagement: the Utopian, Marxist, or existential radical begins in detachment, but annuls this detachment in favour of a new commitment. The end of commitment and engagement is the community: the end of detachment, then, is clearly the individual. This is not however an antithesis: nobody ought to be a mere creature of a community, like an insect; nobody can be a pure individual detached from his society. I spoke earlier of the vogue for certain words which seem for a time to have a magical significance. Twenty years ago one such word was 'maturity', now out of fashion for obvious reasons. It does seem to me to have some meaning, if not a magical one. The child, and the adolescent in a different way, oscillates between loyalty to the community of his contemporaries and moods of rebelliousness and introversion. As one matures, one's social mask becomes more difficult to remove, and one becomes resigned to a continuous social role. But that very process of adjusting to society is what makes the genuine individual possible. The barriers designed to protect the individual from encroachment from without have to dissolve before he can realize that he is not a real individual until his energy flows freely into his social relations. What is true of personal life is true of society. Primitive societies are rigidly ritualized ones; only the mature society permits the genuine individual to emerge. By doing so it does not fall apart: it merely transfers more of its order from external compulsion to internal discipline, from reflex response to the habit of learning. The artist, too, often begins as a member of a school, issuing manifestoes and the like, but tends to draw away from such affiliations as he finds his own style. Yet his growing individuality is also a measure of his social acceptance.

If we take a second look at our greatest Utopians, Plato and

More, we notice that Socrates in the *Republic* is not concerned about setting up his ideal state anywhere: what he is concerned about is the analogy between his ideal state and the structure of the wise man's mind, with its reason, will, and desire corresponding to the philosopher-king, soldiers, and artisans of the political myth. The ideal state exists, so far as we know, only in such minds, which will obey its laws whatever society they are actually living in. Similarly, More calls his ideal state Utopia, meaning nowhere. Hythloday (the 'babbler'), who has been to Nowhere, has returned a revolutionary communist, convinced that nothing can be done with Europe until it has been destroyed and a replica of the Utopia set up in its place. But More himself, to whom the story is being told, suggests using the knowledge of Utopia rather as a means of bringing about an improvement in European society from within. Plato and More realize that while the wise man's mind is rigidly disciplined, and while the mature state is ordered, we cannot take the analogy between the disciplined mind and the disciplined state too literally. For Plato certainly, and for More probably, the wise man's mind is a ruthless dictatorship of reason over appetite, achieved by control of the will. When we translate this into its social equivalents of a philosopher-king ruling workers by storm troopers (not 'guardians', as in Jowett, but 'guards'), we get the most frightful tyranny. But the real Utopia is an individual goal, of which the disciplined society is an allegory. The reason for the allegory is that the Utopian ideal points beyond the individual to a condition in which, as in Kant's kingdom of ends, society and individual are no longer in conflict, but have become different aspects of the same human body.

Not only does contemporary radicalism include separatist movements, but it is itself intensely separatist in feeling, and hence the question of where one stops separating becomes central. One feels that the more extreme radicals of our time are simply individualists. The more strident the anarchist slogan (e.g.: 'Let's have a revolution first and find out why later'), the more clearly the individualistic basis of its attitude appears, and the more obviously the Utopian attitude is a projection of it. In the Utopianism of Plato and More the traditional authoritarian structure of society was treated as an allegory of the dictatorship of reason in the wise man's mind. We do not now think of the wise man's mind as a dictatorship of reason: in fact we do not think about the wise man's mind at all. We think rather, in Freudian terms, of a mind in which a principle of normality and balance is fighting for its life against a thundering herd of chaotic impulses, which cannot be simply suppressed but must be frequently indulged and humoured, always allowed to have their say however silly or infantile it may be. In short, we think of the mind as a participating democracy: necessary to live with, yet cumbersome, exasperating, and not an ideal but a process. In such an analogy there is no place for the inner-directed person who resists society until death, like Socrates, or More himself: society is divided and the 'individual', despite the etymology of the word, self-divided.

In this process the refusal of all loyalty and authority, the attempt of the individual to assert himself against his whole social context, is one such infantile impulse, to be listened to and ignored. The mature individual, who has come to some working arrangement with his society, is looking rather for a loyalty which is coherent and objective enough to create a community, but commands an authority that fulfils and does not diminish the individual. Such a conception of authority is the kind of authority that education embodies: the authority of logic and reason, of demonstrable and repeatable experiment, of established fact, of compelling imagination. Formerly, the sources of loyalty and authority were the social institutions which formed the civilized context of individual life; but these institutions have really been projected from the total body of reason and imagination represented by the arts and sciences. In our age the mortality of social institutions is what impresses us, and when they can no longer command genuine loyalty or authority, we can only return to their source. Further, when we take a third look at the greatest writers on the social contract and the Utopia, Plato, More, Locke, Rousseau, we begin to suspect that they are not really writing about contracts or Utopias at all, but about the theory of education. Perhaps the social contract and the ideal state are also projections, into the past and the future respectively, of a source of social authority that sits in the middle of our society, and which I shall call the educational contract.

By the educational contract I mean the process by which the arts and sciences, and their methods of logic, experiment, amassing of evidence, and imaginative presentation, actually operate as a source of authority in society. The authority of the social contract is a *de facto* authority: it exists and it may be rationalized, but it lacks a genuinely ideal dimension, and thereby keeps social ideals in an empty world of wish or hope. Conservatives cluster around *de facto* authority and radicals around ideals, but as long as they are kept apart, the revolutionary argument, that the Utopian spirit can only gather force on its side and destroy the existing contract, seems unanswerable. The educational contract makes it possible for both sides to submit their social attitudes to a tribunal that not only respects but includes them both. What is needed is a free authority, something coherent enough to create a community, but not an authority in the sense of applying external compulsion.

This conception of an educational contract was the main contribution made by the great development of educational theory in nineteenth-century England. It is the area of free thought and discussion which is at the centre of John Stuart Mill's view of liberty, and which is thought of as a kind of intellectual counterpart of Parliament. It differs from Parliament, for Mill, in that the liberals can never have a majority, which is why democracy has to function as an illogical but deeply humane combination of majority rule and minority right. In Matthew Arnold the educational contract is called culture, and Arnold is explicit about its being the source of genuine authority in society and at the same time operating in a Utopian direction, breaking down the barriers of class conflict and heading in the direction of a classless society. Newman's distinction between useful and liberal knowledge is parallel, when we realize that it is a distinction between two aspects of education, not two kinds of education. All forms of education are at once useful and liberal: they help us to locate ourselves in existing society and they help to develop us as individuals, detached but not withdrawn from that society. Of course Mill's areas of discussion, Arnold's culture, and Newman's liberal knowledge are conceptions far wider than the university, but the university is obviously their engine-room, and their power can last only so long as the university keeps operating. The university, then, is the source of free authority in society, not as an institution, but as the place where the appeal to reason, experiment, evidence, and imagination is continuously going on.

It is on this basis, perhaps, that we can deal with the demand of student activists for relevance in relation to personal as distinct from social life. Using Newman's distinction, there are two aspects to this demand: a utilitarian aspect and a liberal one. The utilitarian one is for subjects of education to conform to what the student thinks to be his present relation to society, so that, for instance, twentieth-century literature would be more relevant than medieval literature. This is, of course, an immature demand, and should be met with massive and uncompromising resistance. In literature, every major writer may be studied in his relation to his own time, or in his relation to the communicative power that makes him relevant to us. To concentrate solely on the latter distorts him by translating him entirely into our own modes of thought. When we study him in relation to his own time we are led into a different kind of culture, with unfamiliar assumptions, beliefs, and values. But contact with these is what expands our own view of human possibilities, and it is what is irrelevant, in the narrow sense, about what we study that is the liberalizing element in it. The same principle enabled the classical training of humanism, from the sixteenth to the nineteenth centuries, to be a far more genuinely liberal education than it is often given credit for being. The study of an essentially alien civilization, even one which was at the historical roots of our own, was probably a much better preparation a century ago for civil service in India than cost accounting or personnel management.

The other conception of relevance needs to be more seriously considered. It rests, in the first place, on a division between two types of academic discipline, often identified with the humanities and the sciences, though not quite coterminous with them. The word 'scientific' implies among other things a desire to escape from controversy, to rest one's case on evidence, logical and mathematical demonstration or open experiment, which are, as far as possible, beyond the reach of the kind of argument that attacks the validity of its postulates. The assumption is that while what is true today may be insufficiently true tomorrow, still anything that has ever been true—really true, not just believed—will always be continuous with whatever is going to be true. But there are other subjects which deal, not with the world around man (the sciences), but with the world that man is trying to create. These subjects can never escape from controversy or radical questioning, because existential values are built into them. I should call them the mythological subjects: they include large areas of history, political theory, religion, philosophy, psychology, anthropology, and sociology, and the key to them is literature, the laboratory of myths. It is these subjects with which student activism today is largely concerned. The sciences are to a degree impersonal, but the mythological subjects have to be more personally taught. There is always something of Mark Hopkins and the log about them, whereas the sciences can never dispense with complicated apparatus, and have nothing to do with any logs that do not roll.

We have to start again with the decline of the sense of continuity and teleology, already mentioned. Knowledge is, of course, and always must be, continuous and structured. A generation ago, this feature of knowledge was taken for granted, and the continuity of the university was accepted, even by the most radical, as a part of the general continuity of human existence. Much student unrest today springs from what is actually a very ancient conception, though not expressed now, so far as I know, in its traditional terms: the superiority of wisdom to knowledge. Knowledge is knowledge *of* something: wisdom is a sense of the potential rather than the actual, a practical knowledge ready to meet whatever eventualities may occur, rather than a specific knowledge of this or that subject. Formerly, wisdom was associated with seniority, it being assumed that experience carried with it a residual continuity which gave older people a fuller perspective. Or, as Yeats says, carrying the same principle one logical step further: 'Wisdom is the property of the dead.' The loss of belief in any form of continuity has led to a feeling of the necessity of breaking through the habits of knowledge. What many students today want is some guidance in how to deal with their own sense of the discontinuity in experience. Knowledge for them is propaedeutic: one needs only the minimum of knowledge that will introduce one to the great existential issues. After the three R's, the three A's: anxiety, alienation, absurdity. Instead of entering into a structure of knowledge, one seeks the higher wisdom through 'unstructured' means, chiefly informal discussion. In this quest the word 'dialogue' has acquired a portentous verbal magic, like the ninety-nine names of God.

This movement began with the impatience of students with instructors who regarded their teaching as a second-rate activity and an obstacle to research. As research is largely a matter of specialization, this meant that the instructor who was bored by his teaching was really attaching social status to his ignorance rather than to his knowledge. The feeling that the quest for the esoteric needs to be pulled down periodically into the ordinary area of communication was undoubtedly normal and healthy, and throws a very different light on what Sir Charles Snow, in his account of the two cultures, stigmatized as the 'Luddite' attitude of the humanities. Humanists have to be Luddites to some extent, but what they are breaking are sometimes not machines but the cells of specialization that are walled in from the human community.

But as the student protest has gone on, it has tended to take an anti-intellectual form, to become, in its most extreme versions, a repudiation of the educational contract itself, a refusal to appeal to reason or experience or history or anything except emotional reflex. In its anti-intellectual form it joins on, naturally, to the anti-intellectualism of the past. Fifty years ago we had Stephen Leacock and his recipe for starting a university with informal discussions among students, going out to 'hire a few professors' when he got around to it. This in turn reflected the old Oxbridge mystique of the commonroom, the myth of the Sitting Bull, the rationalization of the fact that for an ascendant class, as such, the point of a university education was in its social contacts rather than in its intellectual training. Its reappearance in our day is part of the general confusion among students about whether they want to be a privileged class or an intellectual proletariat.

What seems not to have been noticed is the fact that there is really no such thing as 'dialogue'. Just as some children try to behave like the heroes and heroines in the stories they read, so 'dialogue' is a literary convention taken to be a fact of life. The literary convention comes from Plato, and we notice how clearly aware Plato is of the fact that unstructured discussion is a collection of solipsistic monologues. The etymology of the word symposium points to the fact that the presence of liquor is necessary to make the members of such a group believe in their own wit. Nothing *happens* in Plato until one person, generally Socrates, assumes control of the argument and the contributions of the others are largely reduced to punctuation. This means, not that dialogue has turned into monologue or democracy into dictatorship, but that Socrates has discovered a dialectic, and has committed himself to following it wherever it may lead. From there on, Socrates and his listeners are united in a common vision of something which is supreme over both.

Education can take place only where there is communication, which means the conveying of information from A to B, or a discussion united by the presence of a specific subject. Such discussion is educational in proportion as it is structured. This takes us back to the principle that everything connected with the university, with education, and with knowledge, must be structured and continuous. Until this is grasped, there can be no question of 'learning to think for oneself'. In education one cannot think at random. However imaginative we may be, and however hard we try to remove our censors and inhibitions, thinking is an acquired habit founded on practice, like playing the piano. How well we do it depends on how much of it we have done, and it is never autonomous. We do not start to think about a subject: we enter into a body of thought and try to add to it. It is only out of a long discipline in continuous and structured thinking, whether in the university, in a profession, or in the experience of life, that any genuine wisdom can emerge. The fox in Aesop was wiser than he knew: grapes prematurely snatched from the highest branches really are sour.

What is it, then, that the more restless and impatient students of our time are trying to break through their university training to get? I suggested earlier that they are seeking guidance to the existential questions which have largely overwhelmed what confidence they ever had in the discipline of thought. In other words, their quest is a religious one, and they are looking for answers to religious questions that the university, *qua* university, cannot answer. I do not mean by this that such students should be sent to the churches: the number of people there who can deal with their questions is no greater than it is in the universities, and they start from postulates that relatively few students accept. The scholar can only deal with these questions as a person, not as a scholar, but no one who would turn away a serious student on the ground that these questions were out of his field deserves the title of teacher. The professor in our day is in the same position as the modern doctor who has to try to cure *Weltschmerz* as well as bellyaches. The doctor may long for the simple old days when hysteria and hypochondria were specific disturbances of the womb or the abdomen, but he is not living in those days, and must struggle as best he can with the intangible.

Nothing seems less likely today than a return to the introspection of the Eisenhower decade, yet I cannot help feeling that such a return is just around the corner. Student unrest is not a genuinely social movement: it has no roots in a specific social injustice, as Negro unrest has. Like the beatniks, who have gone, the hippies, who are on the skids, and the LSD cults, which are breaking up, student unrest is not so much social as an aggregate of individual bewilderments, frustrations, disillusionments, and egotisms. It takes patience to grant students everything that can be granted in the way of representation on decision-making bodies which are restructuring the curriculum, and to look with a friendly eye on the founding of 'free' universities, which, as just said, are really religious organizations. The reward of the patience is that students soon come to realize that these things are not what they want, and that, after every possible effort to climb over the walls has failed, there is no avenue of real escape except the open door in front of them.

The Renaissance of Books

I suppose one may spend one's whole life with books, without thinking particularly about the different kinds of emotional impact that books may have, not only because of what they are, but because of what they symbolize or dramatize in society. I can trace in my own earlier life several kinds of such symbolic influence. There had been a clergyman in our family, and the bookcases in our house included several shelves of portly theological tomes in black bindings. These were professional books, of course, and their equivalents would have been, and still would be, found in other such homes. But on a child they gave an effect of immense and definitive authority, of summing up the learning and wisdom of the ages. They appealed to that primitive area of response before reading was a general skill in society, when "gramarye" meant magic, when there were few Prosperos and many Calibans to say of them:

> remember
> First to possess his books; for without them
> He's but a sot, as I am, nor hath not
> One spirit to command. . . . Burn but his books.

And yet when I was old enough to begin to try to use these books myself, I became aware of another important principle connected with books: the principle of the mortality of knowledge. Apart from two which I am still using, a Cruden's Concordance to the Bible and a Josephus, there was hardly a statement in any of these volumes which had not become demonstrably false, meaningless, or obsolete. I remember opening a huge commentary on the first page, the introduction to Genesis, and reading there: "Nothing is more certain than that this book was written by Moses." Alas, I already knew that if there was one thing more uncertain than the authorship of Genesis, it was the existence of Moses. The black bindings were appropriate: the books were coffins of dead knowledge. Their impressiveness as physical objects was grotesquely inconsistent with the speed at which scholarship moves, and it was clear that books ought to have a very different sort of appearance if they are to symbolize the fact that genuine knowledge is always in a state of flux.

In the same house there were sets of Scott and Dickens, and sets of lesser writers as well, for in those days even a best-selling novelist with a temporary vogue might achieve a collected edition in twenty volumes. There were also poets—Elizabeth Browning, Longfellow, Whittier—bound up in some repulsive substance that at the least hint of sustained use began to split, crack, and come off on the fingers. Sinclair Lewis in *Main Street* refers to the "unread looking sets" of authors in the homes of Gopher Prairie, and doubtless many such sets were unread. But being read may not have been their only, perhaps not even their primary, social function. I still possess a set of *The World's Best Essays,* bound in red leather and illustrated by steel engraving portraits of the authors. I hesitate to give it away, because it really is an extraordinary collection: I could hardly have believed that so much of Baudelaire, for example, was so available to North American homes around 1910. But the physical conditions of the set make it difficult to read, and almost impossible to use.

I am not trying to characterize the reading habits, or non-reading habits, of an earlier generation: I am trying to illustrate the symbolic impact of certain types of books in middle-class households up to about 1920. As physical objects, such books assumed the role of a cultural monument, representatives of the authority of tradition. They are well evoked in an early poem of T. S. Eliot:

> Upon the glazen shelves kept watch
> Matthew and Waldo, guardians of the faith,
> The army of unalterable law.

However, this poem is also about a girl who smoked and danced the modern dances, implying that even Matthew and Waldo may not have been altogether with it, at least not in that physical form. The word "glazen," meaning, of course, that they were in formally designed bookcases with glass covers, indicates that, whether they were read or not, being looked at when they were not being read was an integral part of their function and value.

I went to Toronto for my university training, and Toronto, in the nineteen-thirties, still had a good deal of the British midland town about it, including a number of second-hand bookshops. Here was a quite different kind of emotional appeal connected with books. I should put this statement in the plural, for many emotions clustered around the second-hand bookshop. One was the emotion of nostalgia, on finding the favorite books of one's earlier life. Alexander Woollcott has an essay about a woman who discovered on a Paris book-stall the identical copy of a book she had possessed as a child: he speaks of this experience as "catching nature in the act of rhyming." Then there was the reflection on the vanity of human wishes, in coming, say, upon a book by an unknown author with a sad little inscription on the fly-leaf presenting it to a friend. More central, of course, was the excitement of the treasure hunt. This could be literal and commercial, the rare exhilaration of carrying out from under the bookseller's nose something that was more valuable than he realized. But that was for experts: as a rule, one was content with the feeling that the book itself might be a hidden treasure, an unlocked word-hoard. This feeling, however often disappointed, is quite as primitive and essential as the impression of magical authority, already mentioned. Such shops have now largely disappeared from Toronto, as from other cities: even the forlorn books that used to go the rounds of church rummage sales have been bought up by librarians of new universities, at least in enough quantity to remove them from the orbit of the book-searcher's interest. The second-hand bookshop however represents something irreplaceable in one's literary experience, and it is bound to revive sooner or later, if only as an aspect of the junk-antique business.

I was in London, on my way to Oxford as a student, when Penguins began to appear. At that time they were sixpence apiece, and could be got out of slot machines. They were aggressively advertised, at least for British mores at that time: I remember an advertisement contrasting a new Penguin with a battered and dog-eared copy of a book from a public library, with the caption: "You don't know who had it last." I did realize that this reflection on public libraries had some social significance, the public libraries being so major an influence on the book market throughout the nineteenth century, able to exert collateral forms of pressure like censorship. But I did not realize that I was seeing the birth of something like a revolution. After all, why should it have been one? Why should putting out books in brightly colored soft covers, with the pages glued instead of sewn, be an important cultural change? It is surely not comparable with other physical changes in the history of the verbal arts, such as the change from scroll to codex around the beginning of the Christian era, to say nothing of the invention of the printing press itself.

The reason, I think, is once again the fact that books are significant not only for what they are but for what they dramatize or symbolize in society by their appearance. The paperback was partly a reaction to the book as cultural monument, and by being that it helped to dramatize the importance of the book as an intellectual tool. It suggested a higher degree of expendability, and so acknowledged the mutability of scholarship and literary taste. The psychological effect of studying such a work as Hegel's *Phenomenology of Mind* in paperback seems to me to be quite different from studying the same book in a hard cover. And by dramatizing the book as intellectual tool, the paperback also dramatized the extraordinary effectiveness of the book, the fact that, familiar and unobtrusive as it is, the book is one of the most efficient technological instruments ever developed in human history.

There are signs, naturally enough, that the paperback vogue is waning and that it will come to dominate the book world less exclusively in the future. One has to see it in its proper context, as one of several revolutions in verbal media. Others are the development of photocopying and the immense growth of facsimile reprints: I should add to this also what seems to me to be an unprecedented increase in the volume and range of translation. All these are part of the same cultural expansion that has produced reproductions in paintings and recordings of music, and like them they have greatly expanded the range of possible influence on contemporary culture. Just as any freshman in a conservatory may learn from records more about pre-Mozartian music than Mozart himself ever knew, so any student in a small college may have access, potentially, to a range of materials formerly available only in the biggest libraries. Even when books are produced in the scale and size of the cultural monument, they show the effects of these revolutions. An example is the type of book usually called, rather deprecatingly, the coffee-table book. This is normally a collection of photographs of pictures or buildings, and is designed, not to stand on shelves with an army of unalterable law, but to lie down enticingly and alone, like a mistress.

Paperbacks and photocopied materials reflect also a major change in the academic perspective. As an undergraduate I was taught philosophy by G. S. Brett, a scholar greatly admired by his students, and most deservedly so, for his vast learning. He was the author of a *History of Psychology,* still a standard work on the subject; he had no degree except an Oxford M.A., and was Dean of the Graduate School, a task he took with little seriousness because he thought graduate research was mostly a lot of nonsense. He represented a generation of scholars whose life work was expressed by a single major book, or a very restricted canon of such books. But even in his last teaching years, the cataract of papers, off-prints, and other manifestations of the publish-or-perish fetish in academic life had begun, as a part of the cultural change of which the paperback and the reprint are other symbols. Philosophers like A.J. Ayer began mounting attacks on metaphysics, partly, I think, because metaphysics represented the structural aspect of philosophy, the aspect which made large books possible. In their wake came the "productive scholars" of a new school, who tended to be suspicious of all books that were not collections of brief papers. Robert Musil, in *The Man Without Qualities*, surveys the situation with his usual double-edged irony:

> Philosophers are violent and aggressive persons who, having no army at their disposal, bring the world into subjection to themselves by means of locking it up in a system. Probably that is also the reason why there have been great philosophic minds in times of tyranny, whereas times of advanced civilization and democracy do not succeed in producing a convincing philosophy, at least so far as one can judge from the lamentations one commonly hears on the subject. That is why nowadays there is a terrifying amount of philosophizing done in small slices. . . . There is, on the other hand, a definite mistrust of philosophy in large chunks, which is simply considered impossible.

I have always been very touched by the preface to the third and last volume of Paul Tillich's *Systematic Theology*. This was a work on which Tillich had spent many years, because, he says, he had always wanted to write a systematic theology. I can think of no better reason for writing anything, but the ambition itself was typical of a certain period of culture. By the time he reached his last volume the fashion in theology had changed, the younger intellectuals had turned to much more simplistic versions of existentialism than the one that he held, and he was being told on all sides that the phrase "systematic theology" no longer made any sense, in fact was a contradiction in terms.

Similar changes naturally affected literature itself, especially poetry, which up to about 1950 symbolized a good deal of cultural authority whether it was read or not. When we speak of such nineteenth-century poets as Longfellow as "popular," we are using the term in a somewhat retrospective sense: Longfellow was widely read, but he was also a scholarly poet, and most of those who read him felt that they were engaging in a fairly high-brow enterprise. Even writers of inspirational doggerel might be regarded, on a popular level, with the kind of awe implied in another phrase from Lewis' *Main Street:* "they say he writes real poetry." The great poets of the first half of this century—Eliot, Yeats, Pound—had the somewhat aloof authority conferred by their erudition, even though they often felt the pull of the desire to be genuinely popular. We have the Eliot of Sanskrit quotations and the Eliot of practical cats; we have the Yeats of Rosicrucian symbolism and the Yeats of the luminously simple ballads in the *Last Poems.* Allen Ginsberg's *Howl* is usually taken as the turning point towards a neo-Romantic poetry which has been popular in a way hardly known to previous generations. Much of this poetry has turned back to the primitive oral tradition of folk song, with the formulaic units, topical allusions, musical accompaniment, and public presentation that go with that tradition.

The changes in prose fiction are even more significant from our present point of view. In Canada, as in many other communities, there lingered for a long time the myth of "the great Canadian novel," the hope that somebody some day would produce a novel in Canada as monumental as *War and Peace.* The word "the" implies that whoever did it would do it only once, but, even so, the achievement would have a redemptive force for the whole Canadian community: the authority of such a work would confer authority on the society that produced it. This means, among other things, that a monumental novel reflects a relatively coherent social order, as the Victorian three-decker, the book one could live inside of, manifested the prestige of Victorian society. Even Tolstoy's Russia, despite our hindsight, afforded a good deal of stability to the novelist of this kind. Hence the most highly regarded novels, in the period up to say 1940, were predominantly realistic, for realism had the dignity and the moral force that goes with the ability to study and interpret a civilization. Such realism was central to what F. R. Leavis calls "the great tradition," which he studies, in a book with that title, in George Eliot, Joseph Conrad, and Henry James.

However, when empires start building walls around themselves it is a sign that their power is declining, and "the great tradition" is now not much more than a tradition. Tolkien's *Lord of the Rings* came out in the mid-fifties, to the accompaniment of a chorus of readers saying "of course I can't read fantasy," usually with an air of conscious virtue. The success of Tolkien's book, however, indicated a change of taste parallel to the post-Ginsberg change in poetry, towards the romantic, the fantastic, and the mythopoeic. Science fiction, which is really a form of philosophical romance, has taken on a new importance, and the mythical elements in Pynchon or Vonnegut do not revolve around a realistic center, as they do in *Ulysses.* Romance, fantasy, and mythopoeia are the inescapable forms for a society which no longer believes in its own permanence or continuity. I know several writers who acquired early in life an intense desire to be novelists of the "great tradition" type: they are dedicated and highly intelligent people, but they find heart-breaking difficulties in getting published, and when they are published suffer from a feeling that the parade is now going down some other street.

One curious feature of the realistic development of prose fiction, from *Don Quixote* down to the last generation, is that it so frequently took the form of a parody of romance formulas. This is explicit in *Don Quixote* itself, but many other novels, *Joseph Andrews, Northanger Abbey, The Eustace Diamonds,* even *Waverley,* began as parodies of well known types of romance. In Jane Austen's other novels the realistic study of character and setting is related, somewhat quizzically, to a romantic story with a conventional happy ending, and in the later novels of Dickens a great pageant of vividly "lifelike" characters move within a melodramatic plot so incongruous with them as to be almost an anti-narrative. We notice that characters confused by romantic values —Emma Bovary, Lord Jim, Anna Karenina, Dorothea Brooke, Isabel Archer—often occupy the central place in a realistic narrative. There seems something inherently paradoxical about the structure of a genre of literature that avowedly imitates life. The reason is not really so hard to grasp. Life has no shape; literature has. A realistic story must get its shape from somewhere, and ultimately the only place it can get it from is romance, a form of fiction in which the story is told for its own sake.

The change of taste in favor of the romantic and mythopoeic in fiction, therefore, is parallel to the movement away from representation in painting. Fantasy presents the reader with the kind of situations that occur only in stories: it belongs to a conception of literature as a self-contained and autonomous art. But literature, as long as it uses words, can never be as purely abstract as painting or music, and a more far-reaching principle still is involved. Modern criticism, as such, begins with Oscar Wilde's dialogue, *The Decay of Lying,* the main object of which is to point out the shortcomings of any kind of literature that accepts the obligation to imitate "nature," or "real life." The speakers in Wilde refer to Charles Reade, who wrote one outstanding romance, *The Cloister and the Hearth,* followed by a number of inferior realistic stories, as an example of the fact that the popular notion of the greater weight and dignity of realism can often mislead a writer. They also say that *Romola* is a better novel than *Daniel Deronda,* not a statement that many admirers of George Eliot would accept, but again expressing a preference for romance over realism. Literature, we are told, does not necessarily gain in seriousness or value when it imitates nature or real life, but nature and real life do gain in seriousness or value when they imitate literature, that is, when something like a literary shape can be discerned in their chaotic phenomena. Wilde's argument is presented as a good-humored paradox, but for us to go on thinking of it as one is living in the past: it expresses a simple truth reflected in many aspects of our cultural situation, especially from the mid-fifties to our own day.

The principle of life imitating literature explains why the growth of fantasy and mythopoeia in fiction is accompanied by such works as Truman Capote's *In Cold Blood* and Norman Mailer's *Armies of the Night,* which are not realistic fiction but are documentary reports on events that seem to have in themselves a narrative shape. In some films the boundary line between imaginative artifact and documentary is even more difficult to find, the former often being disguised as the latter. This development is important in the growth of the communication media that have the social function of stabilizing the non-reading public. The non-reading public includes, of course, the reading public whenever it is not reading. But it also includes the very large group of people who cannot get a sufficiently vivid stimulus from the printed word to rely much on it for their imaginative participation in society. This group has finally settled mainly on television, to which films, radio, and picture magazines have all become subordinated. All these media are concerned with news and commentary as well as entertainment, and the principle of life imitating literature is present in both aspects.

Our waking existence is a continuum: sleep and dreams have beginnings and ends, but when we wake up again we rejoin the continuum. Our lives also begin and end with birth and death, but birth and death, both of which are often described in terms of sleep or dream, respectively attach us to and drop us off the unending continuum of the living, the dead, and the unborn, in Edmund Burke's phrase. The function of the news media is to present a verbal imitation of this continuum, and television is the most efficient of all the media at doing so. Ritual is one means of keeping the continuum punctuated: we dramatize the stages when we join it or leave it or make a major change in our relation to it. News, in the stricter sense, is whatever breaks into the continuum, which is why so much news consists of disaster, and why all disaster is news. But besides the images of breaking, air crashes and the like, there are images of confrontation. Intellectual news, or the discussion of "issues," consists very largely of a polarizing of attitudes, for and against, which is why news media are so fascinated by the conception of the "controversial." In the "issue" the continuum appears to stop for an instant and focus on a simultaneous vertical contrasting of opposed attitudes.

Television is consequently most effective when it presents such rituals as public weddings and funerals, or the ritualized confrontations of football and hockey games, and it presents "issues" in the same polarized way. Such direct pro-and-con opposition, with all neutral or middle ground eliminated, is also what the revolutionary aims at: the revolutionary strives for situations in which everyone opposed to his group can be equally characterized as "counter-revolutionary." Hence the treatment of issues in democratic mass media consists very largely of a kind of unconscious and undirected revolutionary strategy. The time when the impact of television really hit American society, in the later sixties, produced exactly this kind of undirected revolutionary confrontation, in student demonstrations and the like, which achieved practically nothing of any real social importance and stopped as suddenly as it began.

This combination of ritual, game, and polarized issue brings into television a quality of literary imitation, a "story line" with a beginning, a prescribed direction, and a conclusion. The three elements are most completely merged in the great public trial or investigation scenes, where ritual, game, and the polarizing dialectic of legal prosecution and defence are all most fully employed. The Watergate sequence belongs to the same quasi-literary genre as the Joseph McCarthy hearings of the fifties: evidently a modern society needs a continuous supply of such dramas if the imitation of literature by life is to be kept at its most effective pitch. And unless life takes on something of the shaped quality of a literary structure it will not be deeply interesting to watch. For, as indicated above, it is by our imaginations, the mental response we make to literature, that we primarily participate in society.

By itself, of course, this imitation of literature by the news media could become a very sinister tendency. There is no difference between Watergate and the Stalin purge-trials of the thirties so far as the genre being employed is concerned. Besides, moral issues are not related to literature in the same way that they are related to actual life. We ask an actor to put on a good show, not to tell the truth, and when, say, a senator remarks approvingly that the President was very "believable" in his last interview, he reflects the confusion of standards. Such a confusion returns us to the Machiavellian principle of pure appearance, the basis of what we now call propaganda. It is not important that the prince should be virtuous; it is important only that he should seem so. Such an attitude is imaginative in a perverted sense. Literature is phenomenal: it presents reality entirely through appearance, but in "real life" what is "real" is normally hidden or disguised by the appearance. In trying to get out of the bind that this imitation of literature by life gets us into, we have to return to the book, or at least to the verbal documents of which books form a major part.

Newspapers and the electronic media have carried much further a tendency which was begun by the book: the tendency to break down the distinction between private and social experience. It always was true that poetry, for example, could never become the exclusive possession of one person in the way that an easel painting could be. Wherever there is a literature, there is a community of shared imaginative experience; and yet, wherever there are books, there is the opposite tendency of individualizing the audience. When society still contained a number of illiterates, or habitual non-readers, a village community, say, would form around a man who could read aloud to them the news, or what passed for news, and current literature. A certain amount of Richardson in the eighteenth century, even of Dickens in the nineteenth, was transmitted in this way. But of course in proportion as the ability to read increased, the audience of hearers decreased. In Elizabethan times there were several popular theatres, but the fateful action taken by Ben Jonson in 1616, of publishing his plays in a book, and so suggesting that one could stay home to read the play instead of risking catching the plague in an audience, began an erosion of the public theatre that by Victorian times had threatened to remove drama from serious literature altogether. Similarly with religion: although Protestants insisted on public attendance at church as strongly as Catholics, their simultaneous insistence on the supreme authority of a sacred book did much to advance the decay of church attendance which is still with us. The concert hall has met similar difficulties with the recording of music. In the age of television it is a common experience to attend a public function and then go home to get on television a more comprehensive and comprehensible view of what one has just been engaged in. So what is the comparative value of the two experiences?

Traditionally, the individual is thought of as having a primary duty to support the institutions of society. The permanence and continuity of church, court, lawcourt, political party, classroom, even, in lesser degree, of theatre and concert hall and museum, give dignity and importance to the individual's life by representing something older and longer lasting than he is. Hence the feeling of obligation about many forms of public attendance. The kind of development we have been tracing, from the earliest books to television, reverses this tendency by increasing the range of private life. It is significant again that the impact of television in the late sixties carried with it a cult of nearly anarchic individualism. Yet the individual, qua individual, can hardly get much beyond the spectacular perspective on public life which makes it potentially a series of theatrical events. There must be some other form of activity that enables us to get closer to what underlies these spectacular representations.

The permanence of social institutions is often symbolized by public monuments, buildings, statues and the like, built for the astonishment of posterity out of stone or metal. There is of course a lurking irony in such productions of the kind crystallized in Shelley's "Ozymandias" sonnet: anything that can be set up can be knocked down, and doubtless will be sooner or later. The history of verbal documents is rather different, even though they too can become monumental, as we saw. There is a dramatic episode in the Book of Jeremiah, in the Old Testament, where Jeremiah's secretary Jehudi is reading from the prophet's scroll, to the king, a prophecy consisting largely of denunciations of the royal policy. At the end of every paragraph or so the exasperated king cuts off the read portion of the scroll with a knife and throws it into the fire. This must have been a papyrus scroll: parchment or vellum, besides being probably beyond the prophet's financial means, would have been tough enough to spoil the king's gesture. The king's palace disappeared totally in a few years, but the Book of Jeremiah, entrusted to the most fragile and combustible substance produced in the ancient world, remains in reasonably good shape. The vitality of words written on papyrus, as compared with the hugest monuments of perennial brass, has perhaps some analogy to the fact that life, precarious and easily snuffed out as it is, is still at least as strong a force as death.

In our own civilization, as explained earlier, information changes quickly and needs more fluid media, and paperbacks, talked and taped books, interview books, print-outs, microfiche, and documents coded for feeding into computers are all parts of the result. So are the great mountains of photocopied papers, which among other things have thrown the copyright law into a complete chaos. But by doing so, photocopied materials have illustrated the importance of a moral issue connected with the verbal arts which is even more important than copyright.

In a primitive society, where there is no general dissemination of the ability to read or write, the poet becomes the teacher of the community. The reason is that a society without writing depends a great deal on memory, and the poet is better able to remember than other men because he can hitch things into verse, and verse is easier to remember than any prose arrangement of words. In such a society there is of course no sense of the poet's having exclusive possession of his material, any more than any other teacher would have. Later, the conception of literature develops as a body of great traditional themes held in common. Gradually literature became assimilated to the conditions of the capitalistic market: the individual author's work had to be sufficiently distinct for him to patent it and prevent others from appropriating it. The right of an individual author to benefit from the marketing of his work is of course an unquestioned moral principle, and is likely to remain one. Still, copyright, or the private possession of literary work for the purposes of making a living from it, is not the primary moral principle connected with literature, or the verbal arts generally. That primary principle is rather the principle of public access to the work.

I think once more of the Old Testament. We are told that during the repairing of the Temple in Jerusalem, a "book of the law" was discovered and brought to King Josiah:

> And when the king heard the words of the book of the law, he rent his clothes. And the king commanded . . . saying, Go ye, inquire of the Lord for me, and for the people, and for all Judah, concerning the words of this book that is found; for great is the wrath of the Lord that is kindled against us, because our fathers have not hearkened unto the words of this book.

What is significant here is the king's conviction that it was a matter of the utmost importance for the community as a whole to know what was in a written document. Naturally the first categories of verbal documents that need to be publicly known are the laws, so it is not surprising that a book of the law should first be open to public inspection. Most scholars think that the book thus discovered was, or was closely connected with, the existing book of Deuteronomy, which in the present arrangement of books looks like a supplement to or repetition of the law, as its name indicates. But it seems more likely that Deuteronomy was the kernel of the conception of a sacred book, out of which the whole Bible eventually grew. What was new was the feeling that this sacred book should be known by the whole community instead of being locked away among temple records. We see history in the process of turning a corner here, making a decisive and permanent change in human conditions. In such an event as the Protestant Reformation, two thousand years later, we can see how important still for the future was the insistence on the general accessibility of the acknowledged sacred book.

This leads to a much more far-ranging general principle, one that has been expounded by the Canadian scholar Harold A. Innis in such works as *The Bias of Communication.* Control of communications is one of the primary aims of an ascendant class: whatever tends toward democracy must have, as one of its primary aims, the openness and sharing of communications.

This principle goes along with another one, that the more fully a communications medium is concentrated on the passing show, on recording events as they occur, the more it tends to become a one-way street of messages in which the ordinary consumer has a passive role. In our day radio and television tend naturally to become monologues of this kind, despite the efforts made through cable and open-line programmes to give the consumer a chance to talk back to his set. The electronic media are in any case so set up that, given a revolutionary situation, it is relatively easy for the group in power to seize control of them. Wherever there are dictatorships, the radio is the main instrument of expression: it is, in fact, highly significant that everything we regard as anti-democratic should be summed up by the word "dictator," that is, an uninterrupted speaker, who can expatiate for five hours on the glories of his regime and have the same speech bellowing from every street corner. Television is sometimes thought to be a "cooler" medium, but it isn't: we may compare the role of the "telescreen" in Orwell's *1984*. In the democracies, of course, radio and television reflect the economic anxieties of selling and making profits through consumer goods rather than the political anxieties of censorship and thought control, but the cultural consequences have many parallels. Newspapers also become one-way streets in proportion to their preoccupation with headlines and deadlines: however, the competition of television is now forcing them to become something more like journals of opinion. Even *Time*, the most dictatorial of all journals, was recently startled by Watergate into producing an editorial.

In this situation it seems clear that, however important it may be to have a "free press" and extend the principle of that freedom to radio and television as well, the main battles of freedom are not fought on the news front. They are fought further back, in an area where issues have acquired some temporal dimension and some historical context. If it were really true, as McLuhan and others have urged, that print is a "linear" medium, carrying the eye forward and hypnotizing all responses except the purely visual one of reading, there would be no difference between print and any other medium. But this thesis confuses the reading process with the consulting process, and overlooks the fact that print has a unique power of staying around to be read again, presenting, with unparalleled patience, the same words again however often it is consulted. It is therefore public access to printed and written documents that is the primary safeguard of an open society. We notice how drastic the alteration of the degree of freedom in society is when we are at war and a large group of documents have to be treated as "top secret," thereby inculcating a facile habit of secrecy which carries on into peacetime. We said earlier that there is no difference between Watergate and the Stalin purge-trials of the thirties so far as the genre is concerned: open inspection of the relevant documents is one of the major moral distinctions between them, one quite as important as the physical treatment of the witnesses.

The relevant documents are, of course, difficult to interpret, and in raw form are as esoteric to most people as though they were locked up. We are brought back to the book, more particularly the book which is an expository treatise, as the ordinary means of expressing and understanding the general conflict of opinion in society, so far as that opinion is not simply a snap response to current events but a sustained and supported argument. The written expository treatise looks at first sight like a dictatorial monologue, but this is a misunderstanding. Nothing of the hypnotic rhetoric of speech to a present audience is left in it: the author is forced, by the nature of his medium, to put all his cards on the table, to take his reader into his confidence, to appeal to nothing but the evidence of the argument itself. And so, however often it may fail in meeting the standards prescribed by its own physical shape, the expository or thesis-book remains the normal unit of impersonal social vision, and the normal medium by which communication draws us together into a community. Now that society, after some years of reeling from the impact of television, is beginning to bring it under control, we can see more clearly that the book is the chief technological device that makes democracy and the open society continuously possible.

The Times of The Signs

To say the solar chariot is junk

Is not a variation but an end.
Yet to speak of the whole world as metaphor
Is still to stick to the contents of the mind

And the desire to believe in a metaphor.

[WALLACE STEVENS: *The Pure Good of Theory*]

The seventy years of the life of Copernicus were, as we all know, the time when the Middle Ages ended and the modern world came into being. Educated men had known for many centuries that the earth was a sphere, and that one could get to the east by sailing to the west. Perhaps a jealous God would see to it that one got to hell instead, as he did Ulysses in Dante: when there is no reason for crossing the Atlantic, there are any number of reasons for not doing so. But with the voyages of Columbus, da Gama and Magellan, humanity as a whole began to realize that the earth was round, and to order their lives on that assumption. Up till then, the centre of the world had been, as the word itself makes obvious, the Mediterranean, and the people who sat like frogs around a pool, in Plato's phrase, on the shores of the sea in the middle of the earth. But after 1492 the nations on the Atlantic sea-board began to realize that it was they who were now in the middle of the world.

In an age which went through this gigantic spatial displacement, it was appropriate that someone should put forward the thesis that the earth is not the unmoved centre of the universe, but one of the planets or wandering stars, and that we must look for another centre for the earth. In the age of Humanism and the increased authority of ancient writers, it was also appropriate that someone should revive the ancient Greek doctrine, propounded by Aristarchus of Samos in the third century B.C., that the earth went round the sun. So when Copernicus published a tentative summary of his views, the *Little Commentary (Commentariolus)*, he attracted a good deal of friendly attention, including the encouragement of the Pope. But as the Reformation began to split Christendom down the middle, the mood changed, and Copernicus changed with it. His later book, *On the Revolutions of the Heavenly Bodies,* which appeared in the year of his death, began with a weaseling preface, not by Copernicus, explaining that it contained only hypotheses to be studied by mathematicians, and that what it said was perhaps not true or even probable, only a device to simplify the calculations. Although Copernicus' central thesis eventually destroyed the old Ptolemaic picture of the world, Copernicus himself clung to the two Ptolemaic principles of circular motion and uniform speed for all heavenly bodies. Hence the book, though its essential idea is a simplifying one, got into bewildering complications, and it has been very little read. The first English translation (a very bad one, apparently) was published in 1952, as part of a relentless search for "Great Books" carried out by a then fashionable programme at the University of Chicago.

So Copernicus had little impact on his own time, and nearly a century had to pass before the work of Kepler and Galileo consolidated his thesis and removed most of the serious objections to it. It is at this point that the first references to Copernicus begin to enter English literature. Most of the references are in a context of utter disbelief: the heliocentric view was not universally accepted in England until Newton's time, two centuries after Copernicus was born. Francis Bacon refers to Copernicus very slightingly, almost contemptuously, as promoting a tremendous hypothesis on very inadequate grounds. Bacon was wrong, but he was wrong for some good reasons. In his *Novum Organum* he enumerates four great fallacies, which he calls "idols", that stand in the way of scientific advance. One, probably the subtlest, of these fallacies is the idol of the theatre, or aesthetic thinking, the desire to impose elegantly symmetrical patterns on an untidy mass of facts, instead of patiently waiting to see what general principles really do emerge from them. Copernicus, for Bacon, was typical of the kind of pseudo-scientific speculator who gets a hunch and rebuilds the universe on the strength of it, making the earth go around the sun only because the mathematics of that situation look nicer. And when we remember that curious preface to Copernicus' book, we can at least see what Bacon means. It may even be true that Copernicus was not primarily an observer of the stars, but primarily a speculative mathematical philosopher.

By that time there were strenuous efforts being made to stop the new philosophy. Bruno was burned alive in 1600, and Copernicus' book placed on the Index in 1616, the year in which the first attempt was made by the Inquisition to silence Galileo. As always happens in revolutionary situations, there was a swarm of revisionists putting forward compromise solutions, such as keeping the earth at the centre but having the other planets revolve around the sun. In the superb "Digression of Air" in the *Anatomy of Melancholy*, Robert Burton, whose tremendous erudition never blunted the edge of his sense of humor, began to suggest that some of the resulting complications had a funny side. He is speaking of an astronomer named Roeslin, who had attacked Copernicus (Burton himself seems to have been, however reluctantly, rather impressed with Copernicus):

> Roeslin censures all, and Ptolemaeus himself as insufficient . . . In his own hypothesis he makes the earth as before the universal centre, the sun to the five upper planets, to the eighth sphere he

> ascribes diurnal motion, eccentrics and epicycles to the seven planets, which hath been formerly exploded; and so, *Dum vitant stulti vitia in contraria currunt,* as a tinker stops one hole and makes two, he corrects them and doth worse himself, reforms some and mars all. In the meantime, the world is tossed in a blanket amongst them, they hoist the earth up and down like a ball, make it stand and go at their pleasures; one saith the sun stands, another he moves; a third comes in, taking them all at rebound, and, lest there should any paradox be wanting, he finds certain spots and clouds in the sun, by the help of glasses . . .

The situation reminds one a little of the various atomic cosmologies in physics during the early part of this century.

A third reference to Copernicus in the English literature of this period is, to my mind, the most deeply significant of all. It occurs in John Donne's anti-Jesuit satire, *Ignatius His Conclave,* where Copernicus clamors for entry into a distinguished place of authority in hell. He says to Lucifer:

> I am he, which pitying thee who wert thrust into the Center of the world, raised both thee, and thy prison, the Earth, up into the Heavens; so as by my means God doth not enjoy his revenge upon thee. The sun, which was an officious spy, and a betrayer of faults, and so thine enemy, I have appointed to go into the lowest part of the world. Shall these gates be open to such as have innovated in small matters? and shall they be shut against me, who have turned the whole frame of the world, and am thereby almost a new Creator?

The full implications of this passage may not have been clear to Donne himself, but it will serve me as a text. The dispute between the geocentric and the heliocentric views of the solar system looks to me, being a literary critic, essentially a collision between two mythologies, two pictures or visions, not of reality, but of man's sense of the meaning of reality in relation to himself. The geocentric or Ptolemaic view had on its side the religious feeling that the moral and natural orders had been made by the same God, that man was the highest development of nature, that

God had died and risen again for man, and that therefore the notion of a plurality of worlds could be dismissed. It was too much to ask anyone to believe that Christ had had to die again to save the inhabitants of the planet Jupiter, much less accept an infinite number of inhabited worlds.

The Ptolemaic view was also supported by the powerful mythical analogy of the macrocosm. Man, the microcosm, was the epitome of the universe: he contained everything that it contained, and hence the universe was really a larger body like that of man. The Ptolemaic universe, with its onion shape and its concentric spheres, nevertheless had a top and a bottom, like the human body. The regular circling of the stars overhead suggested planning, order, intelligence, everything that goes with a human brain; down below was a world of death and corruption leading to hell. And hell had many characteristics of the less highly regarded aspects of the body: there was always a strong smell of sulphur about the devils, and their horns and tails suggested the kind of erotic interest that we should expect to find among such low forms of spirituality.

Further, the macrocosm was finite in both time and space. Just as man lives for only seventy years, so the universe was created to last for seven thousand years, six thousand years of history and a thousand years of millennium, corresponding to the six days of creation and the Sabbath of rest. Creation took place four thousand years before the birth of Christ, who was born in 4 B.C.: therefore the millennium will begin in 1996. Some of you will be around to check up on the statement. As for space, the universe was certainly thought of as vast, and Ptolemy himself had said that the earth was only a point compared to the whole natural order. The phrase is still echoing fifteen centuries later in the Elizabethan poet Thomas Campion:

> Earth's but a point to the world, and a man
> Is but a point to the earth's compared centre;
> Shall then the point of a point be so vain
> As to triumph in a silly point's adventure?

But still the universe was finite, and the finite is always comprehensible, no matter how big.

However, the heliocentric view had some mythological trump cards too. The sun is the source of light, and therefore the symbol of consciousness. And the Renaissance brought with it a new and expanded sense of consciousness, a feeling that consciousness represented something that tore man loose from the lower part of nature and united him with a higher destiny. For such a feeling the centrality of the sun, a much "nobler" object than the earth, was an obvious focus. The earth is rather a symbol of man's fall into nature, and at its centre, according to Dante, is the devil, or more precisely the devil's arse. This heightened sense of consciousness is not necessarily, as is so often said, a new sense of the dignity of the individual. The sun consciousness of Descartes is quite consistent with the absolutism of the Sun King, Louis XIV. It was rather a new sense of aggressiveness, a feeling that man was capable of dominating nature, exploring it and forcing his own logical patterns on it, the higher mechanism of the awareness which knows that it knows.

Of course, it happens to be true that the earth goes around the sun, and not true that the sun goes around the earth. When mythologies collide, it is doubtless an advantage to have the truth, or more of the truth, on one's side. But it is not a clinching advantage. The words "sunrise" and "sunset" are as familiar to us as ever: we "know" that what they describe is really an illusion, but they are metaphorically efficient, and man can live indefinitely with metaphor. It is fascinating to read medical treatises of the pre-Harvey period and see the complete authority and lucidity with which they diagnose diseases in terms of what we should call the metaphor of the four humors. The psychoanalytical treatises of our day are based on hydraulic metaphors of drives and channels and blocks and cathects, and will no doubt look equally quaint in a few years, but they are no less implicitly accepted now. The autonomy of science goes along with its reliance on mathematics, which can apparently penetrate much further into the external world than words can do.

For mythology is not primarily an attempt to picture reality:

it is not a primitive form of science or philosophy, however crude. It is rather an attempt to articulate what is of greatest human concern to the society that produces it. Myths tell us the names, functions, and genealogies of the gods; they explain how certain features in the social structure and organization came to be as they are. They do this mainly by stories or fictions. Mythology is a form of imaginative thinking, and its direct descendant in culture is literature, more particularly fiction, works of literature that tell stories. There is thus also a central place in literature for schematic thinking, an emphasis on design and symmetry for their own sakes. Such pattern-making is also inherited from mythology.

As society develops, however, mythology tends to project itself on the outer world, which means that science, at a certain stage of social development, finds itself imprisoned in a schematic, symmetrical, mythological framework of pseudo-scientific presuppositions. This is Bacon's idol of the theatre, already mentioned. Science cannot proceed further without destroying every trace of this mythological thinking *in its own area.* I emphasize the last four words because there is no reason why mythological thinking should be destroyed in areas where it belongs. Bernard Shaw remarks that if William the Conqueror had been told by a bishop that the moon was seventy-seven miles from the earth, he would have thought that a very proper distance for the moon, seven being a sacred number. This is an excellent example of mythological thinking in a place where it has no business to be. Dante uses all he can get of the science of his own day, and many passages in the *Commedia,* such as the early cantoes of the *Purgatorio,* where Dante and Virgil are looking at a different set of stars on the other side of the earth and discuss what time it would now be in Jerusalem, are pure science fiction. But still Dante's universe was held together by the Scotch tape of symmetrical correspondences, such as the correspondence of the seven planets with the seven metals that they were supposed to engender in the ground. There is not much left of Dante's science today, but the feature that makes his science obsolete is also one of the features that make his poetry as contemporary as it ever was.

Why does a mythology keep such a stranglehold on the scientific impulse, and for so long a time? The simplest answer is that the mythology provides a humanly comprehensible structure, which for most people is far more important than a true or valid structure. It seems self-evident that man and his concerns are at the centre of time and space, and that time and space should be the narrative and setting respectively of a story told by God to instruct man, a story beginning with the Creation and ending with the Last Judgement. Then again, if God made the world, the principles on which he made it would be drawn from human art, the only model for conscious creativity that we know. It is "natural" that there should be seven planets and twelve signs of the Zodiac: after all, our music is based on a diatonic scale of seven tones and a chromatic scale of twelve semitones. This analogy of music, astronomy and mathematics was built into the medieval "quadrivium". If a circle is the central human symbol for eternity, the heavenly bodies must move in circles: why would so conscientious an artist as God have them staggering around in ellipses? This principle, that the fundamental laws of the universe must be aesthetically satisfying, was incorporated into Plato's *Timaeus,* which may well have done more to retard science than any other piece of writing in history:

> Now if so be that this Cosmos is beautiful and its Constructor good, it is plain that he fixed his gaze on the Eternal; but if otherwise (which is an impious supposition), his gaze was on that which has come into existence. But it is clear to everyone that his gaze was on the Eternal; for the Cosmos is the fairest of all that has come into existence, and He the best of all the Causes.

The growth of science however destroys only what is unscientific: mythology has its own sphere and its own function, and what takes place is a separating of the two, not the replacing of one by the other. Dante was able to use the science of his day in his epic poem because the science of his day was still mythological in shape. As the two areas separated, symmetrical patternmaking went underground into the area generally called occult science, the area of alchemy, astrology, kabbalism, and magic. When we look at the sources of nineteenth-century poetry, we find that occultism has had a far more pervasive influence on poetry than actual science has had. The reason is not difficult to understand: occult thought is schematic thought, like the thinking of poetry.

As an example of the gradual separating of poetic and scientific modes of thinking, let us take astrology. Astrology is, like the science of astronomy, a study of the stars, but it studies the stars from a geocentric point of view: it is interested mainly in the "influence" (this word was originally a technical term in astrology) that the movements of the stars have, or are believed to have, on human concerns.

1473. Astrology and astronomy are much the same subject, and most of those who study the stars are interested primarily in astrology.

1573. The situation is not very different, despite Copernicus. There had always been theological reservations about astrology, mainly on the score of an implied fatalism, and these had been increased by the Reformation and Counter-Reformation. But still astrology was generally accepted as a reasonable hypothesis, and in the next generation Kepler was an energetic caster of horoscopes.

1673. This is the age of the Royal Society, and by now most of the star-gazers are interested only in astronomy. The astrologer is becoming a figure of fun in contemporary comedies (e.g., Congreve's *Love for Love*), and Swift's ridicule of the astrologer Partridge (1708) is a turning point in popular acceptance.

1773. With the discovery of Uranus imminent, belief and interest in astrology is abandoned by most educated people.

1873. Astrology is firmly consigned to the scrap-heap of exploded superstitions.

1973. Astrology is a major industry, with newspapers printing horoscopes, a large number of books expounding the subject, and a great many practising astrologers plying their trade. At the same time astrology has separated from astronomy: the two studies are carried on by different people and their literatures are addressed to different publics. There are many who "believe in" astrology, i.e., would like to feel that there is "something in it", but I should imagine that relatively few of them are astronomers.

It is conceivable that astrology will eventually validate its claim to be a coherent subject, and, if so, 2073 may see it reunited with astronomy, as it was when Copernicus was born. In the meantime, the popularity of astrology indicates a growing acceptance, by society as a whole, of the schematic and symmetrical type of pattern-thinking which the poets use. Let us look a little more closely into this process of separation.

What Copernicus began was a revolution in perspective. If we confine his achievement to him, disregarding the long-term developments through Galileo and Newton, his revolution was a shift from an earth-centered to a sun-centered mythology, but it does not take us outside the area of mythological synthesis. For Copernicus still assumed the sun to be fixed and to be at the centre of the entire universe. Naturally these notions soon went by the board, and in proportion as they did so the shadow of something much more frightening began to appear, the shadow of a universe so huge, so totally unrelated to any human principles of construction at all, as to be, in human terms, alienating and absurd. This is of course the feeling encapsulated by Pascal's famous aphorism: *Le silence de ces espaces infinis m'effraie.* But Pascal was exceptional here as elsewhere. For most people, including most poets, it was not until well into the nineteenth century that the new view of nature became imaginatively oppressive.

Dante's colossal vision ends with "the Love that moves the sun and the other stars". The word "moves" indicates why Aristotelian physics kept such a grip on the medieval mind. To that mind, moving things don't just go on until something stops them, as they do in Newton: motion for the Middle Ages was purposeful, directed toward a *telos* or end, and the ultimate end of all movement was the Great Unmoved Mover at the circumference of the universe, identified with the Christian God. The possibility of undirected movement begins with the Copernican hypothesis. One of the more reasonable objections to Copernicus was: if the earth rotates, why do we keep seeing the same stars in the sky, with no perceptible change in their positions except for the planets? The answer put more of a strain on the human imagination than it had ever been subjected to before, perhaps. It was all very well to say "Earth's but a point to the world"; it was all very well for Copernicus to say that the distance from the earth to the sun was insignificant compared to the distance from the earth to the stars. But to have to think concretely in terms of billions of miles was something else again. The next step, of course, is the possibility of reversing Dante's final phrase. If the sun is one of the stars, it is at least conceivable that the stars are suns, centres of other systems with no relation to man. The espousal of this doctrine by Giordano Bruno was one of the reasons why he seemed so horrifying a figure to the jittery Church of 1600.

Over the next three centuries we may see the three figures of Kepler, Newton and Swedenborg as representing three stages in the gradual separation of science and mythology. Kepler backed into the discovery of his laws of planetary motion by way of an *a priori* theory that the distance of the five planets from one another was in proportion to the five solid figures of geometry. He eventually got away from this, but he never abandoned his astrological and other schematic beliefs. Newton was keenly interested in Biblical numerology, even in alchemy, and psychologically these interests must have been connected with his science. But as far as publication was concerned, he kept these interests in separate compartments. Still, it could be said that Newton's religious interests had a good deal to do, not merely with his popular appeal in the eighteenth century, but with the cushioning of the shock of the emotional effect of the new scientific universe. That God was a good Anglican could be taken for granted, but that Newton was a good Anglican, if a somewhat heterodox one, was much more profoundly reassuring. By 1773 one of the leading spiritual influences in Europe was Swedenborg, who started out as a scientist, but changed completely over to visionary religion, Biblical commentary, and various occult doctrines. He represents a stage of culture in which the mythological and the scientific views are mutually exclusive, even if they co-exist in the same mind.

If we compare Milton's epic synthesis with Dante's, we can see that poetic mythology has made a minimal accommodation to the new science. Milton disapproves of Dante's devil-centered earth, on the ground that the earth had not been cursed before the fall of Adam, which came later than Satan's fall, and so Milton puts heaven and hell outside the order of nature, whereas Dante had put them inside. Then again, the only person outside the Bible who is repeatedly and pointedly alluded to in *Paradise Lost* is Galileo, whose telescope is brought in several times, in rather curious contexts. Milton is well aware of the view of the universe that Galileo held (he had met Galileo in Italy), and sometimes, in discussing the movements of the heavenly bodies, he puts the Ptolemaic and the Copernican explanations beside each other without committing himself. But it is clear that the older model has more of his sympathy, and from what we have said we can see why: the Ptolemaic universe, however rationalized, is a mythological and therefore essentially a poetic construction; hence it makes poetic sense. Galileo's world is much more difficult for a poet to visualize.

In Book I of *Paradise Lost* we are introduced to the shield of Satan. Epics have to have shields, because of the shield of Achilles in the *Iliad*, which is most elaborately and minutely described. The shield of Achilles depicts a world of security and peace, and forms a most effective contrast to the weary gut-cutting which goes on through most of the action. Satan's shield has the opposite effect: it is an ironic anticipation of the catastrophe which is to follow with the fall of Adam:

> The broad circumference
> Hung on his shoulders like the moon, whose orb
> Through optic glass the Tuscan artist views
> At evening, from the top of Fesole,
> Or in Valdarno, to descry new lands,
> Rivers, or mountains, in her spotty globe.

According to the Ptolemaic view, the moon has spots because it is nearest the "sublunary" world of death and corruption: it would not have been a "spotty globe" before Adam's fall. The heavenly bodies above it are too far up to have spots: we remember that Burton, in the passage quoted from the *Anatomy of Melancholy,* regarded the discovery of sunspots as the last word in paradox. So Milton's comparison of Satan's shield to the moon gazed at by Galileo implies (a) that Galileo's kind of knowledge is an insecure knowledge founded on the fallen state of nature and (b) that such knowledge is potentially idolatrous (hence the association with Satan), because it concentrates on the visible work of God without instead of on the invisible word within.

This attitude comes into focus in Book VIII, where Adam is being instructed by the angel Raphael. It occurs to Adam to ask whether other worlds than his own are inhabited by intelligent beings: after all, as even Raphael admits, it seems unlikely that the only function of the stars is to shine for man, considering how many of them there are and how little light each one gives. There follows what from one point of view might be considered as repulsive and ridiculous a passage as English poetry affords. Raphael obviously hasn't a clue what the answer is, but instead of honestly saying so he harrumphs, hums and haws, and finally tells Adam that he needn't, and therefore shouldn't, ask such a question. "Solicit not thy thought with matters hid", he says: one shouldn't pry into God's secrets. And Adam is "cleared of doubt", satisfied with the answer. The view that it is a sin, or at least a part of original sin, to want to know merely for the sake of knowing had been deeply entrenched in the Christian tradition since Augustine at least. But for the revolutionary Milton to be conniving at such notions seems very strange.

Yet, before we dismiss Milton, who is clearly endorsing Raphael's attitude, as a tedious obscurantist, we should look at the historical context of this dialogue. It is, in effect, the first clear example in English literature of the drawing of battle lines between mythological and scientific world-outlooks, and the first clear statement that the poet belongs on the mythological side. Leave Galileo alone with his telescope, and he will eventually discover a universe in which man's place gets smaller and smaller, until it seems so insignificant as to make it of no importance what he does or desires. Such a view must be counterbalanced by a more practical and existential view of things in which human life and human concerns are still central. Adam's primary task is to preserve his state of freedom against the coming assault of Satan: if he does that, knowledge, including knowledge of the stars, will take its rightful place. For us, the most important thing is to attain the freedom which, according to Milton, God wants us to have, and the practical reason that helps us to do this is superior to the speculative reason that contemplates the non-human world.

However, Milton looks back to an earlier age: his younger contemporaries were beginning a policy of accommodating themselves to the new science by appeasement. When Milton was writing *Paradise Lost,* one of his chief rivals in poetry was Abraham Cowley, who wrote odes on Harvey, the discoverer of the circulation of blood, on the philosopher Thomas Hobbes, and on the Royal Society, in which he described Bacon as the Moses who had led the modern age out of superstition into reason. He was very much a man of the new age. In his unfinished epic on King David *(Davideis),* Cowley describes David as a youthful musician playing his harp before Saul to cure Saul's melancholy, in a passage which I quote at some length because of the number of traditional symbolic *topoi* or commonplaces which it includes:

> As first a various unform'd hint we find
> Rise in some god-like poet's fertile mind,
> Till all the parts and words their places take,
> And with just marches verse and music make;
> Such was God's poem, this world's new essay;
> So wild and rude in its first draft it lay;
> Th' ungovern'd parts no correspondence knew,
> An artless war from thwarting motions grew;
> Till they to number and fix'd rules were brought
> By the eternal mind's poetic thought.
> Water and air he for the tenor chose,
> Earth made the bass, the treble flame arose,
> To th' active moon a quick brisk stroke he gave
> To Saturn's string a touch more soft and grave.

> The motions straight, and round, and swift, and slow,
> And short, and long, were mix'd and woven so,
> Did in such artful figures smoothly fall,
> As made this decent measur'd dance of all.
> And this is music; sounds that charm our ears,
> Are but one dressing that rich science wears.
> Though no man hear't, though no man it rehearse,
> Yet will there still be music in my verse.
> In this great world so much of it we see;
> The lesser, man, is all o'er harmony.
> Storehouse of all proportions! Single choir!
> Which first God's breath did tunefully inspire!
> From hence blest music's heavenly charms arise,
> From sympathy which them and man allies. . . .
> Thus the strange cure on our spilt blood applied,
> Sympathy to the distant wound does guide.
> Thus when two brethren strings are set alike,
> To move them both, but one of them we strike,
> Thus David's lyre did Saul's wild rage control,
> And tun'd the harsh disorders of his soul.

Ever since Christianity had elaborated its doctrine of the Fall of man, the stars in the sky had been the image of the original unfallen order of nature, as God had created it and designed it for man. I said earlier that human art supplies the models for the belief in a divine creation, and an integral part of the traditional imagery of the starry spheres was the analogy of music. The spheres gave out a "harmony" which symbolized their unchanging order, and Cowley associates the four elements of the creation with contrapuntal part-writing. The music was also often symbolized, as here, as an unending dance, into which Cowley manages to accommodate the new scientific realization that the heavenly bodies moved at different speeds. He goes on to make the commonplace analogy between the harmony of the spheres and the harmony which characterizes the soul of the good and wise man, the analogy based on the doctrine of the microcosm. David's method of curing Saul was the Biblical proof of the genuineness of these metaphors of "harmony", and of the therapeutic value of music. Cowley even accounts for the popular contemporary belief in sympathetic magic on the same principles.

Cowley shows us very clearly how dense the texture of this symbolic cosmology was, and how many values and beliefs were still bound up with it. And yet we cannot help wondering whether this highly enlightened and with-it poet really believes much of what he is saying. He provides immensely erudite footnotes to his poem, and in one of them he makes it clear that the "music of the spheres" is really a metaphor for the fact that the universe can be studied mathematically: "This order and proportion of things", he says, "is the true music of the world, and not that which Pythagoras, Plato, Tully, Macrobius, and many of the Fathers imagined, to arise audibly from the circumvolution of the Heavens". But if all this business about "harmony" is only metaphorical, can we really attach anything more to the conception of the microcosm, also invoked in this passage? Are there really only four elements? Does Cowley really believe in cures by sympathetic magic? We consult his footnotes again, and find that his footnote on the last point is exceedingly detached: "There is so much to be said of this subject, that the best way is to say nothing of it". It is difficult to resist the conclusion that poets talk a good deal of nonsense because nonsense sounds well in poetry. If so, perhaps the language of poetry itself represents something that the human mind may soon outgrow.

This possibility is not consciously present in Cowley's mind, but it is implied in some of the intellectual assumptions of his age. The imagery of music in the starry heavens, even if only metaphorical, suggests that, as Sir Thomas Browne had said earlier in the century, "Nature is the Art of God". If so, the art of man has a very restricted scope: this had always been true in theory, but had not affected the practice of the arts until the rise of science began to raise questions about the adequacy of the traditional mythological language of poetry. For the contemporaries of Newton, Pope and Swift, there seem to be two kinds of reality: the scientific kind, dealt with by reason and evidence, and the religious kind, which is a matter of revelation and is accepted by faith, but is interpreted by the same rational faculties of the mind. Poetry, strictly speaking, belongs neither to revelation nor to science, and its mythological language is hardly appropriate to either. It is puerile to go on repeating the exploded fables of the Greeks and Romans, and pretentious to assume that the poet can say anything about true religion that more conceptual language cannot say better. As Boileau, a great influence on English poetry in this period, had remarked:

> De la foi d'un Chrétien les mystères terribles
> D'ornemens égayés ne sont point susceptibles.

The poet's proper sphere is a social and human one, and in this sphere we may look for a slow but steady improvement, as social manners continue to refine. We can see the influence of science here: science does improve, in the sense that it builds on the work of predecessors. One of the speakers in Dryden's dialogue *Essay on Dramatic Poesy* remarks: "if natural causes be more known now than in the time of Aristotle, because more studied, it follows that poesy and other arts may, with the same pains, arrive still nearer to perfection". The analogy is a false analogy, because literature cannot improve in the way that science does, but an age fundamentally satisfied with its cultural standards may assume that it is doing so. In fact this illusion of the improvement of the arts arises in every generation, whether consciously formulated or not, but its effect is invariably to develop an *élite* and in-group literature, and make that elitism a critical standard for assessing literature in general.

From about 1750 on, poets, critics and literary scholars were in increasing revolt against this elitist conception of poetry. New discoveries in early Norse and Celtic literatures, new ways of looking at the poetry of Homer and the Old Testament, the collecting of ballads and the poetry of the oral tradition, all helped to popularize a new sense that there is something socially primitive about poetry. Poetry thrives on the simple sensational language which nature inspires in human emotion: myth, legend, the fabulous, superstition itself, are the very lifeblood of poetry.

In his *Ode to the Royal Society,* Cowley had praised Bacon for his revolution in language:

> From words, which are but pictures of the thought . . .
> To things, the mind's right object, he it brought.

But for the poets and critics of a later age it seemed rather that the pure and original language was the metaphorical language of poetry, and that Bacon's effort to make language descriptively accurate was a later, secondary and derivative development of it. Still, what does all this do except confirm and make explicit the latent suspicions that poetry is falling out of line with social advance, and is fit only for the scrapheap of discarded notions and beliefs?

Let us go back to the traditional belief that the visible heaven is the appropriate image of the invisible one, that the sky symbolizes the world as it was originally created, and is now all that is left of that original. The impact of the new science on poets was, at first, to confirm them in this belief. Addison paraphrases the nineteenth Psalm in language reflecting a confidence that his own age is updating its great vision:

> The spacious firmament on high,
> And all the blue ethereal sky,
> And spangled heavens, a shining frame,
> Their great Original proclaim.

And yet other imaginative influences were already at work eroding this acceptance of the sky as the symbol of divine order. To "proclaim" a personal creator one needs intelligent beings or angels, such as earlier cosmologies from Plato to Dante had liberally supplied, guiding the planets in their ordained courses. But now the starry heaven was dead, and the law of gravitation, however remarkable an intellectual achievement, could not bring it to life. The stars had not been made out of immortal quintessence, but out of the same substances as our own earth; they do not move in perfect circles around the earth, but attend to their own concerns in the vast depths of empty space. It was not that the symbolism was becoming untrue—truth and falsehood do not apply to mythology in this direct way—but that it was becoming emotionally unconvincing. What we appear to have, up in the sky, is an essentially mechanical order. Can an infinite personality be appropriately symbolized by a mechanism, however complex and well running? By the time we get to the Prologue to Goethe's *Faust*, the conception of God as the infinitely skilful juggler of planets is only a subject for parody. For an English equivalent, we may cite Byron's *Vision of the Last Judgement:*

> The angels all were singing out of tune,
> And hoarse with having little else to do,
> Excepting to wind up the sun and moon,
> Or curb a runaway young star or two . . .

Much more is involved here than the vitality of one particular poetic image. Once the starry heavens begin to go as a symbol of divine intelligence, we begin to wonder if the traditional images of divine and demonic do not need reversing. If the symbol of divine order is an empty, dead mechanism, perhaps the idealized cosmological image is merely a front for a political one, a rationalization of conservative authority. Perhaps the erotic and the rebellious are potentially good things, indications of a greater and fuller human freedom. And if the language of poetry seems to be a primitive language, may not that language be the language of human freedom itself, which is now smothered over by the autocracy of civilization and by the rationalizing parasites of that autocracy?

This way of looking at things, which gathered force after the American and French revolutions, was seized on particularly by William Blake, who, though without influence in his own time, saw more deeply and clearly into the mythological situation of his day than anyone else. In his great poem *Europe* (1794), Blake summarizes the history of Europe from the birth of Christ to the French Revolution. In the Roman world at the time of Christ, the gods had finally become identified almost entirely with the stars. The spirits of the spheres, called intelligences in Plato and angels in the Middle Ages, are really, according to Blake, the exploiting ascendant class, their "dance" an expression of the carefree leisurely lives that are supported by the slavery and misery of others. In the symbolism of the music of the spheres, the trumpet spoken of by Paul as announcing the Last Judgement would be the last musical sound. In Blake's poem the last trumpet is blown by Isaac Newton, after several unsuccessful attempts by an angel. Blake means that after Newton's time it is no longer possible to worship the sky as an image of deity. For worship there must be what in our time Martin Buber has called an "I-Thou" relationship, and science turns everything in nature, sooner or later, from a "Thou" into an "It". It is natural for primitive people to worship the sun, but difficult to feel worshipful about a blast furnace ninety million miles off, however impressive it may be otherwise. And even though Christianity had transformed the idolatry of star worship into the iconology of star-imagery, the principle remains: we cannot go on associating God with a subhuman mechanism. Newton has taught us too much about the deadness and remoteness of the objects in the sky. So after Newton, the reign of autocracies founded on a symbol of unchanging order is over, and the French Revolution, Blake thinks at this time, indicates an entirely new feeling spreading over humanity.

We remember that John Donne, in *Ignatius His Conclave*, had represented Copernicus as calling himself a "second Creator", and as having put the earth at the top and the sun at the bottom of the creation, reversing the traditional order. He has thus emancipated the devil, he claims, because the devil's habitation is conventionally at the centre of the earth. Donne is thus, however unconsciously, looking forward to an imagery in which the sky will be associated with Satan rather than with God, and in which a suppressed demonic figure may prove to be the image of human freedom. Paul had already associated the devil with the sky in the New Testament, calling him "the prince of the power of the air". The poetry of English Romanticism, beginning with Blake, greatly developed this symbolism. Blake was a painter and engraver as well as a poet, and his poems are illustrated by himself. The frontispiece to *Europe* depicts a naked old man with a pair of compasses (deriving from the description of Wisdom in the Book of Proverbs) setting bounds both to nature and the human mind. His name in Blake's mythology, Urizen, is from the same root as "horizon". The traditional Christian view is that the world was created by the Word of God, starting with the command "Let there be light", and that this Word became incarnate later as a young God put to death by a reactionary society. Blake's figure is the kind of cloud-gathering Zeus, or crabby old man in the sky, that all authoritarian religions eventually collapse on.

The same type of figure appears in Shelley as the Jupiter of *Prometheus Unbound.* Jupiter again is the old symbol of divine intelligence which is really a symbol of a political establishment relying on the belief in such a God for its support. The psychological effect of contemplating a symbol of changeless order as an image of deity is to make us feel that whatever happens is inevitable, and to accept all evil and disaster as the will of God. Poetry, which helps us to create rather than simply contemplate what is there, is for Shelley a powerful agent in helping to free the Prometheus in the human mind from the tyranny of Jupiter. A later poet, Thomas Hardy, is never tired of showing us what an imbecile God turns out to be if we create him in the image of the starry order. Hardy has a poem called "God's Education", in which God is represented as learning from the misery of man, in the manner of middle-class people reluctantly coming to realize that some people are not only poor but poorer than they should be. He has another called "By the Earth's Corpse", where God remarks, at the end of time, that he wishes he had never started on this creation business, for which he clearly has so little talent. The novels take the same view: here is the narcissistic and rather stupid heroine of *The Return of the Native:*

> Eustacia Vye was the raw material of a divinity. On Olympus she would have done well with a little preparation. She had the passions and instincts which make a model goddess, that is, those which make not quite a model woman. Had it been possible for

the earth and mankind to be entirely in her grasp for a while, had she handled the distaff, the spindle, and the shears at her own free will, few in the world would have noticed the change of government. There would have been the same inequality of lot, the same heaping up of favours here, of contumely there, the same generosity before justice, the same perpetual dilemmas, the same captious alternation of caresses and blows that we endure now.

Blake and Shelley belong to the Romantic period, but Hardy comes on the other side of Darwin, and it was Darwin who completed the revolution in perspective that Copernicus had begun. Copernicus started the displacing of man from the spatial centre of the universe, and by the nineteenth century his place in that universe looked small indeed. But for long it was still assumed, however vaguely, that the universe was finite in time: that there must have been a creation, and therefore at some time a conclusion to the whole operation. Thus Dryden, writing an ode in honour of St. Cecilia, the patron of music, begins with the customary image of the world as created from "heavenly harmony", and ends with the corresponding image of the end of time:

> The trumpet shall be heard on high,
> The dead shall live, the living die,
> And music shall untune the sky.

This passage rather frightened Samuel Johnson, who remarked that the image is "so awful in itself, that it can owe little to poetry; and I could wish the antithesis of music untuning had found some other place". By saying that it owes little to poetry Johnson means that Dryden's conclusion is for him a simple statement of fact about a situation in which we shall all certainly find ourselves. Another result of this uneasy compromise was eighteenth-century Deism, which was essentially the doctrine that we need a creating God but not a sustaining one: the natural order runs itself automatically, though the perfection of that automatism guarantees its divine origin. Deism had a good deal of influence in America after 1776, as it seemed to provide a formula for uniting most religious groups around the argument that if the world exists, somebody must have made it.

The strength of millennial and apocalyptic movements in the same country seems to indicate something rather exhilarating in the notion of an approaching end of the world, despite Samuel Johnson's attitude. For beginning and ending are human, finite, and comprehensible notions, and when the stars in the sky have become increasingly the image of something demonic and alienating, the sense of a beginning and an end becomes proportionately more attractive. I say this because it seems to me that in the various apocalyptic symbols of our time, annihilation warfare, the atom bomb, the increase of population and shrinking of natural resources, there is something that appeals to self-indulgence as well as genuine concern, and a latent nihilism that may prove to be more dangerous than the problems themselves.

The doctrine of evolution made time as huge and frightening as space: the past, after Darwin, was no more emotionally reassuring than the skies had come to be. Once the starry heavens become an image of mechanism, we are left with the organism as the highest development of existence we know of. But the behavior of organisms in nature exhibits a process of cut-throat competition very similar to that of the worst aspects of the human community. Then again, by showing a creative process forming itself within nature, evolution made it unnecessary to assume a personal Creator outside it: it made nature not only alien but autonomous, a self-regulating process needing no God to start it or man to improve it.

What conclusions are we to draw from the long historical process that we are here tracing back to the hypothesis of Copernicus? In the first place, man lives in two worlds, the worlds traditionally called the worlds of nature and art. We live in an actual world, our physical environment in time and space, and this is the world studied mainly by the natural or physical sciences. At the same time we keep trying to create a culture and civilization of our own. This represents the world we want to live in, as well as the world we are creating out of our environment.

It is where our values and desires and hopes and ideals belong, and this world is always geocentric, always anthropocentric, always centered on man and man's concerns.

It is obvious that the basis of the world we want to live in is mythological. That is, the world we construct is built to the model of a common social vision produced by the imagination. Poetry, which is at the heart of all mythology, finds its function in providing verbal imaginative models for human civilization, and seeing reality in terms of human desires and emotions. In the science that studies nature there is, of course, an essential place for the imaginative and creative powers, but still the ultimate end of science is verification, coincidence with an external reality. Similarly, in the mythology that expresses human vision, there is an essential place for reality: we do not believe the poet as such, but we applaud him for producing something credible. Yet the end of mythology is the conceivable, not the real, or, as Aristotle said, the impossible made probable.

We have to separate these two worlds in our minds, rigorously and completely, before we can address ourselves to the next question, of how to unite them again. Of course everything we do is in one aspect an attempt to unite them, but unless we distinguish them first we shall not know what we are trying to unite. On one side is the world of vision, the world presented to us by poetry and myth, which has being but not existence: it is real but it is not there. On the other side is the world that is there, presented to us in the constructs of science. This world has existence, but it is, so far as we can see, a sub-human, sub-moral, sub-intelligent world, with nothing in it that directly responds to human desires or ideals. In between is the world that we create, or try to realize, out of the merely internal reality of the one and the merely external reality of the other. We want a human community that will conform to our hopes and ideals and our sense of what might be; we need a knowledge of our environment that will give it foundations and keep it from being a castle in the air.

It seems clear that the uniting area must be something like an area of belief. But belief in this sense has to be rather precisely characterized. A genuine belief is an axiom of behavior: whatever we may believe we believe, our behavior shows what we really believe, and a belief which cannot become an axiom of behavior is useless lumber in the mind. Thus genuine belief is the source of whatever is positive or creative in one's life. It may be founded on the flattest truisms: a preference of life to death, freedom to slavery, happiness to misery, gentleness to brutality, truth to falsehood, cleanliness to filth. But it is genuine belief if it makes creative behavior possible. If I believe something, then I should order my life on its practical consequences, and if I cannot do so, I must either discard the belief or recognize that it is discarding me. Assent to verified facts is not belief in this sense: I know that the earth goes round the sun, but it would be unbearably pretentious to say that that was part of my faith. Traditionally, belief has been connected with religion, and often conceived as an uncritical and unquestioning trust in something unproved or unprovable. But it is hard to see how belief in this sense can be a virtue. Neither does it seem to be the original emphasis in religion. Whenever faith is spoken of approvingly in the New Testament, for example, it seems to have something to do with the concentrating of one's imagination or will power. It is defined in the Epistle to the Hebrews as the *hypostasis*, the substantial reality, of what is hoped for; the *elenchos*, the proof or evidence, of unseen things. Belief so defined seems to be much the same thing as creativity, the power of bringing into existence something that was not there before, but which, once there, brings us a little closer to our model vision.

In Copernicus' day the uniting force was unquestionably religion, and there was still a good deal of prestige attached to the great medieval dream of uniting the two worlds by making the axioms of faith, given by revealed religion, major premises from which to deduce a trustworthy philosophy and science. This dream is still with us, and revives in each generation, but things fall apart: *that* centre, it seems, cannot hold. At present, at any rate, it seems that religion has its roots in the model or mythological world only. This is the reason for the curious and persistent relationship between the language of poetry and the language of religion. They are both developments of mythology, verbal constructs made out of myth and metaphor. As long as God was assumed to have a functional place in scientific thought, as the Creator of the order of nature, this fact was concealed. But it seems clear now that for us, in our generation, the conception of God as a Creator has been projected from the fact that man makes things. The revolution that began with Copernicus has clearly ended in the abolition of the conception "God" from the world of time and space, so far as science deals with that world.

At the same time that the Romantic movement had begun the final separation of mythology and science, the industrial revolution was making technology a central factor in society. Both Marxism and the theory of progress in the democracies seized on industrial production as the central uniting force of society, and the realizing power of civilization. Their conception of technology was much the same: they differed only on whether a capitalist or a socialist economy should control it. The great advantage of having technology in such a role was that it seemed to develop automatically, with the minimum of reference to the nagging mythological question: is this really what man most wants and needs? Marxist poets were urged to celebrate the glories of technology under socialism as their ancestors had celebrated gods and heroes. A magnificent Hungarian poem by Ferenc Juhasz, *The Boy Changed into a Stag Cries Out at the Gate of Secrets,* translated by the Canadian poet Kenneth McRobbie with Ilona Duczynska, thus describes the apotheosis of its transformed hero:

> There he stood on the renewing crags of time,
> stood on the ringed summit of the sublime
> universe, there stood the lad at the gate of secrets,
> his antler prongs were playing with the stars . . .
> Mother, my mother, I cannot go back:
> pure gold seethes in my hundred wounds . . .
> each prong of my antlers is a dual-based pylon
> each branch of my antlers a high-tension wire,
> my eyes are ports for ocean-going merchantmen, my
> veins are tarry cables, these

teeth are iron bridges, and in my heart the surge of
 monster-infested seas,
each vertebra is a teeming metropolis, for a spleen
 I have a smoke-puffing barge
each of my cells is a factory, my atoms are solar systems
sun and moon swing in my testicles, the Milky Way
 is my bone marrow,
each point of space is one part of my body
my brain impulse is out in the curling galaxies.

There seem to be some lurking ironies even here, and in any case poets, at least in the democracies, have not responded to pylons and factories with much enthusiasm. Most of them appear to agree with the humanists who were scolded by Sir Charles Snow, in his famous "two cultures" lecture, for being what he called "Luddites", reactionary machine-breakers, who for Snow were such a contrast to the scientists who "have the future in their bones". It is instructive to turn to William Morris, because he was one of the relatively few English poets who was a socialist, even something of a Marxist, if a somewhat unorthodox one. We find that he quite explicitly prefers medieval to modern London:

Forget six counties overhung with smoke,
Forget the snorting steam and piston stroke,
Forget the spreading of the hideous town;
Think rather of the pack-horse on the down,
And dream of London, small, and white, and clean,
The clear Thames bordered by its gardens green . . .

This is supposed to be Chaucer's London, though Chaucer himself might have been startled to hear it described as "clean", but it is not the reference to the past which is important. There are doubtless people even yet who would dismiss such writing impatiently as escapist fantasy, but it is just barely possible that in the age of pollution and the energy crisis we may feel that the poets may have some of the future in their bones too. In any case the real reason for the "Luddite" attitude of so many poets to technology is of some interest.

Technically, a machine is an extension of organic life: a telescope is an extension of the eye, an automobile of the feet, a computer of the calculating aspect of the brain. A car can run faster than a human body and a computer calculate faster than a human mind, but the machine left to itself has no will to do these things, despite all the science-fiction horror stories about malignant computers and insurgent robots. Nevertheless, there is a sinister tendency in the human mind to project itself into its mechanisms. The demonic is, like the divine, something within the human mind, not something out there, but it is peculiarly characteristic of the demonic to build itself an external prison in order to have the fun of crawling into it. The civilization produced by the automobile, with its network of highways, the blasted deserts of its parking lots, the grid plan of cities, and the human sacrifices offered to it on every holiday, clearly raises the question of who is enslaving whom. Again, every social system or structure, as these words imply, is essentially a mechanism for providing a human community, but the impulse to make a social structure into a divinely sanctioned prison has run consistently through history from Pharaoh's Egypt to Stalin's Russia. We remember that the great technological invention of primitive man was the wheel, and that the wheel promptly became in mythology a symbol of external compulsion, an emblem of fate or fortune.

When Blake or Morris or D. H. Lawrence attack or repudiate our technological culture, therefore, they are really saying that if man is too lazy to mould his world according to his real beliefs, and tries to abdicate his responsibilities by trusting to some kind of automated progress, he is actually releasing the most sinister and vicious impulses in himself, and the end of it is logically either the total destruction made possible by modern physics or, far worse, the unending tyranny made possible by modern communications. Hence the preoccupation of so many writers with the themes of mad scientists and parody-Utopias like *1984*. One thinks particularly of Mary Shelley's *Frankenstein*, whose monster is popularly supposed to be a symbol of man's enslavement to the mechanisms he has created. Actually the monster is portrayed with a good deal of sympathy: the many references to Milton's *Paradise Lost* in her story make it clear that her real theme is the responsibility that man takes on when he recognizes the extent of his own creative powers. If what he creates is monstrous, merely viewing it with horror is hardly enough. The moral of such fables is that man can never avoid the challenge to examine his own beliefs, his desires and his visions of society at every step of new discovery. The future that is technically possible is not necessarily the future that society wants or can accept. To be fatalistic about this, to assume that whatever can happen must happen, is the way to develop "future shock" into a coma.

The central issue of our own time, five hundred years away from Copernicus, is often described as a crisis in belief. I have no quarrel with this way of putting it, but I have a rather skeptical suggestion to make about it. Just as we have a principle of economy of means in the arts, and of economy of hypotheses in the sciences, so we need a principle of economy of belief. It is no light matter to adopt a real belief, or axiom of behavior, and the loss of influence today of the traditional religions seems to me connected with a widespread feeling that a good many "believers" are rather frivolous people. I have a friend who taught for a year at a college in India, and was told by a genuinely worried student that because he ate beef the best he could hope for in his next incarnation was to be reborn as a dog. Now, of course, one cannot prove that one will not be reborn as a dog in one's next incarnation, or even that one will or will not have another incarnation. But still his attitude was an impatient "to hell with all *that* stuff". What is significant is that this is the only attitude for which one could possibly have the slightest respect.

It is relatively easy for us to see this when the beliefs are unfamiliar, but the general principle is inescapable that when belief is a matter of uncritical acceptance of the unprovable, the less we believe the better. Sin is traditionally countered by faith, but when we see Bunyan's Christian, in *The Pilgrim's Progress,* staggering off towards the Gate of Good Will under the burden of his sins, we cannot help wondering if the burden of his beliefs was not even heavier, and perhaps worse for him. The self-pitying moans exhaled from many nineteenth-century and later writers about the tragedy of their loss of faith never quite conceal an underlying exhilaration. In our time we are about to be faced with new scientific developments, in such fields as genetics, which will affect human life profoundly, and which will have to be met with genuine belief in what we can accept or reject for our own social life. To try to encounter such problems as clonal reproduction with a clutter of vestigial superstitions and polemical pseudo-beliefs inspired by an over-active superego, by resentments (e.g., "I feel this must be true because my parents, or my children, deny it"), or by expediency, is like trying to rely on the vermiform appendix for digesting our food.

My opposition of mythology and the physical sciences will of course remind you that we have developed the ability to study our own civilized institutions in the same detached and objective spirit with which we study nature. This development has given us the social sciences, which are obviously a powerful element in the process of realizing the kind of society we want. The social sciences are still gravely handicapped, it seems to me, by not realizing that they are also the applied humanities, but the importance of bringing the scientific spirit to bear on man himself is undeniable. What they represent is the power of criticism in society. We often speak glibly of the need for questioning and challenging our beliefs: it is the kind of thing we say to avoid any real thought or action. But of course the criticism of a genuine belief is not a negative activity, but is the same thing as the recreation and renewal of that belief.

This takes me back to the epigraph from Wallace Stevens with which I began this paper:

> To say the solar chariot is junk
>
> Is not a variation but an end.
> Yet to speak of the whole world as metaphor
> Is still to stick to the contents of the mind
>
> And the desire to believe in a metaphor.

Stevens is also opposing mythology to science, and is telling us that we cannot live wholly within either construct. The scientific perspective on reality is one that destroys mythology in its own field. In science there can never be any sun gods or solar chariots: they are scientifically junk. It does not follow that they have no place in mythology, though it is true that as science extends our knowledge of the sun, poets get tired of solar chariots as no longer effective metaphors, so that they eventually become junk in poetry too. We cannot however live in a world where there is no mythology, where everything the imagination produces is junk. Yet there is no escape in running to the other extreme and retreating to a self-contained world of the imagination. Such a world, Stevens' believed-in metaphor, would be not imaginative but imaginary, a narcissistic mirror of our own minds, a facile conquest of the unreal.

Ever since Copernicus began the displacement of man in space, we have been progressively discovering that the physical environment seems to be an order of existence without human value, including the supreme human value of finiteness. Hence it is easy for poets to call it alien or absurd, a world which, however we may have blundered into it, is not ours, except for the tiny piece that we have made ours for the time being. It may be better to think of it, however, as something other, something not ourselves which none the less extends and expands us. It is one of the primary functions of science to remind us of how much we still do not know, to present to us a universe of infinite scope and infinite possibilities of further discovery. Mythology does not expand and progress in the way that science does, but it keeps constantly transforming itself, as though there were a power of renewal within it as infinite as the galaxies. If the Royal Society of Canada survives to 2073, mankind may by that time have realized more clearly that there may be an otherness of the spirit as well as of nature, and that a tiny part of that too may become ourselves.

Part Two

THE MYTHOLOGICAL UNIVERSE

Expanding Eyes

This article grew out of a profound disinclination to make the kind of comment that I was invited to make on Angus Fletcher's article in a previous issue. I felt that such a writer as Mr. Fletcher, who clearly understands me and, more important, himself, ought to be allowed the last word on both subjects. Besides that, I have a rooted dislike of the "position paper" genre. In all the arts, adhering to a school and issuing group manifestoes and statements of common aims is a sign of youthfulness, and to some degree of immaturity; as a painter or writer or other creative person grows older and acquires more authority, he tends to withdraw from all such organizations and become simply himself. Others in the same field become friends or colleagues rather than allies. I see no reason why that should not be the normal tendency in criticism and scholarship also. About twenty years ago I was asked, in a hotel lobby during an MLA conference, "What is your position relatively to Kenneth Burke?" I forget what I mumbled, but my real answer was, first, that I hadn't the least idea, and, second, that anyone who could really answer such a question would have to be a third person, neither Burke nor Frye.

The sense of being something of a loner has always been in any case rather exceptionally true of me, with my introverted temperament, indolent habits and Canadian nationality. When I published a study of Blake in 1947, I knew nothing of any "myth criticism" school, to which I was told afterwards I belonged: I simply knew that I had had to learn something about mythology to understand Blake. When I published *Anatomy of Criticism* ten years later, I had never heard the word "structuralism": I realized only that structure was a central concern of criticism, and that the "new critics" of that day were wrong in underrating it. I have had some influence, I know, but I neither want nor trust disciples, at least as that term is generally understood. I should be horrified to hear of anyone proposing to make his own work revolve around mine, unless I were sure that that meant a genuine freedom for him. And if I have no disciples I have no school. I think I have found a trail, and all I can do is to keep sniffing along it until either scent or nose fails me.

I have often been urged to produce a revision to *Anatomy of Criticism,* but that does not seem to me to be a revisable book. Apparently it is by no means out of date, but it is still a book of its own period, the mid-fifties, and to try to dress so middle-aged a production in the unisex jeans of the seventies would be an indignity and not a renewal of youth. My work since then has assumed the shape of what Professor Jerome Bruner would call a spiral curriculum, circling around the same issues, though trying to keep them open-ended. This may be only a rationalization for not having budged an inch in eighteen years, but the most serious adverse criticisms of me still seem to me to be based on assumptions too remote from mine for revision to meet them. Neither, of course, would revision stop the flow of abusive nonsense which has also been directed at me, because most of that comes from people who know quite well what nonsense it is, but have their minds on higher things. Emerson, as we know, deprecated what he called a foolish consistency, but there is always one form of consistency which is not foolish, and that is continuity. With some people continuity takes a revolutionary and metamorphic direction: a philosopher may repudiate everything he has written up to a certain time and start afresh. Even so, I doubt if he can start afresh until he discovers the real point of contact with his earlier work. With me, continuity has taken a more gradual direction, not because I insist that everything I have said earlier, in *Anatomy of Criticism* or elsewhere, must be "right", but because the principles I have already formulated are still working as heuristic assumptions, and they are the only ones available to me.

In *Anatomy of Criticism* I made two polemical suggestions. One was that literary criticism seemed to me to be a potentially scientific discipline; the other was that the emphasis on value-judgements was mistaken, and the attempt to make criticism into an axiological subject both futile and perverse. I have not changed my views on either point, but the amount of reaction they have provoked has got them over-exposed and out of proportion, especially the second. Perhaps it would be better, instead of restating arguments for readers who still believe that they have caught me out in a contradiction whenever I say that Shakespeare is a great writer, to try to locate what appears to be the real basis of such reactions.

Literary criticism in its present form grew up in the nineteenth century, under the shadow of philology. Philology had many spokesmen who were in the direct line of Renaissance humanism, but it often became interpreted in a much more superficial way. Still, in a modified and expanded form, the philological program became the standard method of graduate training in the humanities departments of modern universities. The literary scholar learns to operate, in graduate school, a research machinery that enables him, for the rest of his life, to organize and convey information about literature and add to our stock of knowledge about it. I cannot imagine how one would frame a definition of social science that would exclude this kind of activity: it was, after all, set up on an analogy with science, though, as I think, a more simplistic analogy than the one I tried to propose. Whenever a graduate student is encouraged to do something that "hasn't been done before", which so often in practice means finding a new angle or gimmick for something done hundreds of times, some connection with the division of labour in a scientific activity is assumed. Humanists, of course, are supposed to write much better than social scientists, and some of them do. The real trouble—and this has always been the other half of my contention—is rather that social scientists do not yet understand that their subjects, besides being sciences, are also the applied humanities, and that the myths and metaphors of literature inform them somewhat as mathematics informs the physical sciences. Or, more accurately, the myths and metaphors of literature inform what is specifically verbal in them, as distinct from what is quantifiable or measurable or dependent on repeatable experiment.

The humanist, at the same time that he learns these techniques of scholarship, is haunted by two other feelings. One is that this kind of activity does not represent his real commitment: he clings to the idea of value partly because he knows that his scholarship does not manifest what he feels to be the worth-whileness, for him existentially, in the study of literature. The other is that he is harassed and bedevilled by the dismal sexist symbology surrounding the humanities which he meets everywhere, even in the university itself, from freshman classes to the president's office. This symbology, or whatever one should call it, says that the sciences, especially the physical sciences, are rugged, aggressive, out in the world doing things, and so symbolically male, whereas the literatures are narcissistic, intuitive, fanciful, staying at home and making the home more beautiful but not doing anything really serious, and are therefore symbolically female. They are, however, leisure-class females, and have to be attended by a caste of ladies' maids who prepare them for public appearance, and who are the teachers and critics of literature in schools and universities.

Such superstitions have a long history in social anxiety. Religious and political movements almost invariably assume that the real function of literature is or should be to persuade the emotions or the imagination to agree with the truth of their doctrines, in the way that a wife is traditionally supposed to use her "feminine intuition" to agree with her husband. This is still true of, for example, Marxism, where the anxiety is rationalized by arguments about the impossibility of remaining detached from the for-or-against dialectic of revolution. The humanist, even when he can see that such anxieties have only an external and inorganic relation to his subject, is still apt to be impressed by the air of relevance to the real world that they appear to exhibit.

Let us go back to the student in graduate school, learning to operate the machinery of literary scholarship. If he has a genuine vocation, we said, he will feel that his real commitment is something other than this, however important it may be in itself. His larger commitment is usually revealed by his choice of period, or by his special affection for one or two writers. In the study of literature the element of personal authority, surrendering one's own imagination to that of some master of it, cannot be eliminated, and the relation of master and disciple always remains at its centre, though the master is more commonly a writer of the past than an actual teacher. What gets the serious student really hooked into the study of literature is likely to be a feeling of a common element in life-style with some author whose interest for him is not exhausted by the scholarly work he does on him (he may of course work on something quite different). I got hooked into Blake in this way very early, partly because I had been brought up in much the same evangelical sub-culture that Blake had developed from, and because he made an amount of imaginative sense out of that sub-culture that I had never dreamed was possible. Other people would find, and have found, very different points of contact with Blake: this happened to be mine.

Similarly, a woman scholar may become interested in a woman writer because of a point of contact in the specifically feminine problems of social relationship. Or a homosexual scholar may find his contact in the particular kind of sensibility that a homosexual writer often has, or a black scholar may find his in that of a black writer, and so on. Of course, it is barbaric to say that women writers can only be fully understood by women scholars, black writers by black scholars, Catholic writers by Catholic scholars. That breaks up the community of verbal imagination into a group of exclusive cliques. What I have suggested is simply a normal starting point: as a scholar gains maturity and experience, he can branch out where he likes, at any time. There may be only one such influence on a scholar or there may be a sequence of them; a scholar may remain under such an influence all his life, or may quickly dispense with all such influences. The above principle could also work in reverse: a Jewish scholar might get interested in a writer who showed anti-Semitic tendencies, and for serious reasons. However it operates, there is always a sense in which criticism is a form of autobiography, implicitly dedicated to a guru or spiritual preceptor, even if the guru is the Anonymous who wrote the great ballads, or a cultural composite like "Augustan" or "Romantic", or a series of writers forming a psychological "tradition".

All this indicates where the engaged or committed aspect of literary scholarship has its origin. The personal dependence of scholar on poet does not mean that scholarship is a second-class or parasitic activity: it is merely a special case of the way literary tradition always works. The poet in his turn became a poet in precisely the same way: in fact the process of personal apprenticeship and influence can be seen much more clearly within literature itself. But, as my illustrations have already made obvious, the conception of "personality" in the study of literature, or the further practice of it, moves its centre of gravity very quickly from the ordinary to the poetic personality, from the actual man to the body of what he has written, or what was written in his age.

It is hard to talk about this without resorting to what sounds like paradox. The poet has no identity, says Keats, and is trying to escape from personality, says Eliot; yet it is precisely his identity and his personality that he finds again by writing. Similarly, the relation between poet and scholar modulates into a relation between two mental attitudes or ways of thinking and imagining, in the course of which the scholar in his turn finds his own real personality. It is this core of the impersonal within the personal that distinguishes, in fact contrasts, the discipleship I am speaking of here and the kind I spoke of at the beginning in connection with myself. However grotesque it may sound to suggest that one may come to absorb or contain an influence the size of Shakespeare or Milton or Dante or Blake, still there is something in these creators that can be contained and possessed, something that expands, instead of restricting, the individuality of those who follow after them.

The real function of literary scholarship and criticism is so little understood, even by those who practise it, that it is hard not to think of it, even yet, as somehow sub-creative, in contrast to the "creative" writing of poems and novels, as though creativity were an attribute of those genres rather than of the people using them. Part of the problem is the narrowness of the academic set-up. To take an analogy from philosophy: no one doubts that it is essential to produce commentaries, explications and reinterpretations of the great philosophers of the past, or to study the history of philosophy. But if there were nothing else clearly visible in academic departments of philosophy, one might well ask, where is actual philosophy still being carried on? The corresponding question for literary scholars is: what is the real activity that Samuel Johnson and Coleridge and Matthew Arnold were concerned with? Asked who the influential thinkers of our time are, a literary critic might find it difficult, not merely to name a literary scholar whom he could regard as a leading thinker, in the sense of having influenced anyone outside his immediate field, but even to conceive the possibility of any literary critic's having so central a place in modern thought at all. As for the public, humanists may be making the same mistake that leaders in religion have made, of examining their consciences so publicly that the public at length, and not very reluctantly, comes to believe their admissions of inadequacy.

The academic pigeonholes are of course splitting open on all sides. In the "Tentative Conclusion" to *Anatomy of Criticism*, written several years before the publication of the book in 1957, I said that a number of disciplines appeared to be converging in areas contiguous to the "myth criticism" to which so much of the preceding text had been devoted. My examples of what seemed to me then to be converging look very quaint now; but the prediction itself, in a more general way, has come true with such force that if I were writing such an essay today I should have to lean in the opposite direction.

Doubtless more knowledge would modify my present attitude,

and in such matters I had rather be wrong than right. But structuralism, hermeneutics, phenomenalism, sociolinguistics, cultural anthropology and the philosophy of language have, as I think, made a rather disappointing contribution so far to the understanding of literature, however relevant the context for it that they have set up. Their emergence certainly indicates that the rationale of modern criticism is coming closer to formulation, but their practitioners seem to be under some spell like that of the sexist myth just referred to. They still seem only incidentally interested in literature itself and in what it does or can do to people: like many historians and philosophers, they tend to resist identification with the humanities, as though they felt that they represented, or would like to associate themselves with, some Herculean force in modern thought that would not be content to remain spinning for a poetic Omphale.

In examining the relation of one subject to another, the initial choice of metaphors and conceptual diagrams is a fateful choice. The metaphors and diagrams chosen should never be vertical, concerned with foundations and superstructures. Such metaphors invariably take some form of determinism, where one subject is assumed to provide the basis for explaining another subject. And yet, when I caution my students against trying to "base" literary criticism on something else, I usually run into the most strenuous objections. It seems utterly obvious to one student that poems come out of certain mental processes, and therefore psychological conceptions must underlie or form the foundation for any study of literature. It is equally obvious to another student that a poem is a product of specific historical and social conditions, and therefore, etc. Nothing in my teaching is more difficult to get across than the simple: "throw that metaphor away; it's the wrong metaphor". It always means that we have to get something established in another subject "before" we can study literature, which of course means that we never get to study literature at all.

We seem to have passed through the worst of the age of sublimated imperialism, when there was so strong an attraction toward building some Tower of Babel on a Marxist, Freudian or Thomist model, with a determinism for its foundation and a confusion of tongues for its ground floor. But horizontal metaphors of connecting, uniting, reconciling or bridge-building are even more dangerous, and are derived from an origin much harder to locate in oneself, the indefinite continuity that the ability to write in prose confers. Suppose that Critic A writes an essay on someone, Carlyle or Arnold or Newman or Edmund Burke—call him X. Critic A doesn't like X much, and the point of his essay is to say that idea G in X's work is utterly inconsistent with idea L. Along comes Critic B, also interested in X. He likes X much better, and is not averse to scoring a point or two over A. So he writes another essay in which he says that perhaps ideas G and L in X's work may prove to be, under more careful analysis, not inconsistent at all. What this means is that the verbal formulas H, I, J and K, which would connect G with L, have not been supplied by X, nor, of course, by A, but that he, B, can supply them. The general principle involved is that if we only write enough sentences, any statement whatever can be reconciled, or united or connected or made consistent with, any other statement. When two such statements are in different disciplines, trying to connect them destroys both their contexts.

I have explained elsewhere that I think the word "interpenetrate" a safer metaphor. For example, I consider that I know no psychology and have never studied the subject, though I must have read several hundred books that would be classified as psychology in a library. But I have read these books for whatever help they could give me as a literary critic: they interpenetrate my critical work, but keep their own context in their own discipline. For a contemporary critic interested in Freud or Wittgenstein or Lévi-Strauss, such writers, like medieval angels, do not travel through space from another subject: they manifest themselves from within his subject. These may sound like old and tired problems, but I start with them because there seems to me no other way of getting the autonomy of literary scholarship clear.

II

Literature, like other subjects, has a theory and a practice: poems and plays and novels form the practical side, and the centre of criticism is the theory of literature. Such a theory merges on one side with the theory of words in general, and so is inseparable from linguistics and certain areas of philosophy, and on the other side it merges with the theory of the other arts. My own contributions to literary theory are innocent of any knowledge of either linguistics or general aesthetics, but even these deficiencies may indicate that they are possibly somewhere in a central area. They came originally, of course, out of my study of Blake's "private mythology", where I learned, not merely that Blake's mythology was not private, but that the phrase itself made no sense.

Blake was, even by the standards of English literature, a remarkably Biblical poet, but his interest in the Bible was primarily critical. He realized that the Bible had provided a mythological structure, which had expanded into a mythological universe, stretching from creation to apocalypse in time, from heaven to hell in space, and that this universe had formed a framework of imagery for all European poets down to his own time. It had either destroyed or absorbed other mythological structures, including the Classical, the Celtic and the Norse, and provided the basis for the cosmologies of Dante and Milton. The existence of such a universe in Western culture was neither incidental nor accidental. Some such universe must always exist wherever any human culture does. Man lives in two worlds, the world of nature which forms his external environment, and the constructed world of civilization and culture which he has made himself because he wants to live in such a world. The mythological universe is a model of the latter world: it is usually believed to be, at least in its earlier stages, the structure of the former world also, but it is ultimately not a proto-scientific construct, even when it develops or tries to develop a science. It is a world built in the image of human desires and anxieties and preconceptions and ideals and objects of abhorrence, and it is always, and necessarily, geocentric and anthropocentric, which the actual environment is not.

By Blake's time two things had happened to the traditional Christian universe. First, the rise of science, more particularly astronomical science, had begun to make it clear that this universe was an imaginative construct only, and had no scientific validity. Second, its isolation as a construct showed up the fact that it was an intensely conservative and authoritarian construct, and had been consistently, if often unconsciously, so used in European culture. Blake was the first poet in English literature, or so far as I know in the world, to understand how drastic an imaginative change was taking place in his time, and in his Prophecies he was trying to restructure what C. S. Lewis calls the "discarded model" on a basis of human desire and ambition rather than anxiety, and to see it as of human rather than of divine, so far as that means non-human, origin. More generally, he wanted to recover the mythological universe for the human imagination, and stop projecting it on an objective God or similar analogy of the external order. No contemporary poet made a comparable attempt to do this, except perhaps Goethe in the second part of *Faust.* But Goethe, for all his vast philosophical and poetic powers, or perhaps even because of them, did not have so firmly articulated a skeleton of the imaginative cosmos in his mind as Blake, and the curiously miscellaneous structure of the second part of *Faust* reflects the fact.

In Blake's day the main challenge to the older construct had come from the separating of scientific space from mythological space. A universe in which God was up there and Satan down there could no longer hold together: Isaac Newton had blown the whistle, or, in Blake's language, the last trumpet, on that one. The separation of the mythical spatial categories from the actual world made their reactionary shape clear: what was up in the sky was revealed as what Blake called the ghost of the priest and king, and what was underneath was the ghost of exploited humanity. After Blake, Darwinian evolution and the new geology blew the whistle on mythological time, and the old creation-to-apocalypse view was also reduced to a construct. It is only the universes of human imagination, evidently, that can begin or end. Blake foresaw this development, but took little interest in it, in contrast again to Goethe.

Mythological space, as Blake encountered it, consisted of four main levels. At the top was a father-God associated with the sky, who made the world, and must therefore have made a model or perfect world. A myth of artificial creation has to have a myth of man's fall to complete it and account for the contrast with the creation we see now. This provides a second and a third level. The second level, the original home for man that God intended, is the "unfallen" world, Blake's world of innocence; below this is our world of "experience", and below this again a demonic and chaotic world. The first two levels are pervaded by order, harmony, concord, love, peace and stability. On our third level, these turn into authority, hierarchy, and subordination, where God is, before anything else, the supreme sovereign, the top of a pyramid, the beginning of a chain of command that continues to operate through the structures of church and state. For traditional Christianity, the crisis of history came with the Incarnation, the descent of God into the third world, which started a specific movement of authority at a definite time and place.

For Blake the entire construct had a Heraclitean cast, the descent balanced by a rising movement, symbolized by the Resurrection, where we escape from the chain of command by dying in each other's lives instead of living in each other's deaths. Naturally the Resurrection was central in traditional Christianity too, but Blake saw it as the centre of what he called the "everlasting gospel". Accepting such a gospel means, first, realizing that the creation-fall-Incarnation sequence has to be seen outside history, as a myth of the human imagination. The Resurrection meant to Blake, then, the process of abandoning the projecting of this myth, and recovering it for the human mind. Once we do this, we pass from state to community, from exploitation to imaginative work, from culture as the privilege of a few to culture as the inner condition of everyone. The arts, which tell us how the human imagination operates, are thus an untapped source of mental energy, a means of achieving social and individual freedom. Once we have recovered our imaginative birthright, we can look down on the world we have left behind and see that it forms a demonic parody of the world we are now in.

This last point cleared up for me the role of two figures who had been culture-heroes of mine from my student days, Spengler and Frazer. Their conceptions seemed to get into and inform everything I worked on, yet there was never, for me, anything of the apprentice-master relation towards them that I have just spoken of. They both seemed extraordinarily limited and benighted in general intelligence and awareness of their world, and what they had that fascinated me they seemed to have almost in spite of themselves. Eventually I realized that their limitations and their usefulness to me sprang from the same source. They were both literary or cultural critics, without realizing it, and as soon as I got this clear my conception of the real area covered by the word "criticism" vastly expanded. Frazer was a Classical scholar, whose centre of gravity was in his editions of Pausanias, Apollodorus and the *Fasti:* he thought he was a scientist, and collected a great deal of illustrative material from anthropology, but that did not make him primarily an anthropologist, however useful he may also be in that field. Spengler was a cultural critic like Ruskin (who had also come to influence me a good deal): his illustrations were historical, but that did not make him primarily a historian. He did something that no historian can do without ceasing to be one: showed how all the cultural products of a given age, medieval or Baroque or contemporary, form a unity that can be felt or intuited, though not demonstrated, a sense of unity that approximates the feeling that a human culture is a single larger body, a giant immersed in time.

Blake's "everlasting gospel" turns on the quest of Christ, the God-Man who descends from a higher world and returns to it, carrying human society with him in his ascent. Frazer demonstrated the existence in the human mind of a symbolism often latent in the unconscious, perhaps never emerging in any complete form, but revealed through many ritual acts and customs, of a divine man killed at the height of his powers, whose flesh and blood are ceremonially eaten and drunk. This symbolism expresses the social anxiety for a continuity of vigorous leadership and sexual vitality, and for a constant renewal of the food supply, as the bread and wine of the vegetable crops and the bodies of eaten animals are symbolically identical with the divine-human victim. The context of this natural theology is the cycle of the turning year, and it is based on an anxiety about keeping the cycle of nature going. The destroying or renouncing of whatever is most precious in the present moment because of an anxiety about the future seems to be a constant factor in the demonic or lowest level of cultural life, and informs the whole psychology of sacrifice, including the sacrifice of freedom which is postulated in most theories of social contract.

In the Biblical myth there is no complementary creative force to set against the artificial creation of God, no earth-mother or sexual creator, such as we find in many Oriental mythologies as well as the ancient Mediterranean and Near Eastern religions. A female principle, who represents the earth itself, and is therefore the mother, the mistress and eventually the witch-destroyer of the dying god, is at the centre of all the myths studied by Frazer, but Frazer politely overlooks her existence for the most part, and it was left for Robert Graves to incorporate her into contemporary criticism in *The White Goddess.* Blake had set forth the whole story in *The Mental Traveller* and the third part of *Jerusalem,* and it was because he had done so that I knew how important *The Golden Bough* and *The White Goddess* were. They were important because they were books about Orc and Vala; and the two of them together outlined a vision of life as it would be if man really were, as he usually believes himself to be, wholly imprisoned within the cycle of nature. Blake not only provided the vision, but the connecting links: fatalism, the worship of nature as a closed circle, the inherent death-wish or "original sin", the instinctive acceptance of authority and hierarchy, the tendency to look outside oneself for directives. For Blake Jesus is a redeemer, but Christian civilization emphatically was not: it merely set up the old projection figures of gods, angels, priests and kings once again.

The demonic aspect of historical time is clearer in Vico than in Spengler, though Vico came later into my reading. In Vico there is also a projecting of authority, first on gods, then on "heroes" or human leaders, then on the people themselves. Vico lived at a time when there had been no permanently successful example of a democracy, and from his study of Roman history he concluded that the people cannot recover the authority they project on others, and hence the third age of the people is followed by a *ricorso* that starts the cycle over again. In Spengler there is no general cyclical movement of this kind, but there is one latent in his argument. Spengler's sense of a historically finite culture, exploiting and exhausting a certain range of imaginative possibilities, provided the basis for the conception of modes outlined in the first essay of *Anatomy of Criticism.* I soon scrapped his loaded term "decline" for a more neutral conception of cultural aging, but his vision of cultural history superseded the onward-and-upward people I had read still earlier in youth, such as Bernard Shaw and H. G. Wells, who had obviously got it wrong.

In ordinary life all our hopes and desires focus on the point of renewal in the cycle of nature, the turning of winter into spring, of darkness into dawn, of age into renewed youth. But the next step in the imagination shows what a donkey's carrot this is. The exclusion of hope from Dante's hell means that his hell is an illusion: it is the hell with hope in it that is the real hell. I noticed that the acceptance of theories of recurrence seemed to accompany either neurotic obsession, as in Nietzsche, or projected forms of self-interrogation of the most dubious kind, as in Yeats' *Vision.* Also that cyclical images seemed to be central and indispensable to fascist and nazi views of history. I could understand too why reincarnation found no place in the Biblical myth. We do not know what is "true" in such matters, but reincarnation has two reactionary elements built into it. It makes possible a lessening of seriousness about the efforts to be made in this life, and, if one's own life happens to be lucky, one may rationalize that as due to one's virtue in a previous life, instead of realizing that being lucky means something very wrong in a world where most people are unlucky.

The descending movement of history is permeated by two forces expressed in mythology as Adonis and Hermes, a power and a wisdom or imagination that find their fulfilment only in death. These are the forces visualized by Frazer and by Spengler respectively. On the rising side are the forces of Prometheus and Eros, social and individual freedom. Christianity and Marxism are intensely Promethean myths—the Promethean imagery in Marx himself would make a fascinating study. In the traditional Christian universe, as we saw, the rising movement hinges on the Resurrection, which is not renewal or rebirth in time, even when it uses such imagery, but rather the opposite of rebirth, a movement upward into a different world. However, the great religions of the West, Christianity, Islam and Marxism, have developed from the revolutionary basis of Judaism, and as they attained social power they tended to the opposite extreme, of distrusting any kind of liberation that their institutions could not control. The myth of Christianity provided only the most rigidly sacramental basis for rising out of the "fallen" state, and Marxism also apparently cannot cope with the real needs of the humanities, whenever those needs reach a point that transcends the socially predictable. In the Stalinist days, when I was working on *Anatomy of Criticism*, Marxist critics could talk about nothing but Marxism, which included nothing recognizable as a direct response to literature. Since then, some Marxist thinkers have made impressive contributions to criticism, but two significant conditions appear to be necessary for them. One is living outside the countries where Marxism has come to power; the other is a separation of theory from practice, Marxist vision from Marxist tactics, which official Marxism still calls a heresy.

Similarly, anxiety about authority, whether Christian or Marxist, finds it very hard to come to terms with Eros. Even the greatest Eros poets, Plato and Dante, though they clearly understand that any driving force that lifts man upward has to be Eros-based, still accompany their visions of that rising movement with the most thorough-going forms of sublimation. In Dante the journey to paradise is made by a soul floating out of Dante's body: the Christian doctrine of bodily resurrection is accepted in theory, but postponed until after the action of the poem. The mythological universe of Christianity retained a close analogy with the human body: God was associated with the sky and the brain, the devils with the organs of excretion below. Any rising movement, attempting to leave the demonic world behind, would have to determine what and how much would have to be symbolically excreted. Because of the close anatomical connection of the genital and excretory systems, and even more because of society's constant fear of Eros, sexual love, even the physical body itself, was often included among the things that had to be left behind.

It is clear that in literature the descending order, the worlds of Adonis and Hermes, is the order that tragedy and tragic irony present from the inside, the story of fallen greatness and the subordinating of human desire and ambition to the power of the gods. The ascending order of Prometheus and Eros is similarly the order of comedy, and my special interest in comedy, which Mr. Fletcher speaks of, is connected with my constant effort to follow up Blake's conception of the socially emancipating role of the arts. Of modern thinkers, Freud knows most about Eros, but his conception of Eros, like his conception of society, is a deeply tragic one: he sees it as squirming helplessly underneath the "reality principle", even though much of the reality may have been created by Eros in the past, and as ending finally in death or Thanatos. More recently, Freud has been made into the prophet of a gospel of revolutionary optimism, just as Marx has been made into a prophet of neo-humanism: these developments indicate, for me, the strength and solidity of Blake's imaginative vision, because they fit that whether they fit Freud and Marx or not.

III

We have long since weathered the Newtonian crisis of separating mythological from natural space, and the Darwinian crisis of separating mythological from natural time. A third crisis, more difficult and subtle, is succeeding it: the distinguishing of the ordinary waking consciousness of external reality from the creative and transforming aspects of the mind. Here the distinction between the scientific and the mythological ceases to operate, for science is a creative construct like the arts. And it seems clear that there is nothing on the rising side of human life except what is, in the largest sense, creative. The question therefore resolves itself into the question of the relation of ordinary life, which begins at birth and ends at death and is lived within the ordinary categories of linear time and extended space, to other possible perspectives on that life which our various creative powers reveal.

This is a question that the great religions have tended to dodge, except in special areas. Marxism deliberately excludes it, and the traditional religious myths project it, pushing it into an "after life" in heaven or hell or purgatory or this world, conceptions which, to say nothing of their inherent crudity, betray an obvious political motivation. The area to be explored is thus reduced to methods of intensifying imaginative experience. Hence, today, the drug cults; hence the vogue for techniques of meditation, including yoga, magic, and various kinds of divination like astrology. I had noticed, ever since working on Blake, how large a part, after the decline of the "discarded model" of the Ptolemaic universe, occult schematisms had played in literature, so large as to make it clear that something more than a temporary fashion is involved now.

The current interest in such matters brings a third figure into focus within the area of cultural criticism, and that is Jung. Without belittling Jung's achievements in psychology, it is possible that he too, like Spengler and Frazer, is of greatest significance as a critical and cultural theorist. At the centre of his vision of life is a progress from the "ego", ordinary life with its haphazard and involuntary perceptions of time and space, to the "individual", who works with far more co-ordinated and schematic modes of perception. In Jung the symbol of the "individual" perception is the mandala, as he calls it (perhaps he should have called it a yantra), a symmetrical diagram recalling the geometrical cosmologies so common in the Middle Ages and the Renaissance. The view of literature set out in *Anatomy of Criticism* has many points in common with a mandala vision, so much so that many people have drawn up mandalas based on the book and have sent them to me, asking if this was what I really had in mind. I generally reply, with complete truth as far as I am concerned, that they have shown much more ingenuity in constructing their models than I could achieve myself. A mandala is not, of course, something to look at, except incidentally: it is or should become a projection of the way one sees.

I am continually asked also about my relation to Jung, and especially about the relation of my use of the word "archetype" to his. So far I have tended to resist the association, because in my experience whenever anyone mentions it his next sentence is almost certain to be nonsense. But this may actually be a reason for welcoming it. When one finds that very perceptive people are describing one as the exact opposite of what one is, one may feel that one has hit a fairly central area of social resistance. And when I, who have fought the iniquity of mystery in criticism all my life, am called a neo-Gnostic and a successor of Proclus and Iamblichus, both of them pagans, initiates of mystery-cults, and very cloudy writers, perhaps I should feel that I am well on the road to identification. Even granting the human tendency to look in every direction except the obviously right one, it seems strange to overlook the possibility that the arts, including literature, might just conceivably be what they have always been taken to be, possible techniques of meditation, in the strictest sense of the word, ways of cultivating, focussing and ordering one's mental processes, on a basis of symbol rather than concept. Certainly that was what Blake thought they were: his own art was a product of his power of meditation, and he addresses his readers in terms which indicate that he was presenting his illuminated works to them also, not as icons, but as mandalas, things to contemplate to the point at which they might reflect "yes, we too could see things that way".

One of the central principles in *Anatomy of Criticism* is founded on an analogy with music, though the usual objections to mixing up the arts, formulated in Lessing's *Laocoon* and elsewhere, do not apply to it. I am by no means the first critic to regard music as the typical art, the one where the impact of structure is not weakened, as it has been in painting and still is in literature, by false issues derived from representation. For centuries the theory of music included a good deal of cosmological speculation, and the symmetrical grammar of classical music, with its circle of fifths, its twelve-tone chromatic and seven-tone diatonic scales, its duple and triple rhythms, its concords and cadences and formulaic progressions, makes it something of a mandala of the ear. We hear the resonance of this mandala of musical possibilities in every piece of music we listen to. Occasionally we feel that what we are listening to epitomizes, so to speak, our whole musical experience with special clarity: our profoundest response to the B Minor Mass or the Jupiter Symphony is not "this is beautiful music", but something more like "this is the voice of music"; this is what music is all about. Such a sense of authority, an authority that is part of one's own dignity and is not imposed from outside, comes mainly from the resonance of all our aural experience within that piece of music. I am sorry if this sounds obscure, but such a response does happen, and words like "classic" and "masterpiece" really mean very little except the fact that it happens. One difficulty here is that the response itself may be to anything at any time, even to a bird asserting his territorial rights. The classic or masterpiece is a source of such a response that won't go away, and will not elude us if we return to it.

Anatomy of Criticism presents a vision of literature as forming a total schematic order, interconnected by recurring or conventional myths and metaphors, which I call archetypes. The vision has an objective pole: it is based on a study of literary genres and conventions, and on certain elements in Western cultural history. The order of words is there, and it is no good trying to write it off as a hallucination of my own. The fact that literature is based on unifying principles as schematic as those of music is concealed by many things, most of them psychological blocks, but the unity exists, and can be shown and taught to others, including children. But, of course, my version of that vision also has a subjective pole: it is a model only, colored by my preferences and limited by my ignorance. Others will have different versions, and as they continue to put them forth the objective reality will emerge more clearly.

One prevailing assumption in criticism is that the work of literature is an object set over against us, as something to be admired and studied. So it is, and if criticism ended there, there would be little point in trying to substitute a vast schematic abstraction, however impressive, as the end of literary experience, instead of actual plays and poems and novels. But, first, I am not suggesting that all works of literature are much the same work, or fit into the same general scheme. I am providing a kind of resonance for literary experience, a third dimension, so to speak, in which the work we are experiencing draws strength and power from everything else we have read or may still read. And, second, the strength and power do not stop with the work out there, but pass into us. When students complain that it will kill a poem to analyze it, they think (because they have been told so) that the poem ought to remain out there, as an object to be contemplated and enjoyed. But the poem is also a power of speech to be possessed in his own way by the reader, and some death and rebirth process has to be gone through before the poem revives within him, as something now uniquely his, though still also itself.

Jung being a psychologist, he is concerned with existential archetypes, not imaginative ones: with the recurring characters and images that turn up on the way to "individuation". His most significant book, from our present point of view, is his *Psychology and Alchemy,* in which he treats the "great work" of the alchemists as an allegory of self-transformation, a process of bringing an immortal body (the stone) to birth within the ordinary one (the *materia prima*). Such a work of transformation is the work specifically of saints, mystics and yogis. However the alchemists managed, it seems to require teachers, oral instruction, and joining a school, and it is so unimaginably difficult that very few get far along the way, though they undoubtedly make a big difference to the world when they do. The transmission of such teaching, however, is often accompanied, especially in the East, by a total unconcern for society as a whole, or else, especially in the West, by an over-concern with the preserving of the unity of the transmitting body. In any case some powerful force of social entropy seems to affect it wherever it appears.

One of the most impressive figures in this tradition in our own century, Gurdjieff, distinguishes two elements in man: the essence and the persona, what a man really is and what he has taken on through his social relationships. Gurdjieff clearly thought of the kind of training that he could give as essentially a developing and educating of the essence. Perhaps there is also a way to development through the persona, through transforming oneself into a focus of a community. This includes all the activity that we ordinarily call creative, and is shown at its clearest in the production of the arts. What is particularly interesting about alchemy is the way in which it uses the same kind of symbolism that we find in literature to describe the "great work" of the mystic. If spiritual seeker and poet share a common language, perhaps we cannot fully understand either without some reference to the other.

Here we return to the point we started from: the nature of the commitment to literature. We remember Yeats:

> The intellect of man is forced to choose
> Perfection of the life, or of the work,
> And if it take the second must refuse
> A heavenly mansion, raging in the dark.

It seems to me that the first two lines express a profound insight, and that the next two are self-dramatizing nonsense. Those who seek perfection of the work, though called creators, are really, as they keep telling us, more like receptors: they are nursing mothers (the female metaphor we began with has, we see, a proper application) bringing to birth something not themselves, yet more genuinely themselves than they are. The something, call it a poem, is made out of both conscious and unconscious materials: the unconscious is something that nobody short of a bodhisattva can control, but in certain mental places it can find its own mode of expression. When it does so, it forms a kind of transformer of mental power, sending its voltage into its readers until, as Blake says, the expanding eyes of man behold the depth of wondrous worlds.

It is at this point that the question of the social function of the arts becomes so important. Some people find it a shock to discover that, say, the commandant of a nazi death camp can also be someone with a highly developed taste in music. If he had a thorough knowledge of organic chemistry, there would be no shock; but—well, the arts are supposed to have or be based on values, aren't they? But that is precisely the trouble. We find it hard to escape from the notion that the arts are a secondary social luxury, something to turn to after the real standards of living have been met. On that basis they become subject to evaluation, like jewels: they are enjoyed and possessed by what Jung calls the "ego", and something even analogous to price develops. The arts approached in that way can add pleasure and refinement and cultivation and even some serenity to life, but they have no power to transform it, and the notion that they have is for the birds.

It would be better to think of the arts as, like physical exercise, a primary human need that has been smothered under false priorities. If we look at any culture that has reduced its standard of living to the barest essentials, like that of the Eskimos, we see at once how poetry leaps into the foreground as one of those essentials. Not only so, but the kind of poetry that emerges has precisely the quality of primitive simplicity that keeps eluding the poets of a more complex society, however earnestly they seek it. One might start drawing morals here about what kind of society we should reconstruct or return to in order to achieve such simplicity, but most of them would be pretty silly. I merely stress the possibility, importance and genuineness of a response to the arts in which we can no longer separate that response from our social context and personal commitments. As for the danger of poetry becoming a "substitute" for religion, that again is merely bad metaphor: if both poetry and religion are functioning properly, their interpenetration will take care of itself.

The descending side of our world-picture is the side of the past, the chain of authority and subordination that has persisted all through history. In its most concentrated form it is a closed circle, all efforts to break with it, like revolutions, ending in real revolution, that is, the wheel turning again. Thus it is the world of the future, of hope and expectancy for the not yet, as well as the record of the no longer. The ascending side is the power of creation, directed toward the goal of creating a genuinely human community. Tragedy presents the descending world from the inside, but it is, no less than the comedy which presents the activity of creation itself, a recreation of memory and frustrated desire, where the spectres of the dead, in Blake's phrase, who inhabit the memory take on living form. The central symbol of the descending side is metamorphosis, the fall of gods or other spiritual beings into mankind, of mankind, through Circean enchantments, into animals, of all living things into dead matter. On the ascending side there is a reversal of metamorphosis, a disenchanting journey back to our original identity that ends when the human creator recovers his creations from his Muses, and lives again, like Job, with the daughters of his memory transformed into a renewed presence.

Charms and Riddles

The study of genres, or the differentiating factors in literary experience, is not yet begun. Despite a book called *Beyond Genre*, we have not got to the subject yet, much less beyond it: we do not even know where the conception stops. But clearly there are different kinds of genres, and perhaps a botanical analogy may be helpful in approaching their variety. There are genres of imagery, the roots of literature, a vast subterranean tangle of metaphors and image-clusters, attached to and drawing in sustenance from experience outside literature, yet showing typical forms of relationship to that experience. There are genres of narrative, the stems and branches, typical ways of beginning, proceeding, and ending. There are genres of structure, the leaf-flower-fruit cycles of literature: these are based on what we call conventions, and are where all the familiar generic terms, such as epic and drama, belong. And finally, there are generic seeds or kernels, possibilities of expression sprouting and exfoliating into new literary phenomena. Two of these last, charms and riddles, I should like to consider here, picking up and expanding a theme in my *Anatomy of Criticism*.

Charm is from *carmen*, song, and the primary associations of charm are with music, sound and rhythm. The native word for charm is "spell," which is related, if somewhat indirectly, to the other meaning of spell in the sense of reading letter by letter, or sound by sound. Riddle is from the same root as read: in fact "read a riddle" was once practically a verb with a cognate object, like "tell a tale" or "sing a song." And just as the connections of charm are closer to music, so the riddle has pictorial affinities, related to ciphers, acrostics, rebuses, concrete and shape poetry, and everything that emphasizes the visual aspect of literature. Emblem books are a flourishing development of riddle poetry, and any picture that needs a verbal commentary to make its point may be said to be a pictorial riddle. Hieroglyphics and Chinese characters have a large element of riddle-reading obviously built into them: alphabetic systems also have it, though less noticeably.

Hence charm and riddle illustrate the fact that literature, with its combination of rhythm and imagery, is intermediate between the musical and the pictorial arts. They also represent the contrasting aspects of literature that we call sound and sense, rhyme and reason. These two factors, taken together, show that the riddle, in particular, illustrates the association in the human mind between the visual and the conceptual. What is understood must, at least metaphorically, be spread out in space: whatever is taken in through the ear has to form a series of simultaneous patterns *(Gestalten)* in order to be intelligible. Factors which inhibit this, such as too high a speed of utterance, prevent understanding. We may illustrate by a dialogue in *Through the Looking Glass:*

> "Can you do Addition?" the White Queen asked. "What's one and one and one and one and one and one and one and one and one and one?"
>
> "I don't know," said Alice. "I lost count."

The White Queen is not employing a charm, but she illustrates the overwhelming of sense by sound, which is where charm starts.

Charms have their roots in magic, and the central idea of the magic of charm is to reduce freedom of action, either by compelling a certain course of action or by stopping action altogether. The technique is hypnotic: if A charms B, B is compelled to do what A wants; if a woman charms a man, the man, according to convention, becomes her slave. One very simple kind of charm is a formula to get rid of a disease or some parallel evil. You may compel the evil by possessing a name: you can compel a devil to clear out either by knowing his name or the name of someone like Jesus he's afraid of. Or you can compel by the force of rhythm and sound alone, by getting the right words into the right order at the right speed, and so setting up a kind of movement that the thing being charmed will be forced to imitate. The fiddle that compels everyone who hears it to dance is a familiar folktale theme, and expresses one of the central conceptions of charm very clearly. Thus in a fourteenth-century charm against rats:

> I command all the ratons that are here about
> That none dwell in this place, within ne without,
> Through the virtue of Jesu Christ, that Mary bare about,
> That all creatures owen for to lout,
> And through the virtue of Mark, Matthew, Luke and John,
> All four Evangels corden into one . . .

The basis of this charm, obviously, is the reciting of powerful names which set up an energy capable of driving out everything opposed to them. At the same time, when you drive something out, you cleanse or protect the space that the enemy has vacated. The invoking of the evangelists reminds us of the bedtime charm:

> Matthew, Mark, Luke and John,
> Bless the bed that I lie on

where there have to be four protectors, one for each corner of the bed, to keep hostile powers away. The outlining of the protected space is as important as the driving out of the enemy: this frequently means that the enemy may have a counter-spell that also has to be kept at bay, as in the song for Titania in *A Midsummer Night's Dream:*

> Never harm
> Nor spell nor charm

Come our lovely lady nigh.
So good night, with lullaby.

The rhetoric of charm is dissociative and incantatory: it sets up a pattern of sound so complex and repetitive that the ordinary processes of response are short-circuited. Refrain, rhyme, alliteration, assonance, pun, antithesis: every repetitive device known to rhetoric is called into play. Such repetitive formulas break down and confuse the conscious will, hypnotize and compel to certain courses of action. Or they may simply put to sleep, which is one of the primary aims of hypnotism: one obvious example of charm poetry is the lullaby, which we have just met in the *Midsummer Night's Dream* song. Drowsy and narcotic repetitions of sound, with analogies to lullabies, turn up frequently in Spenser among others:

And more, to lulle him in his slumber soft,
A trickling streame from high rocke tumbling downe
And ever-drizling raine upon the loft,
Mixt with a murmuring winde, much like the sowne
Of swarming Bees, did cast him in a swowne:
No other noyse, nor peoples troublous cryes,
As still are wont t'annoy the walled towne,
Might there be heard: but carelesse Quiet lyes,
Wrapt in eternall silence farre from enemyes.

The assonance of "noyse" and "annoy," which would be a mere blunder in an incompetent poet, is here a carefully calculated discord designed to express the mingling of mental impressions that precedes the coming of sleep.

The association with less freedom of action leads us from the lullaby to the more sinister sleeping song, the siren song that may lure one to one's death. Spenser again has many passages of this type: the context of the one just quoted is sinister, and the first book of *The Faerie Queene*, from which it comes, reaches a rhetorical climax of sinister charm with the temptation of Despair. Falling asleep in a world of echoic associations is in turn close to the elegiac tone in poetry, the kind of rhetoric appropriate for talking about death or the vanishing of things into the past, as in the *ubi sunt* convention in medieval poetry. Here is another Spenserian example: as often in Spenser, the alexandrine at the end of a stanza announces the theme of the following stanza, which is a rhetorical exercise on that theme:

> Wrath, gelosie, griefe, love this Squire have layd thus low.
>
> Wrath, gealosie, grief, love do thus expell:
> Wrath is a fire, and gealosie a weede,
> Griefe is a flood, and love a monster fell;
> The fire of sparkes, the weede of little seede,
> The flood of drops, the Monster filth did breede:
> But sparks, seed, drops, and filth do thus delay:
> The sparks soone quench, the springing seed outweed,
> The drops dry up, and filth wipe cleane away:
> So shall wrath, gealosie, griefe, love dye and decay.

This passage was quoted in a rhetoric book before it was published, but the point is not simply rhetorical virtuosity. The use of repeated sound, alliteration, rhyme, assonance and refrain, invokes a meditative mood cutting through the normal waking responses. Similarly with poems that pick up echoes of the "dust to dust" formula of burial services:

> Erthe toc of erthe erthe wyth woh;
> erthe other erthe to the erthe droh;
> erthe leyde erthe in erthene throh.
> Tho hevede erthe of erthe erthe ynoh.

Perhaps there was originally, in such elegiac rhetoric, a magical attempt to quiet down a restless ghost. Certainly there is something protective in it against a much deeper anxiety. Elegiac poetry includes the danse macabre, a form like that of the theme and variations in music, where Death is the theme and a number of people who die are the variations. Here the repetitions, like the refrain in Dunbar's "Lament for the Makaris," "Timor mortis conturbat me," express, not a charm imposed by Death—Death is too powerful to need charms—but the poet's anxiety about dying. Anxieties, when they become sufficiently obsessive, often generate an uncontrollable mechanism of verbal dissociation, in which (to use an example I once encountered) one may spend a night pondering the implications of "break up" and "break down."

Such states of mind, where one experiences the real horror and malignancy of being under a spell, are usually states of nightmare or insomnia, and from this point of view the charm techniques associated with sleep and death are really counter-charms, modes of escape from them. They may be projected as a fear of witches, or, more profoundly, a fear of hell, a world where one can never sleep or die. The vision of "Corps pourriz et ames en flammes" is central in Villon, whose favorite form is the testament, where the speaker is about to die and disintegrate into aspects of himself which he distributes to others, and whose ballades sometimes use repetitive techniques to the point of suggesting obsession. In English literature the repetitive rhetoric of anxiety appears in Donne's *Devotions Upon Emergent Occasions*, more particularly in the terrible fifteenth "Expostulation," under the rubric "I sleep not day nor night."

Charms can also be social, and one use of repetition is to bind the community into a single enterprise. Political oratory depends on patterns of repetition ("of the people, by the people, for the people"), and so do sermons and similar types of communal exhortation. If we look through a Protestant hymn book, we may notice that the more evangelical and aggressive the sect that the hymn has originated in, the more likely it is to throw its emphasis on a refrain or chorus. Yet even in community songs there may still be something of the cleared and protected place, with charms to keep off those who threaten it, even if they merely withdraw from it. In one of the most festive drinking songs in English, for instance, it is interesting to see that the main emotional focus is not on the convivial group at all:

And he that will this toast deny,
Down among the dead men,
Down among the dead men,

Down,
Down,
Down,
Down,
Down among the dead men let him lie.

The compulsion inherent in charm means that authority and subordination are integral to it. Words of command in an army are not in the usual sense of the term charming, but they are highly stylized in rhetoric, and they depend for their effectiveness on a long training in what is essentially a form of hypnosis, automatic response to a verbal stimulus. When the television commercial comes on, and the ordinary viewer goes to the bathroom, the literary critic should stay where he is, listening to the alliteration, antithesis, epigram (i.e., slogan-writing) and similar rhetorical devices that invade the sound track as soon as the subject becomes really important. The products are presented as magical objects, and the hypnotic voice of the announcer compels us to go straight down to the store and demand that product, not forgetting the name. Here the tone of giving orders to a mesmerized subordinate is naturally disguised, but the mood is still imperative and the rhetoric repetitive.

In English poetry of the 1590–1640 period, particularly, all areas of order and authority are thought of as protected areas, dependent on something analogous to a spell to keep off the powers of anarchy. Love, similarly, had a cosmological aspect as the charm that created order out of chaos, and love in turn was, in its Christian context, part of the creation by the Word of God itself, which pronounced the original spell to keep chaos away. The Book of Job expresses this spell as "hitherto shalt thou come but no further; and here shall thy proud waves be stayed." Similarly with the beginning of the creation in Milton:

"Silence, ye troubled waves, and, thou deep, peace!"
Said then th'omnific Word: "your discord end!"

The word "discord" emphasizes the connection of the creative Word with music, the "harmony" which was also of the essence of the original charm imposed on chaos. The spells of love, harmony and the Word of God come down to us from a superior world: if we wish to assert our authority over, say, rats, we invoke this higher authority and join ourselves to it. As a result the rhetoric of charm incorporates an analogical formula of an "as that, so this" type.

In the word "spellbound," the conception of "binding" suggests inhibition generally, but also implies a mythical system of some kind invoked by specific names and other formulas. The charmer is bound into this system and gets his power from it; whatever is charmed is externally bound by it. In the second Idyl of Theocritus *(Pharmaketyriai)*, a girl is performing a rite to bring back her lost lover. She melts a waxen image, and says: as this puppet melts, so may Daphnis melt (i.e., into affection for me). This is uncomplicated sympathetic magic, where the "as that, so this" formula merely connects two objects. But she then says, in a negative formula: as Theseus forsook Ariadne, so may Daphnis forsake the girl he's got now. Here we have an extension of the binding notion: something in a myth is used as an archetypal model to be followed by the present situation. Exorcism incorporates this pattern: as Jesus compelled the devils to leave possessed men, so I compel these rats to leave this house. The whole principle of sacramental imitation in religion, the binding of one's life into a pattern following the model prescribed by scripture or the life of a saint, flowers out of this. The vow, the verbal formula that binds one to a certain course of life, is a self-administered charm of the same type. Here we have, of course, moved out of the orbit of magic, but, as we shall see in a moment, the literary devices employed are very little changed.

The girl in Theocritus turns a wheel which she addresses as "iynx," the name of a bird who was doubtless in the original rite, if not in this one, pinioned to the wheel and turned with it. The magic involved here is that of gaining power by imprisoning some spirit or force of life. Such a conception gives us a nonreligious motive for the popularity of the crucifix in the Christian world, as well as for the belief in its peculiar efficacy against demons. The address to the iynx and the wheel forms a refrain, which as we saw is one of the technical devices typical of charms. Whenever we find this combination of refrain, elegiac mood, efforts to reinforce one's own power, and archetypal allusions on the "as that, so this" model, we have charm poetry, as in the Old English "Complaint of Deor".

When we drive out rats in the name of Christ and his evangelists, we are using a magic that keeps in with the establishment, so to speak; when a young woman invokes Hecate, as the speaker in Theocritus does, to bring back the affections of her lover, something else is involved. Divine charms founded the orders of creation and of human society; magic that starts at the human level, searching for powers greater than itself, is more likely to turn to the mysterious beings in the lower world, who in the Christian centuries were nearly all demonic, and had been sinister and dangerous long before that. Such beings, expressions of man's fear of an indifferent and powerful natural order, may operate on their own initiative to work disaster for us. The typical response to this kind of threat is the negative or ironic charm that says, in effect: there is nothing here for you; please go away. This wistful little Eskimo chant is, we are told, a charm to ensure fine weather:

> Poor it is: this land,
> Poor it is: this ice,
> Poor it is: this air,
> Poor it is: this sea,
> Poor it is.

Sinister charms, which may operate on us from the unknown, or which we may gain possession of to control others, are normally powers pushing us or our enemies into a lower state of existence. The typical form of this movement is descending metamorphosis, the changing of a conscious being into an animal or vegetable or inanimate form, as the charms of Circe changed men to animals. (The reason for inserting the word "descending" will be clearer when we come to riddles.) We notice in the elegy over the dead squire in Spenser the imagery of elements dissolving back into chaos. The lower state is often symbolized as a subterranean or submarine world, where, like Narcissus, we pass from substance to shadow or reflection. What Narcissus was to the eye his mistress Echo was to the ear, and the echo song is a standard literary development of charm poetry. The "harmony" of the music of the spheres is reproduced, or, much more frequently, parodied, in the harmony of the siren or Lorelei song. Thus the crucial temptation in Spenser's Bower of Bliss takes the form of a five-part madrigal, where a strong emphasis is laid on harmony and concord:

> For all that pleasing is to living eare,
> Was there consorted in one harmonee,
> Birdes, voyces, instruments, windes, waters, all agree.
>
> The joyous birdes shrouded in chearefull shade,
> Their notes unto the voyce attempred sweet;
> Th'Angelicall soft trembling voyces made
> To th' instruments divine respondence meet:
> The silver sounding instruments did meet
> With the base murmure of the waters fall:
> The waters fall with difference discreet,
> Now soft, now loud, unto the wind did call:
> The gentle warbling wind low answered to all.

We may note the concord of the identical rhyme on two meanings of "meet," very possibly the only word in the English language that would have been meet for such a purpose.

The last line quoted from the rat charm, "All four Evangels corden into one," illustrates the upper dimension of harmony. The fact that the four Gospels are a harmony is a central Christian doctrine, and of course one gets four times as much power over rats by using all four names. But beyond this there is the sense of a concord or harmony brought into play which the rats cannot disrupt. Such magic may be reversed in direction when we want not to expel something, but to make something or somebody appear. Thus in the invocation to Sabrina in Milton's *Comus:*

Listen, and appear to us,
In name of great Oceanus,
By the earth-shaking Neptune's mace,
And Tethys' grave majestic pace;
By hoary Nereus' wrinkled look,
And the Carpathian wizard's hook;
By scaly Triton's winding shell,
And old soothsaying Glaucus' spell;
By Leucothea's lovely hands,
And her son that rules the strands;
By Thetis' tinsel-slippered feet,
And the songs of Sirens sweet;
By dead Parthenope's dear tomb,
And fair Ligea's golden comb,
Wherewith she sits on diamond rocks
Sleeking her soft alluring locks;
By all the nymphs that nightly dance
Upon thy streams with wily glance;
Rise, rise, and heave thy rosy head
From thy coral-paven bed,
And bridle in thy headlong wave,
Till thou our summons answered have.
Listen and save!

The average reader has to look up something like seventeen Classical allusions in the notes to make sense of this passage. If he does, he may miss the point that the vagueness and mystery of the names is one of the reasons for using them. But if he does not, he may miss the equally important point that the names are being used with great precision. The simple archetypal parallel of "as that, so this" has greatly expanded here: a whole mythological construct is being set up, one assumed to be so powerful that Sabrina will be compelled to manifest herself within it. The address is to a water-nymph, a benevolent and not a sinister one, but connecting with the same Lorelei imagery of webs, veils, shrouding hair, and other threshold images of sinking into sleep, as well as of a reflecting water-world like that of Narcissus. In the *Pervigilium Veneris,* where the refrain, the elegiac tone, and the theme of compelling love to return make it clear that the poem is generically a charm poem, the imagery takes on similar qualities:

> In spring lovers form harmonies (concordant); in spring the birds mate, and the grove unbinds her hair (nemus comam resolvit).

The traditional realm of magical power is normally the area symbolized by the *diva triformis* or threefold goddess, the Hecate of the lower world, invoked in Theocritus, the Diana of the woodland, and the moon. The power of drawing down the moon is a conventional attribute of magicians and witches, and has been constantly alluded to since Virgil's Eighth Eclogue, which is partly an adaptation of Theocritus' charm poem, popularized it ("carmina vel caelo possunt deducere lunam"). What is meant by it is not so much actual control of the lunar cycle as the acquiring of magical powers from the highest level of our "sublunary" world, the moon beneath whose mirror-reflection we are all imprisoned. The link of the upper mirror of the moon and the lower mirrors of seas and lakes runs all through the poetry of charm. Edgar Allan Poe is full of images of reflections, from the moon itself to the house of Usher crumbling into its mirror in the "tarn." Sometimes what we have is a "wilderness of mirrors," in Eliot's phrase, reflections reflecting reflections:

> And now, as the night was senescent
> And star-dials pointed to morn—
> As the star-dials hinted of morn—
> At the end of our path a liquescent
> And nebulous lustre was born,
> Out of which a miraculous crescent
> Arose with a duplicate horn—
> Astarte's bediamonded crescent
> Distinct with its duplicate horn.

One obvious question about charm in its magical context is, who or what can be compelled by a charm? Magicians seem in practice to be confined mainly to elemental spirits, the shades of the dead, and a few very minor lower gods, or, in Christianity, minor devils. Superior powers, even if infernal like Hecate, may be invoked, but not compelled. The language of invocation, however, differs rhetorically very little from the language of compulsion. This is why religious poetry tends to use the same repetitive and dissociative techniques that we glanced at earlier. Here the poet is on the other end of the charm, so to speak, trying to break down his own resistances to the influx of a greater spirit. Examples range from the fourteenth-century *Pearl* to the opening paragraph of the fifth section of Eliot's *Ash-Wednesday,* and include Donne, though the Donne of the sermons rather than of the sacred poetry.

Further, if greater powers cannot be compelled, they can compel us, and hence we should expect similar techniques in sacred scriptures embodying a divine revelation. If we pick up the Koran, for instance, and try to read it as we should read any other book, we may well find its repetitiveness intolerable: surely, we feel, the God who inspired this book was not only monotheistic but monomaniacal. And even this response comes only from a translation: the original is so dependent on the interlocking sound-patterns of Arabic that in practice the Arabic language has had to go everywhere the Islamic religion has gone. Yet, for anyone brought up in the religion of Islam, hearing the Koran from infancy, and memorizing great parts of it consciously and unconsciously, the Koran does precisely the rhetorical job it is set up to do. The conception of the human will assumed is that of a puppy on a leash: it plunges about in every direction but the right one, and has to be brought back and back and back to the same controlling power.

The rhetoric of God, then, according to the Koran, is essentially the kind of rhetoric we have associated with charm. This principle is far less true of the Bible, even though much of the Hebrew text is oracular in style and contains many puns and sound-associations, invocations to God, commandments, proverbs or general maxims of prudent conduct, prophetic oracles, and, in the New Testament, the parables of Jesus which end "go thou and do likewise." But the specific techniques of dissociative writing are still rather rare: the Old Testament, with its fondness for acrostic poems and the like, has more in common with the riddle, and in the New Testament dissociative rhetoric almost disappears. There is some of it in the first Epistle of John:

> That which was from the beginning, that which we have heard, that which we have seen with our eyes, that which we beheld, and our hands handled, concerning the Word of life (and the life was manifested, and we have seen, and bear witness, and declare unto you the life, the eternal life, which was with the Father, and was manifested unto us): that which we have seen and heard declare we unto you also . . .

but it is so isolated as to give almost the effect of senility, which is perhaps why some scholars insist on ascribing it to the apostolic John writing at the age of a hundred and twenty or so.

The more closely the magical aspect of charm is adhered to in poetry, the more likely the poem is to present some kind of specific ritual, as the Theocritus poem does. When the "as that, so this" formula is employed in such a context, the "this" refers to the ritual being performed and the "that" to an archetypal myth which the ritual is not only referring to but re-creating. The ritual is, so to speak, the epiphany or manifestation of myth, as the ritual of the mass in Christianity manifests the myth of incarnation. In highly developed cultures, myths, as I have tried to show elsewhere, stick together to form mythologies, and mythologies eventually expand into mythological universes, as the mythology of Christianity in medieval times expanded into the universe that forms the setting of Dante's *Commedia.* Wherever we turn in charm poetry, we seem to be led back to some kind of mythological universe, a world of interlocking names of mysterious powers and potencies which are above, but not wholly beyond reach of, the world of time and space. This mythological universe may be thought of as a real existence revealed to us in a scripture of divine origin, or it may be simply regarded as an imaginative human construct. But it is artificial, whether the artificer is divine or human: it is not the actual outward environment of man, nor is it a primitive attempt to describe that environment, even when it tries to develop a philosophy and a science. It is a separate world that is reached through imagination or belief or acceptance of traditional authority, not through direct sense experience, or, except in very limited ways, through reason. This is as far as we can take the problem of charm before turning to riddles.

II

Those who consult oracles usually do so with a sense of uncritical awe, but oracles and oracular prophecies frequently turn on puns, ambiguous or double-faced statements, or sometimes, as in *Macbeth*, on quibbles that sound like feeble-minded jokes. There is a point at which emotional involvement may suddenly reverse itself and become intellectual detachment, the typical expression of which is laughter. In Zen Buddhism there is a conventional dialogue form in which an earnest disciple asks a deeply serious question of a master, expecting an oracular answer: he gets a brush-off answer which is designed to push him into this mental reversal. Thus:

> Disciple: Can a dog have a Buddha-nature?
> Master: Bow-wow.

Similarly, the riddle is essentially a charm in reverse: it represents the revolt of the intelligence against the hypnotic power of commanding words. In the riddle a verbal trap is set, but if one can "guess," that is, point to an outside object to which the verbal construct can be related, the something outside destroys it as a charm, and we have sprung the trap without being caught in it. The pun on "meet" that we noted in Spenser is part of the hypnotizing and spell-binding quality of the stanza, where different things are drawn into a single focus by similar sounds. But the puns which answer riddles of the "Why is A like B?" type are jokes, and so emphasize the disparity that a conscious mind perceives between two things.

Charms and riddles, however, are psychologically very close

together, as the unguessed or unguessable riddle is or may be a charm. Amulets, abracadabras, Latin tags, jargon words, formulas like the *in principio* of Chaucer's friar, are all charms, or act like charms, as long as they are not understood. Again, the charm you have may be a riddle for somebody else to smash or solve. In *Beowulf* much is made of wound and twisted and curiously wrought objects, often weapons or pieces of armor. These have affinities with the crucifixes and similar power-imprisoning charms mentioned above, but of course an enemy would be out to destroy them.

Hence riddles often imply some kind of enmity-situation or contest, where you will lose a great deal, perhaps your life, if you don't know the answer. The reversal of a charm can be clearly seen in such contests. In a fifteenth-century dialogue between the devil and a virgin, the devil poses a number of riddles, the implication being that the girl will lose her soul if she can't answer. She prays to Jesus for assistance, gets the answers, and the last one, "what's worse than a woman?" has for answer "the devil." As soon as he's named, the devil flies away. A variant of this type of riddle poem is a dialogue between a "false knight" and a school-boy. The boy is asked questions and various imprecations are hurled at him: again the assumption is, or originally was, that if he doesn't answer the question or can't think of a rejoinder he's done for. In cosier and more domesticated versions, a knight seduces a damsel who protests that he ought to marry her: he says he will if she can guess riddles of the same type: she does and he does.

Hence just as charm is connected with sinking into a lower world with less freedom of movement in it, so riddle is connected with comic resolutions, comic recognition scenes of escape or rescue, or with such folktale themes as performing the impossible task, which occurs in the story of Psyche in Apuleius. The guessing of a name, as in Grimm's Rumpelstiltskin story, may be an impossible task of this kind. The riddle is also connected with the very common type of recognition scene which turns on a shift of identity, where, say, the heroine is proved to have been stolen by pirates in infancy, so that her present social status is lower than the one she ought to have. The idea behind such a device is, more or less, "guess who she is," where the link with the riddle becomes clear. In the enmity-situation or contest, the audience's sympathy is normally on the side of the successful riddle-guesser. He is the antithesis of the magician or charmer, and the magician often takes a demonic role as his opposite. The life of Jesus in the Gospels is full of skilful answers to malignant dilemma-questions which mark an affinity to the same literary type. Oedipus and Samson, on the other hand, are tragic figures because their riddle-solving or propounding powers have disappeared into an irrecoverable past.

With the Old English riddles we come to a form which is not so much a verbal trap as a verbal spider-web: they describe something obliquely, and often end with some such formula as "ask what is my name," implying that the guessing is an integral part of the poetic experience involved:

> My head is forged by a hammer, wounded with pointed tools, rubbed by the file. Often I gape at what is fixed opposite to me, when, girded with rings, I must needs thrust stoutly against the hard bolt; pierced from behind I must shove forward that which guards the joy of my lord's mind at midnight. At times I drag my nose, the guardian of the treasure, backwards, when my lord desires to take the stores of those whom at his will he commanded to be driven out of life by murderous power. (Key.)

> I saw two hard captives carried into the dwelling under the roof of the hall; they were companions fettered fast together by strait bonds. Close to one of them was a dark-haired slave-woman who controlled both of them fast in bonds in their course. (Flail.)

What one notices first of all in such poems is the tremendous energy of movement around the objects: the hard physical effort both in creating them and in using them is what is suggested. Here we are again in a world of metamorphosis, but one of a different kind. Just as a picture may seem to us an arrest of energy, rhythm, and movement suddenly caught for a motionless instant, so these riddles show us a dissolving and reshaping movement that comes into a stationary focus as soon as we guess, that is, infer what the solid physical object is that the swirling energy leads up to. The movement is towards identity rather than, as in Ovidian metamorphosis, away from it. Naming such objects also has analogies to waking up from a dream, in the way that Scrooge's ghost of Christmas Future in Dickens was finally identified as a bedpost.

The two examples quoted show that Old English riddles are of two kinds. The object may be described by the poet, or the object may speak for itself and then challenge the reader to guess its name. The latter uses the figure of speech known as prosopopoeia, and develops into such extended forms as Shelley's *The Cloud.* In descending or charm metamorphosis, where, say, Circe transforms men into animals, something once capable of speech and consciousness is obliged to fall silent. The power of words over things, the central principle of charm, eventually separates the magician who has the power of words from the bewitched creature who has lost it and become a mere object. The speaking object reverses the direction of charm, and from the speaking object it is a short step, in imagination, to the identification of the poet, not only with the object, but with all the energy that, as we saw, is reflected in the object. In the collection of Chinese poems known as the *Ch'u Tz'u* there are many passages like this which, according to the translator, show the influence of shamanism, with its ecstatic and erotic flights up to a higher identity with nature:

> I aim my long arrow and shoot the Wolf of Heaven;
> I seize the Dipper to ladle cinnamon wine.
> Then holding my reins I plunge down to my setting
> On my gloomy night journey back to the east.

The popular Restoration poet Tom Durfey is unlikely to have been in touch with Siberian shamans, so it is all the more interesting that the same type of imagery appears in him:

> I'll sail upon the dog-star,
> And then pursue the morning:

I'll chase the moon till it be noon,
But I'll make her leave her horning.

The difference between charm and riddle is thus mainly in imaginative direction. In the Old English period we have, besides the riddles in the Exeter Book mentioned above, the Latin riddles of Bishop Aldhelm, which begin with an acrostic, make many references to books and writing materials, the visual aspect of the producing of words, and conclude with a long and remarkable poem on the creation, in which the poet sees all the objects he had mentioned as contained within the providence of God's creation. One would think, then, that if the charm takes us, as we said, into the mythological universe of traditional names and mysterious powers, the riddle seems rather to take us into the actual world explored by sense experience, where the eye is overwhelmingly prominent, and the reason. Its context appears to be nature, traditionally regarded in the Christian centuries as a secondary word of God, less dependent on special revelation and more accessible to the unaided intellect. But there are difficulties in this view of riddles, difficulties which are indicated by the strong bias of the riddle toward humor and joking, to puzzle and paradox, to a sense of absurdity in the juxtaposing of visual images and ideas. When a verbal account of an object is followed by the "guess," actual or simulated, at what the object is, we may feel that it provides an avenue of escape into the outer world of sense. But it is something of an illusory escape, as poetry cannot really take us outside the world of poetry. Poem and object are very quizzically related: there seems to be some riddle behind all riddles which we have not yet guessed.

In literature, where there is no attempt at actual magic, a poet may work with either form, and in modern times, at least, a poet interested in charm techniques is likely to be interested in riddle techniques also, if only because both present technical problems. We quoted a stanza from Poe's "Ulalume" which is essentially charm poetry, but Poe also dealt in riddles, and some of his poems are complicated acrostics. Similarly in *Finnegans Wake* we have a kind of language that could be read either as oracular dream language or as associative wit. Joyce's contemporary Gertrude

Stein came to be thought of as the very type of dissociative writer, was often ridiculed or caricatured on that basis, and of course it is true that she was greatly interested in dissociative techniques. Here is an example from *Tender Buttons:*

> A no, a no since, a no since when, a no since when since, a no since when since a no since when since, a no since, a no-since when since, a no since, a no, a no since a no since, a no since, a no since.

But many of the vignettes in *Tender Buttons* are riddles of a fairly conventional type, with the solution, as often happens, provided in the title. Thus under the title "A Petticoat" we have "A light white, a disgrace, an ink spot, a rosy charm."

But with works less relentlessly experimental than *Finnegans Wake* or *Tender Buttons,* we can see shifts in emphasis from one to the other. Charm poetry represents one aspect of what Eliot calls a dissociation of sensibility: a mood is summoned up and everything excluded which would disturb that mood. The polemical context of Eliot's phrase reminds us that charm poetry, shown at its subtlest in Keats and Tennyson and at its clearest in Poe and Swinburne, dominated taste until about 1915, after which a mental attitude more closely related to the riddle began to supersede it, one more preoccupied with the visual and the conceptual. Thus Eliot also contrasted the "clear visual images" of Dante with the musical myopia of Milton, spoke of Swinburne as a poet who does not think, and found a more congenial precedent in Donne's "metaphysical" combinations of concrete and abstract imagery. One of the first products of the newer taste was the imagist movement, with its concentration on visualized imagery and description. The tendency itself was of course not new: here for example is Josh Billings, in the nineteenth century:

> The crane iz neither flesh, beast, nor fowl, but a sad
>   mixtur ov all theze things.
> He mopes along the brinks of kreeks and wet places,
>   looking for sumthing he haz lost.
> He has a long bill, long wings, long legs, and iz long
>   all over.

When he flies thru the air, he iz az graceful az a
windmill, broke loose from its fastenings.

This poem (it is a poem, whatever Billings meant it to be) is not technically a riddle poem, because the object it describes is named in it, but it is clearly an imagist poem. I quote it for two reasons. First, its humorous tone marks its affinity with the riddle tradition more clearly than, say, a poem of Amy Lowell; second, it suggests another feature with some links to the riddle tradition, the rhetorical device of the pseudo-definition, which appears in another riddle-poet, Emily Dickinson:

Renunciation—is a piercing Virtue—

This is also the device on which the character books of the seventeenth century were built. The character books derive from Theophrastus in Greek literature, but develop his fairly sober and straightforward observation into epigram and paradox, written in a kind of sing-song antithetical prose. Thus Samuel Butler:

A Sailor

Leaves his native earth to become an inhabitant of the sea, and is but a kind of naturaliz'd fish. He is of no place, though he is always said to be bound for one or other, but a mere citizen of the sea, as vagabonds are of the world . . .

We noticed that it is common to give the "solution" of riddle poems in their titles, and in such poems we move from work to title. Here is what I have to say about something; guess what it is. In the above technique we move from title to the work. Here is what I'm talking about; you'll never guess what I can find to say about it.

Emily Dickinson shows us another aspect of the rhetoric of riddles in this poem on a hummingbird:

A Route of Evanescence
With a revolving Wheel—
A Resonance of Emerald—

A Rush of Cochineal—
And every Blossom on the Bush
Adjusts its Tumbled Head—
The mail from Tunis probably,
An easy Morning's Ride—

Here the object is described in terms of its energy of movement, and the vivid colors are, as in impressionist paintings, seen as vibrations of light rather than as attributes of a static object. The longer words "evanescence" and "resonance" are obviously used because their sound reinforces the imagery of spinning and humming. But this poet seems to be fond of such words in their own right: in another poem she says of the bluebird:

Her conscientious Voice will soar unmoved
Above ostensible Vicissitude.

We tend to think of long Latin words as gray and abstract, because the concrete metaphors that they originally conveyed have largely faded out. When they were new, in the fifteenth century, they were thought of as "colors" of rhetoric, strange exotic terms belonging to what was called "aureate" diction. Emily Dickinson clearly shares something of this feeling, and so does Poe: the diction of "Ulalume" is also full of Latin words, although, this being a charm poem, the effect of such words as "senescent" and "nebulous" is rather a drowsy and blurring one. Milton also uses a good many Latin words, mainly because they have a large number of unstressed syllables, and relieve the heavy monosyllabic thump of the native vocabulary. Milton is, of course, always well aware of the metaphorical basis of such words: "elephants indorsed with towers" means elephants with towers on their backs. But except for such special cases, poetry has a limited tolerance for words likely to become abstract. Literary practice does not confirm the enthusiasm of Stephen Hawes, in the early sixteenth century, for this type of rhetoric:

In few words sweet and sententious
Depainted with gold, hard in construction,

To the artic [artistic] ears sweet and delicious
The golden rhetoric is good refection
And to the reader right consolation
As we do gold from copper purify
So that elocution doth right well clarify

The dulcet speech from the language rude . . .

This brings us to the other half of Eliot's dissociation of sensibility, the kind of poetry that is made out of ideas and thoughts, that expresses emotion by talking about it. The formula of William Carlos Williams, "not ideas about the thing but the thing itself," sums up several decades of reaction against this kind of rhetoric. We have noted that in the riddle there are two foci of imaginative interest, one visual and the other conceptual. In medieval bestiaries, for example, the alleged behavior-patterns of various animals are described, but we are led, not merely to their names, but to the moral or typological "significance" of their behavior. Similarly with the relation of pictures to commentary in the emblem books. The paradox here is that of a world where, as Wallace Stevens says, "The squirming facts exceed the squamous mind," where human efforts to get control of the external world through mental constructs seem rather desperate. The sense of strain and irony in the relation of the mind to nature becomes highly self-conscious in Donne and the metaphysicals, and gives a humorous twist to the kind of imagery most typical of them. Eliot, noting this quality also in the nineteenth-century French *symbolistes,* suggests that preserving the tone of ironic strain and difficulty is almost a moral duty for a twentieth-century poet. The trouble with Williams' anti-conceptual statement, however, is that in poetry there is, so to speak, no such thing as a thing. Word and thing are frozen in two separate worlds, and the reality of each can be expressed only by the other in its world. This paradoxical deadlock is precisely the essence of the riddle.

Eliot is also clear that such imagery really comes into its own during times of waning spiritual authority. In the Renaissance, Nicholas of Cusa, the inventor of the doctrine of "learned ignorance," also invented a series of riddle-games designed to express certain paradoxes in the nature of God that show up the limitations of the human mind in trying to grasp that nature. God is absent yet present; he is within the world and yet outside it; his eyes follow us everywhere and yet never move, and so on. Some of these paradoxes are made into actual riddles by Ben Jonson and incorporated into his masque *Love Freed from Ignorance and Folly,* where the answers to them are not "God," but King James and the land of Britain. Jonson, however, takes a low view of riddles, which he regards as the refuge of stupidity: his attitude is anti-"metaphysical," here as elsewhere. Hence the "Ignorance" of his masque is identified with the Sphinx, who asks the riddles. But the Cusanus paradoxes are still haunting Eliot in our century, struggling to express the meaning of an incarnation which is neither in nor out of time, and is surrounded by "a white light still and moving".

When Mallarmé says that the poet does not name or point, but describes the mood evoked by the object, he seems to suggest a method of riddle-writing without guessing, which appears to destroy the whole point of the riddle. It may be, though, that he is also suggesting a way of getting past the deadlock we encountered above. In the typical riddle there is a question implied in the poem, of which the guess is the answer. But an answer to a question accepts the assumptions in the question, and consequently consolidates the mental level on which the question is asked. This is adequate for information, where we simply want to stop or neutralize the question. But in religion, in philosophy, in science, all answers wear out sooner or later, because these subjects keep growing and expanding through a series of better formulated questions. Something similar must surely be true of literature, even if the processes of growth and expansion take different forms there.

One of the Old English riddles reads:

> The monster came sailing, wondrous along the wave; it called out in its comeliness to the land from the ship; loud was its din; its laughter was terrible, dreadful on earth; its edges were sharp. It was malignantly cruel, not easily brought to battle but fierce in the fighting; it stove in the ship's sides, relentless and ravaging. It

> bound it with a baleful charm; it spoke with cunning of its own nature: "My mother is of the dearest race of maidens, she is my daughter grown to greatness, as it is known to men, to people among the folk, that she shall stand with joy on the earth in all lands."

The answer is supposed to be "iceberg," which has water for its mother and daughter because it comes from and returns to water. But the answer hardly does justice to the poem: like all interpretations that profess to say "this *is* what the poem means," the answer is wrong because it is an answer. The real answer to the question implied in a riddle is not a "thing" outside it, but that which is both word and thing, and is both inside and outside the poem. This is the universal of which the poem is the manifestation, the order of words that tells us of battles and shipwrecks, of the intimate connection of beauty and terror, of cycles of life and death, of mutability and apocalypse, of the echoes of Leviathan and Virgil's Juno and Demeter and Kali and Circe and Tiamat and Midgard and the mermaids and the Valkyries, all of which is focussed on and stirred up by this "iceberg."

The charm comes out of a mythological universe of mysterious names and beings: the magician derives from that world the power that he applies to things. The poet is a magician who renounces his magic, and thereby re-creates the universe of power instead of trying to exploit it. Riddle goes in the opposite direction, and has to make the corresponding renunciation of the answer or guess. The answer is another way of trying to get control over things, the conceptual way, and renouncing it means, again, being set free to create. As Paul says, we see now in a riddle in a mirror, but we solve the riddle by coming out of the mirror, into the world that words and things reflect.

Romance as Masque

Let us start with the two comic genres of Old Comedy and New Comedy, familiar from Greek literature. The distinguishing feature of New Comedy, the form predominant from Roman times to the nineteenth century, is the teleological plot, in which as a rule, an alienated lover moves toward sexual fulfilment. New Comedy reaches its *telos* in the final scene, which is superficially marriage, and, more profoundly, a rebirth. A new society is created on the stage in the last moments of a typical New Comedy, and is often expanded by a recognition scene and a restoring of a birthright. The recognition is connected with the secret of somebody's birth in the common device of the foundling plot. Simpler and equally popular is the comedy in which a hero, after many setbacks, succeeds in doing something that wins him the heroine and a new sense of identity.

In such a structure the characters are essentially functions of the plot. However fully realized they may be, they are always organically related to the roles on which the plot turns, whether senex, parasite, buffoon, or bragging rival. The *commedia dell'arte* indicates with great clarity how a group of stock characters, related to a stock plot, is the basis of the comic structures of Shakespeare and Molière, as both of these dramatists show many affinities with the *commedia dell'arte.* In Ben Jonson's "humor" theory the New Comedy conception of character as a plot-function is rationalized in a most ingenious way. A character who is, by definition, essentially what his context in the plot makes him to be obviously has something predictable at his basis. The humor is also, by definition, a character dominated by a predictable reaction. But predictability of response is also one of the main sources of the comic mood, as has been noted by a number of theorists of comedy down to Bergson. Therefore, in a "comedy of humors," comic structure, comic characterization and comic mood are rigorously unified. A similar unity forms the basis for the "well-made play" of Scribe and Sardou in the nineteenth century, a type of drama well within the New Comedy tradition. Many of Jonson's plays, unhappily, especially the later ones, were so "well made" that they failed on the stage through over-elaborateness.

New Comedy developed two main forms: the romantic form of Shakespeare and the more realistic and displaced form of the Neo-Classical tradition, in which the greatest name is Molière. The more realistic such comedy becomes, the more it is in danger of becoming a sentimental domestic comedy, like the *comédie larmoyante* of the eighteenth century. A combination of realistic treatment and New Comedy structure has a tendency to sentimentality inherent in it, as its theme approximates very closely the favorite rubric of the agony column: "Come home; all is forgiven." Molière focusses nearly all the dramatic interest on a central "humor" or blocking figure, whose particular folly, whether avarice or snobbery or hypochondria, helps to keep the tone well away from the sentimental. In Sheridan and Goldsmith the effort to achieve a dry and witty texture is more of a strain. The domestic virtues do not appear to have attracted the loyalty of a major dramatic genius, unless we wish to call Beethoven a major dramatic genius: *Fidelio* is a bachelor's tribute to domestic felicity, but the extraordinary unevenness of the music perhaps indicates some doubt in his mind.

Eventually the New Comedy structure deserted the stage for the domestic novel, where a sentimental tone is easier to accommodate. The foundling plot reappears in *Tom Jones,* and is a standard feature of Dickens. The conception of characterization in Dickens is very close to that of the Jonsonian humor, except that the looser fictional form can find room for a great number of peripheral characters who are not directly concerned in the central plot. But when English drama revived towards the end of the nineteenth century, the formulas of New Comedy were used mainly for purposes of parody, parody being the usual sign in literature that some conventions are getting worn out. We begin with mysterious-heir parodies in Gilbert and Sullivan, notably in *Pinafore* and *The Gondoliers;* then we have Wilde's urbane spoof of the foundling plot in *The Importance of Being Earnest.*

Wilde's contemporary Bernard Shaw was well aware of the extent to which some standard New Comedy devices had already been parodied by Ibsen. Shaw's parodies of New Comedy recognition scenes include the ingenious device that enables Undershaft to adopt his son-in-law as his successor in *Major Barbara,* and the discovery in *Arms and the Man* that Captain Bluntschli is of the highest social rank possible in his country, being an ordinary Swiss citizen, besides being made rich enough, by inheriting a hotel business, to upstage his rival Sergius. A more conventional type of New Comedy concealed-parentage plot is parodied in *You Never Can Tell.* In the next generation, the writer who most closely followed the New Comedy structure as laid down by Plautus and Terence was P. G. Wodehouse. In other words, the teleological New Comedy structure seems to have dropped out of the center of "serious" literature in the twentieth century.

In this situation writers of comedy clearly have to do something else, and what they are doing may be easier to understand if we think of Old Comedy, not simply as a form used by Aristophanes which died with him—in fact before him—but as in a larger structural sense a permanent genus of comedy, open in any age to writers bored or inhibited by other conventions, or suspecting that their audiences are. When we look at Old Comedy in this way, it begins to expand into *the* alternative genus to New Comedy.

The structure of Old Comedy is dialectical rather than teleological, and its distinguishing feature is the contest or *agon.* This feature makes for a processional or sequential form, in which characters may appear without introduction and disappear without explanation. In this form, characters are not functions of a plot, but vehicles or embodiments of a contest. The dramatic contest of Old Comedy is as a rule not simply between personalities as such, but between personalities as representatives of larger social forces. These forces may be those of some form of class struggle, as in Brecht, or they may be specific crises like a war or an election, or psychological drives or attitudes of mind. In Aristophanes they are often the forces associated with demagogues in Athens, like Cleon, who were obsessed with prosecuting the war against Sparta. Such a form is an appropriate one for introducing historical or contemporary figures. We recall how Socrates and Euripides appear in Aristophanes; in Bernard Shaw, who shows the transition to Old Comedy conventions very clearly, we have the caricatures of Asquith and Lloyd George in *Back to Methuselah;* and this prepares the way for more recent plays about Churchill, the Pope, and various analogues of Hitler. Such characters may also come from literature: I think, as a random example, of Tennessee Williams' *Camino Real,* which begins with Don Quixote and Sancho Panza entering from the audience in a way curiously reminiscent of *The Frogs.*

We notice in Aristophanes that while the *agon* may conclude with the victory of something the dramatist approves of, it may equally well be a victory of something patently absurd, as in *The Birds* or *Ecclesiazusae.* A comic structure based on a contest in which absurdity is the victor is clearly anti-teleological, and the greatest possible contrast to the more idealistic New Comedy. So, although Aristophanes himself is a high-spirited writer, full of jokes and slapstick, the form he uses, in its larger context, is also an appropriate form for black or absurd comedy. Even in him the hostile personal attacks, while they may have been permitted for what were in origin religious reasons, are not simply all in good fun. We may rationalize the guying of Socrates and Euripides on this basis, but there is still Cleon. The darker tone latent in Old Comedy was recognized in Elizabethan times: Puttenham says, for example: "this bitter poem called the old *Comedy* being disused and taken away, the new *Comedy* came in place, more civil and pleasant a great deal." It was doubtless the sardonic mood of *Every Man Out of His Humor* that made Jonson speak of it as close to Old Comedy, though it is still within the conventions of New Comedy in its structure. In our day the black comedy is normal, but half a century ago, when Chekhov showed characters slowly freezing in the grip of a dying class, many audiences found it difficult to believe that *The Cherry Orchard* or *The Three Sisters* were comedies at all.

New Comedy may go either in a romantic or in a realistic direction; one typical development of Old Comedy is towards fantasy, which now seems to us a peculiarly modern technique. Where characters are embodiments of social or psychological conflicts, the conception of the individual as defined mainly by the "sane" or waking consciousness of ordinary experience is only one of many possible points of view. In New Comedy we are continually aware of the predominance of the sense of experience: we notice this, for example, in the rigid social hierarchy of Shakespearean comedy, which the action of the play never essentially disturbs. Old Comedy, by contrast, may be called the drama of unchained being. In Aristophanes some of the characters may be gods, as in *The Birds*, or the dead, as in *The Frogs*, or allegories, as in *Peace*. A similar tendency to introduce characters who are not coterminous with the bodies of individuals is marked in the theatre of the absurd, especially in Ionesco. One direction of this tendency is the archetypal characterization that we find, for instance, in *Waiting for Godot*, where the two main characters identify themselves with a number of representative figures, such as the two thieves crucified with Christ.

Waiting for Godot is also, in one of its aspects, a parody of the vaudeville dialogues, the long shapeless rigmaroles which used to be packed around the "feature film" in my youth. Such verbal filler occasionally appears in legitimate drama, as in the first scene of Shaw's *The Apple Cart*, which dimly recalls the "well made play" convention of introducing the story and atmosphere through such devices as a heroine-confidante conversation at the beginning. In fact a good deal of the texture of many Shaw plays consists of a type of cross-talk dialogue which bears much the relation to Old Comedy that the *commedia dell' arte* does to New Comedy. In more sophisticated versions of such dialogue, as we have it in certain forms of night club entertainment (e.g., Nichols and May), it becomes more clearly a verbal *agon.* When the contest is one of incident rather than words, we may have the loose sequential structure of some of the early Chaplin films, where there is a series of collisions between the hero and a number of unsympathetic antagonists, very similar in form to, for example, the last part of Aristophanes' *The Acharnians.*

In New Comedy the essential meaning of the play, or what Aristotle calls its *dianoia,* is bound up with the revelation of the plot, but such a meaning may be crystallized in a number of sententious axioms that express reflections arising from the various stages of the plot. These sententious maxims are one of the best known features of New Comedy rhetoric. Old Comedy is less sententious and more argumentative than New Comedy, hence it can find a place for the long harangue or monologue, which tends to disrupt the action of a New Comedy, and appears in it only as a technical *tour de force,* like the speech of Jaques on the seven ages of man. In Aristophanes we sometimes have a direct address to the audience, technically called *parabasis;* in Shaw the *parabasis* is transferred to a preface which the audience is expected to read along with the play; and many recent comedies not only include but are based on monologue, as we see in several plays of Beckett and in Albee's *Zoo Story.*

As we can see from Aristophanes' use of a chorus, Old Comedy, because of its looser processional form, can be more spectacular than New Comedy. In New Comedy, once we go beyond the incidental songs that we find in Shakespeare, music and spectacle tend to caricature the complications of the plot, as in *The Marriage of Figaro.* But Old Comedy is in its nature closer to musical comedy, and we notice how the plays of Shaw, despite their intensely verbal texture, often make surprisingly good musical comedies. Again, the fact that Old Comedy is less preoccupied with the game of love and the rituals of upper- or middle-class courtship makes it a better medium for a franker and more explicit treatment of the workings of the sexual instinct. Even the scurrility which is so conspicuous in Aristophanes recurs in *MacBird* and similar forms of undercover drama.

Of modern dramatists, perhaps T. S. Eliot shows most clearly the conflict between the two types of comedy. Eliot begins his dramatic efforts with the exuberant and superbly original *Sweeney Agonistes,* subtitled "Fragment of an Agon," where, besides the obvious and avowed influence of Aristophanes, many of the features noted above appear, such as the assimilation to musical comedy and vaudeville forms. When he settles down to write seriously for the stage, however, we get such confections as *The Confidential Clerk,* where the main influence is Euripides' *Ion,* usually taken as the starting point of New Comedy. But *The Confidential Clerk* seems, in comparison with *Sweeney Agonistes,* a somewhat pedantic joke, an attempt to do over again what Oscar Wilde (and, for that matter, Gilbert) had already done with more freshness.

Shakespeare's comedies conform for the most part to a romantic development of New Comedy. But Shakespeare was a versatile experimenter, and there is at least one play which comes close to the genus of Old Comedy as we have been dealing with it here. This play is *Troilus and Cressida.* Here the characters are well-known figures from history or literature; the structure is a simple sequential one, built up on the background movement of Helen from Greece to Troy and the foreground movement of Cressida in the reverse direction; the characters are both embodiments and prisoners of the social codes they adopt, and so far as the action of the play itself is concerned, the only clear victor of the contest is absurdity. There is no fantasy in the play, except in the sense in which the Trojan chivalric code is fantasy, but the characterization is archetypal, with a strong sense that the Trojan War, the beginning of secular history, is establishing the pattern for all the history that follows. We find this in the two tremendous speeches of Ulysses on degree and on time, the two primary categories of life in this world, and in Pandarus' remark: "let all pitiful goers-between be call'd to the world's end after my name; call them all Pandars." The reasons why this play seems a peculiarly "modern" one, often performed in contemporary dress, should be clear by now.

New Comedy, especially in its more romantic or Shakespearean form, tends to be an ideal structure with strong analogies to religion. The sense in which Christianity is a divine comedy is a New Comedy sense: the hero of the Christian comedy is Christ, and the heroine who becomes his bride is the reborn society of the Christian Church. Similar affinities between romantic New Comedy and religious myth may occur outside Christianity, as we see in Sanskrit plays, notably *Sakuntala.* Old Comedy is a more existential form in which a central theme is mockery, which may include mockery of the gods, above or below. The presiding genius of New Comedy is Eros, but the presiding genius of Old Comedy is more like Prometheus, a titanic power involved by his contempt for the gods in a chaotic world of absurdity and anguish.

There are two major structural principles in literature: the principle of cyclical movement, from life to death to rebirth, usually symbolized by the solar and seasonal cycles of nature, and the principle of polarity, where an ideal or attractive world, described or implied, is contrasted with an absurd, repulsive, or evil one. In New Comedy the containing form is cyclical: the teleological action moves toward the new life or reborn society of the final scene. The principle of polarity exists within this, as, say, the opposition of a father to his son's desire to marry the heroine. In Old Comedy, where the contest between two contrasting sets of values is usually very prominent, polarity is as a rule the containing form. That is, Old Comedy suggests some kind of social norm implicitly contrasting with its main action in the audience's mind, something in the light of which the absurdity of that action appears properly absurd. There are glimpses of this in Aristophanes, as in the festival of Dionysus in *The Acharnians,* but there is no consistently idealized picture of life presented in his plays. Similarly in New Comedy, idealized life occurs not so much in the action as in the kind of "lived happily ever after" life that is often assumed to begin at the end of the action.

The comedy of the English Renaissance was confined to New

Comedy for many reasons, of which perhaps the simplest and most obvious is censorship, combined with the clerical, and more particularly puritan, disapproval of theatres generally. An age in which *Mucedorus* could be denounced as morally corrupting and *Sir Thomas More* treated like a revolutionary manifesto was clearly not an age for an Aristophanes. We notice that *Troilus and Cressida* was one of the least popular plays of an otherwise quite popular dramatist. Yet the rigid New Comedy frame was also a hampering one, and although romance is equally rigid in its conventions, and masque far more so, romance and masque both represent to some extent two directions of dramatic experiment away from the established form.

II

In the masque the organizing principle is that of polarity, the contrast between the two orders symbolized by the two parts into which it was divided, the antimasque and the masque proper. The antimasque normally came first (Middleton even spells it "antemasque"), and it often depicted the grotesque, the ribald, or whatever the audience was ready to accept as socially substandard. Bacon, in his brilliant little essay on masques and triumphs, lists antimasque figures as "fools, satyrs, baboons, wild-men, antics, beasts, sprites, witches, Ethiopes, pigmies, turquets, nymphs, rustics, Cupids, statuas moving, and the like." The masque proper was a stately and elaborate ceremonial in honor of a distinguished person, frequently royal. The theme was usually allegorical or Classical, of a kind that often required a good deal of explanation when printed, especially when Ben Jonson was the author. Such a theme was appropriate to the elitism of the setting, the Classical deities clearly having been originally created on the analogy of an aristocracy. The actors of the later and more elaborate antimasques were often professionals; those in the masque proper more likely to be lords and ladies whose names were proudly listed in the printed versions. Highbrow anxieties about mingling upper and lower classes in the plays of the popular theatre were seldom ruffled by a masque, which tended to make social distinctions an essential theme in the spectacle. In Jonson especially the general idea is that the antimasque represents a parody or burlesque of something of which the real form is presented later in direct association with the king, or the most eminent figure present.

The masque thus held up an idealizing mirror to its audience, and not only dramatized its stratified social structure, but in its imagery reflected the whole religious and philosophical cosmology which rationalized that structure. In this cosmology the world began with an act of creation in which a divine power imposed an order on the turbulence of chaos. The order is often called a harmony, and is symbolized by music; the creative power is also the power of love, love being, on the purely automatic level of "attraction," the force that enables the warring principles of chaos to separate into the four elements, each of which keeps to its own place. Creation takes the form of a hierarchy or chain of being, and the hierarchy of Jacobean society, the chain of authority depending from the king, continues the natural order of things in its social and political aspects. At every point there is a political and a cosmological parallel: at the bottom of the chain of being is chaos; at the bottom of society are the corresponding elements of anarchy and unrest.

The king, therefore, not only rules by divine right but is a visible emblem of the authority of God. Considering that Jonson remarked to Drummond of Hawthornden that Donne's *Anniversaries* were blasphemous because he said things about Elizabeth Drury that should only have been said about the Virgin Mary, it may seem strange that Jonson sometimes speaks of King James in terms that would be more appropriate to Christ. In *Love Freed From Ignorance and Folly,* the action turns on guessing riddles of which the right answers are Britain and King James: the riddles themselves come from some paradoxes of Nicholas of Cusanus, where the right answer is God. Similarly in *Oberon:*

> 'Tis he, that stays the time from turning old,
> And keeps the age up in a head of gold.

> That in his own true circle still doth run;
> And holds his course as certain as the sun.
> He makes it ever day, and ever spring,
> Where he doth shine, and quickens every thing
> Like a new nature: so that true to call
> Him by his title, is to say, He's all.

But what seems like a rather brutal flattery is consistent with the genre that Jonson was working in, and did so much to create. We may find it hard to realize what a strain these masques must have been on the people in whose honor they were held, not least the king. He, when present, was always at the center of the whole show, being, like Ariel, an actor in it, however passive, as well as an auditor. It is understandable that the few remarks recorded of James at masques should betray an exasperated weariness at being dragged out to so many such entertainments. It is clear that sometimes he would have given his crown to possess the equivalent of that bastion of democratic liberties, the television button, which can turn the whole foolish noise into silence and darkness, leaving not a rack behind.

Prospero's speech after the masque in *The Tempest,* just echoed, expresses with definitive eloquence another characteristic of the masque: its transience. Like a miniature World's Fair, where a whole city is set up and torn down, the masque was an enormously expensive and variegated performance which glittered for a night and disappeared. Some of the printed texts give a sense of trying desperately to salvage something of the intense experience of the original production. "These things are but toys," is Bacon's opening remark in his essay, and the masque does have something of the cultural quality that Fabergé symbolized in a later age, of elaborate "devices" or playthings for a leisure class. The flickering light of candles and torches must have greatly increased the sense of unreality, almost to a point of hallucination. The masque, in short, irresistibly suggests the imagery of magic or summoned-up illusion.

This was the aspect of the masque that got Jonson down: it seems ironic that an author with so strong a sense of the permanence of literature, who was unique in his day for his anxiety to get his plays into print, should have been associated with a fragile and highly specialized dramatic development that had so little significance outside its immediate setting and occasion. Jonson was proud of his ability to write masques, naturally, but the feeling that Inigo Jones, with his endlessly resourceful stage effects, was the real magician, and stole the show from him every time, was hard on his self-respect. To preserve that self-respect he clung to the cosmology which the masque dramatized. For him the masque consisted of a perishable body, created by Inigo Jones, and an immortal soul, the poetry that he could supply. The body was also represented by the antimasque, the epiphany of temporary disorder or confusion obliterated by the real masque, which comes to a focus in the figure in front. The *de jure* monarch in particular, who represents the continuity of order in society, is a visible emblem of permanence, including the permanence of Jonson's fame. Thus in the preface to *Hymenaei:*

> So short-lived are the bodies of all things, in comparison of their souls. And, though bodies oft-times have the ill luck to be sensually preferred, they find afterwards the good fortune (when souls live) to be utterly forgotten. This it is hath made the most royal Princes, and greatest persons . . . not only studious of riches and magnificence in the outward celebration or show . . . but curious after the most high and hearty inventions, to furnish the inward parts. . . .

Unfortunately for this pious hope, the antimasques, along with the elaborate settings, proved to be more popular in appeal to the audience than the highly allusive allegories, buttressed with documentation and footnotes, which Jonson regarded as the soul of the genre. The audience in general, including King James, preferred dancing to talking, and the principle that the dance was the real soul of the masque had much more authority. In a later masque of Shirley's there is an opening announcement that there is to be no antimasque: this provokes protest from one of the characters, who says that the audience will never stand for such a thing, and something like thirteen antimasques follow. Jonson saw in the proliferation of antimasques the degeneration of the form, and in this he was clearly right. Again, the breakdown of the form presaged the fall of the social structure which supported it: one of many examples of the socially prophetic role of the arts.

To return to the cosmology which the masque reflects: we have a descending movement of order and harmony on chaos, which is the original creative act of God, perpetuated in human society by the structure of authority. God could have created only a perfect world, and this original creation formed a second or ideal level of reality. It included the Garden of Eden, and all myths of a Golden Age or an earthly paradise are reminiscent of it. All that is now left of it is, or is symbolized by, the heavenly bodies. The fall of man established a third level, and the fall of Satan a fourth one, which now has the third in its grip. In the original creation the Son of God descended to the second level, walking in the garden of Eden; at the Incarnation he descended to the third, and, after his death on the cross, to the fourth. These descents were followed by a rising movement, through the Harrowing of Hell, the Resurrection, and the Ascension. This rising movement is redemptive, bringing man back from his alienated or fallen state to a condition nearer his original one.

Writers of masques, apart from Milton, are so concerned with the secular occasion that there is little explicit reminder of this cosmology. But the cosmology itself was so firmly fixed in the Jacobean mind that such a form as a masque, where the presence of nobility and royalty suggested in itself a secular analogy to spiritual authority, had to fall into a similar shape. Jacobean Christianity, Jacobean drama, Jacobean masque, all inhabited the same mythological universe. Besides, royalty and nobility were not merely an analogy: they represented, to a very considerable degree, the continuing visible form of spiritual authority, especially in Protestant England, where the Church itself had been put under the headship of the temporal sovereign.

In the cosmology, authority descends from above: any descending movement which is not that of authority represents evil, following its own law of moral gravitation, and sinking through our world towards the demonic level and the bottom of the chain of being. The central symbol for this kind of descent is metamorphosis, in the sense of transformation into a lower state of existence, such as we have in Ovid's *Metamorphoses,* in Apuleius, and in the stories about Circe in the *Odyssey* and elsewhere. This theme often appears in the antimasque, and when it does, the movement to the masque proper incorporates a cyclical progression from chaos to cosmos, unorganized energy to new life, into the polarized structure. The main thrust of the movement to and through the masque proper is therefore upward, in the reverse direction from Circean metamorphosis, and to higher levels of the chain of being.

Both antimasque and masque present unreal worlds, but the masque has at least the reality of an ideal, a dream of a happy island or paradisal garden of perpetual spring, with its providential parental figures of king and queen inhabiting it like the presences in the rose-garden of Eliot's "Burnt Norton." It is significant how often Jonson associates Britain with the legend of the floating island—Delos in Classical myth—which has been caught and fixed for a moment. The magically evoked instant is real for that instant, however quickly it fades. And in that instant Britain is seen as what, according to Christian teaching, it originally was: a green and pleasant land, part of the Garden of Eden or Golden Age of unfallen man. In Jonson the magic which calls this state of innocence into a moment of being is symbolized, in particular, by Mercury and Proteus, gods of magic and metamorphosis, and in *The Fortunate Isles* Proteus says of Britain:

> There is no sickness, nor no old age known
> To man, nor any grief that he dares own.
> There is no hunger there, nor envy of state,
> Nor least ambition in the Magistrate.
> But all are even-hearted, open, free,
> And what one is, another strives to be.

We have to keep the vertical metaphor of the chain of being in our minds to understand the consistency of masque imagery. The descending movement is from the divine through the angelical, human, animal, vegetable, and mineral worlds down to chaos, and the movement itself, when not voluntary or authoritative, is associated with sinister enchantments and the lowering of intelligence and freedom of movement. Human beings turned into animals, statues, or flowers, like Narcissus, are typical images of such enchantment. In masques this kind of movement is often reversed, going through the corresponding disenchantments. In Jonson's *Lovers Made Men,* a simplified form in which antimasque and masque have the same characters, we begin with the lovers in the world of the dead, led there by Mercury in his role as psychopomp. They are not actually dead, but think they have died for love. They drink of the river Lethe or forgetfulness, but what they forget is their death, and they come to life again. Thus the main movement is that of a freeing from enchantment or metamorphosis and a restoration of the original identity. In Campion's *Lords' Masque* we are introduced to Prometheus making women: Jupiter, furious, turns them to statues, but after the proper invocations the statues are brought to life. We recall that "statuas moving" was a common masque theme for Bacon, though he associates it with the antimasque. An anonymous *Masque of Flowers* shows flowers turning into men, in a reversal of the Narcissus theme.

Most of the imagery of the masque, then, is strung along what we may call an *axis mundi,* the center of the vertical line of images held together by the chain of being, and going in an upward direction. This upward movement of *axis mundi* imagery connects the masque with a very similar family of image-sequences that appears in alchemical symbolism, where the alchemical processes symbolize the transformation of the soul from the state of original sin, the *prima materia,* to the state of original identity, the *lapis.* Closely linked, also, is the immensely long tradition in ritual and literature of ziggurat imagery, where the theme is the climbing of a tower or a mountain representing the hierarchies of being. This latter is as old an archetype as civilization affords: it is the basis of Dante's *Purgatorio,* and is going as strong as ever in Yeats, Eliot, and Ezra Pound, whose "Dioce" goes back to

Herodotus and his description of the original towers of Ecbatana and Babylon. Its ancient forms have been studied by Gertrude Rachel Levy in *The Gate of Horn* and *The Sword from the Rock.* In narrative poetry the sequence usually goes up some kind of spiral climb, but this is not very dramatic, and would be difficult to stage even for Inigo Jones. What is symbolically a going up on the *axis mundi* is often represented as a going within. The masque is naturally a proscenium drama, and in the usual arrangement the audience was seated at one end of a hall, the other end displaying a curtain on which the antimasque scene was painted. The scene normally portrayed something low down on the chain of being, just above chaos, such as the slope of a mountain, or simply rocks, rocks being common enough to be recognized at the time as something of a cliché. Afterwards the curtain parted to exhibit one or two inner scenes, spatially thought of as within the mountain or rocks, but symbolically representing an order superior to or on top of them.

Thus in Jonson's *Oberon* we first meet satyrs, then an inner scene shows us two "sylvans" asleep in front of a palace, sylvans being evidently higher in rank than satyrs; then the palace opens to disclose "Fays" or knights, and the masque ends in panegyric of Prince Henry, in whose honor it was held. In Jonson's *Pleasure Reconciled to Virtue* the scene is a mountain (Atlas), beginning with a "grove of ivy" at the bottom, from which Comus, here the genius of gluttony, comes with an antimasque of tuns or bottles. Hercules in this masque has to choose between Vice (Comus) and Virtue; he chooses Virtue and gets Pleasure as well, both of whom are much higher up on the mountain, along with Mercury and the masque dancers. In Campion's *Lords' Masque* we begin with the "lower part" of a divided scene, with Mania, the goddess of madness, in a cave, and from there we move up to the sphere of fixed stars.

The ascending imagery is accompanied by reversals of the stock symbols of descent. Antimasque scenes often begin in a thick mazy wood, a labyrinth where there is no certain direction. In Jonson's *Masque of Augurs* an antimasque dance is said to be "a perplexed Dance of straying and deformed Pilgrims, taking several paths." A symbol of lost direction, the echo song, becomes a standard feature of masques. But there is also a higher labyrinth, the controlled and ordered movements of the stars, and *Pleasure Reconciled to Virtue* introduces a dance imitating these movements, of which the coryphaeus is Daedalus. When a man appears on the stage as an actor he has already undergone a form of metamorphosis: in the junctions of actors and audience in the masque, such as the dance in which the masquers "take out the ladies," the actors come back to their original identity.

What we have called ziggurat imagery often features two things on the top: an idealized landscape or garden, and the body of a bride who is united with her lover at this point, and whose body is often identified with the garden, as in the Song of Songs in the Bible. In Jonson's *Hymenaei*, perhaps the most elaborate of wedding masques, where Juno symbolizes the marriage union, the masquer's dance is compared to "the Golden Chain let down from Heaven" by Jupiter, and the masque is introduced by the figure of Reason, described as "seated in the top of the Globe (as in the brain, or highest part of Man)," indicating that the upward movement through the *axis mundi* has an analogy to the human body also. Then again, the strong association of the masque with magic, and perhaps also the link in imagery with alchemy, help to make occult themes prominent in Jonson—perhaps it is not an accident that Jonson's greatest play is about an alchemist, however much of a scoundrel. In *Mercury Vindicated from the Alchemists* we move from an alchemist's laboratory presided over by Vulcan to "a glorious bower, wherein Nature was placed, with Prometheus at her feet." In *The Masque of Augurs* we move from an antimasque said to have no connection with the main theme to the gods Apollo and Jupiter, the true augurs in the service of the king: again there is a sense of lower and higher mysteries. The Ovidian and Chaucerian image of the House of Fame or Rumor is employed as a symbol of the confusions of the lower states of being: we may compare the dialogue of Truth and Opinion in *Hymenaei*. In *The Fortunate Isles* we are introduced to a credulous Rosicrucian, teased by an "aery spirit" who reminds us of Ariel, and who promises him visions of "gardens in the depth of winter" and a journey from the depths of the sea to the height of the Empyrean. Eventually he is declared to be a gull, but his dreams of an earthly paradise are satisfied by the Britain of King James.

We noted that occasionally the rising on the chain of being is expressed in a cyclical movement from darkness to dawn, winter to spring, age to youth. The fact that Britain is an island in the far west, a land of the region of sunset, enables the action of some masques to begin in a dark world, as in *Love Freed from Ignorance and Folly*. Here the antimasque presents a sphinx who has kidnapped the "daughters of the Morn," journeying from east to west, and also holds Love a prisoner. As mentioned, Love has to guess riddles of which the answers are Britain and King James. The antimasque is danced by "twelve she-fools," and ends with the recognition of James the sun-king, the rising dawn that puts ignorance and folly to flight. A somewhat similar imagery is employed in the *Masque of Blackness*, with its sequel the *Masque of Queens*.

Milton's *Comus* is, of course, not typical of the court masque, but for that very reason it indicates the kind of thing that could have been done with the form to make it a solid and durable dramatic genre. For one thing, Milton is much less preoccupied by the secular occasion and more aware of the cosmological structure of masque symbolism. It has often been noted that the descent of Peace in the *Nativity Ode* is reminiscent of masque devices, and the *Nativity Ode* is based on the same Christianized cosmology that informs the masque, its theme being the descent of a principle of order and control, of divine origin and repeating the creation, which is symbolized by the harmony of music. The Incarnation opens up a polarizing contrast between the paradisal model world of God's original creation, now entering the third level of human life for the first time since the fall of Adam, and the world of the dark demons infesting that fallen order, who represent what corresponds to the antimasque in the poem. The Christ-child is the rising sun that puts these demons to flight, like King James in Jonson. I have spoken elsewhere of the masque-like arrangement of the opening books of *Paradise Lost*, with the vision of hell followed by the blaze of light in heaven. In *Arcades* we have a Classical version of the paradisal order that God originally created, its protection symbolized by the Genius of the wood, the objective counterpart of the lady in whose honor the masque is given.

In *Comus* we begin with the same protected order, symbolized by the Attendant Spirit, who belongs to a world above our own and directly beneath heaven, like the Garden of Eden. *Comus*, however, like *Arcades*, is written in a Classical tonality, and the Attendant Spirit's home is associated rather with the Gardens of Adonis (in the background is the easygoing etymology that derives "Adon" from "Eden"). The fact that the Lady's chastity is identified with virginity means that she is less explicitly Christian than a vestal or pagan saint like the nun in *Il Penseroso* or the ideal poet in the Sixth Elegy, just as the "divine philosophy" of the two brothers is less Christian than Neoplatonic.

The Lady and her brothers descend into a labyrinthine forest symbolizing the lower world, where they lose their way and the Lady sings an echo song, after which we are introduced to the antimasque of Comus and his rout. Comus is the son of Circe, and is consequently not Jonson's fat slob but the presiding genius of the world of descending metamorphosis. He and his followers are demonic fire-spirits like the *ignis fatuus*, parodies of the circling heavenly bodies which they profess to imitate, and which symbolize the higher labyrinth of heavenly order. Comus and his band are connected, like the false gods of the *Nativity Ode*, with everything "fallen" that we associate with the word natural, on its lower or physical level, the level of animals and plants. The Lady's chastity is what is natural to her on the upper, paradisal and originally human level of nature. The emblems of Comus, the cup and the wand, are sexual symbols representing the aspect of the natural in which man tends to lose his human identity. The argument is hardly intelligible without some understanding of the hierarchic cosmology, both Christian and Neoplatonic, in which there are two contexts for the word "nature."

At the end the Lady returns to her own state of higher nature, and is presented, along with her brothers, to her parents. Here we have the junction of audience and actors that is characteristic of the masque form, except that the symbolism is more concrete.

The Lady and her brothers are the only human beings in the play: everyone else is a spirit of the elements of the nature into which the Lady has descended. The action of her descent, like that of Christ in the *Nativity Ode*, polarizes them into the good and the bad, the Attendant Spirit and Sabrina being benevolent spirits of air and water like the Genius of the wood in *Arcades*, the fire-spirits Comus and his followers (along with some earth-spirits, parenthetically referred to in the text) remaining demonic. We notice too the symbolism of a night-world in the far west which we met in Jonson: the setting, near the Welsh border, reminds us also of the sunset world of the Irish Ocean and the mouth of the Dee in *Lycidas.* The release of the Lady by Sabrina, the spirit of the Severn river, belongs to the archaic cyclical symbolism of the dead waters of winter succeeding to the living waters of spring, for even after the Lady has been rescued from Comus she is still "frozen."

The familiar features of Old Comedy, as we have it in Aristophanes, the ribaldry, the sense of an unstructured or substandard society, the fantasy, the dancing, are all features reappearing in the antimasque. The antimasque, as Enid Welsford has noted, goes back to something far older than the masque itself—in fact older than Aristophanes, and an ancestor of his form also. It has affinities with the satyr play, which was the embryo of tragedy, and in Elizabethan tragedy, when the mood turns fantastic or grotesque, we get scenes reminding us of antimasques, especially when the theme includes magic. The witches in *Macbeth* are an obvious instance, and in *Macbeth* also we have other illusions, like the moving wood, which were common masque features. For all the obvious differences, the structural affinities of the masque are closer to Old Comedy, being polarized and based on spectacle, than to New Comedy, which is cyclical and based on plot.

III

In Shakespeare's romantic comic form the structure is taken from New Comedy, but the presence of what I have elsewhere called a green world makes the polarizing element in his comedy much more prominent, being a collision and eventual reconciliation of two opposed worlds or orders of experience rather than of groups of characters. We make a distinction between Shakespeare's comedies and the romances of his final period, implying that this distinction is generic, or has a generic aspect. In terms of what we have been saying, it seems to me that the "comedies" are plays in which the New Comedy structure maintains itself to the end, though in its own distinctively romantic way. In Terence or Molière the hero and heroine wriggle out of the obstacles and prohibitions of the blocking figures and arrive at marriage and a festive ending within the social order that the blocking figures have set up. In the romantic comedy of Shakespeare and of some of his contemporaries and predecessors, the central characters approaching marriage, who have the audience's sympathy, are placed in a different symbolic setting, or what we might call, in this strange world of the nineteen-seventies, a separate reality, usually represented as a forest, which permeates and finally transforms the more "realistic" world of the blocking figures. Here the two worlds have an approximate relation to the worlds of wish-fulfilment dream and of waking consciousness, the former being strong enough to mold the latter into something like its own shape, which implies that it is ultimately more real.

In the romances the two worlds are more sharply opposed: the blocking worlds are an intense contrast to the comic spirit, often forming tragic actions in themselves, as in *The Winter's Tale* particularly. Something in these worlds has to be condemned and annihilated before the festive conclusion can take place, not simply reconciled or won over. What is annihilated is the state of mind, the jealousy of Posthumus or Leontes, the intrigues of Cymbeline's Queen or the Court Party in *The Tempest*, rather than the people in those states, though some of the people get eliminated too, at least in *Pericles* and *Cymbeline*. The structure of the romances thus approximates the complete polarity of the antimasque and masque. The dramatic romances of Shakespeare and his contemporaries, whatever the circumstances of their original performance, have their roots in the popular theatre with its unselected audience. The masque, driven by a steadily narrowing class-consciousness into a brittle spectacle as ephemeral as a firework display, nevertheless has features that make it possible for us to think of romantic comedy as a kind of democratized version of the same form, a people's masque, as it were.

In Shirley's *Love's Cruelty* there is a frequently quoted passage about masques: "in the instant as if the sea had swallowed up the earth, to see waves capering about tall ships, Arion upon a rock playing to the Dolphins . . . a tempest so artificial and sudden in the clouds, with a general darkness and thunder . . . that you would cry out with the Mariners in the work, you cannot scape drowning." The explicit reference is to Jonson, but the modern reader will think of *The Tempest* or *Pericles.* In fact Shakespeare, who never looked at a Quarto proof and left his plays to be gathered up after his death, may have been temperamentally closer to the masque than Jonson was. In any case the romances show an ascending movement from chaos and absurdity to peace and order very like that of the masque, and an actual masque, or masque-like scene, the epiphany of Diana in *Pericles,* the dream of Posthumus in *Cymbeline,* the sheep-shearing festival in *The Winter's Tale,* and the wedding masque in *The Tempest,* appears at the peripety of the action. In drama later than Shakespeare, the most ambitious dramatic romance dealing with themes of redemption and the recovery of original identity, along with a good many alchemical themes, is perhaps the second part of *Faust,* and we can see how that poem flowers out of the two gigantic masques, which dramatically are rather antimasques, of the scene at the Emperor Maximilian's court and the Classical Walpurgis-Night.

As I see it, there are six romances in the last period of Shakespeare's production: *Pericles, Cymbeline, The Winter's Tale, The Tempest, Henry VIII,* and *The Two Noble Kinsmen.* The first and last are clearly works of collaboration, and are not in the Folio, but collaboration does not mean that the plays lack unity. Shakespeare in any case would have been the senior collaborator, more likely to be responsible for the general design and scheme of the play. We may look first at *Henry VIII,* now an unpopular and rarely performed play, so often said to be largely the work of

Fletcher that the statement has come to have the force of an established fact, though it is not one. If we look at it objectively, without worrying about whether it was really the right sort of play for Shakespeare to be ending his career with, we can see how different generically it is from the other histories. It is, in the first place, a pageant: tremendous parades of nobility take place, to such an extent that one contemporary complained that it made greatness too familiar. The coronation of Anne Boleyn in the fourth act is the spectacular climax. When the play was performed at Stratford, Ontario, some years ago, the production was gorgeously costumed, with many resources beyond anything that Shakespeare himself could have commanded; but even Stratford gave up on this scene, and had it simply described as taking place offstage. The spectacular nature of the play is perhaps the reason for the low-keyed quality of the writing. The greater the extent to which spectacle is visually provided, the greater the violation of decorum in having obtrusively magnificent poetry in the text accompanying such spectacle.

The hero of *Henry VIII* is not so much the king as the wheel of fortune. The first turn of the wheel brings down Buckingham, the second turn Wolsey, the third Queen Katherine and others. If we like, we can see a rough justice or even a providence operating: Wolsey's fall is the nemesis for his treatment of Buckingham, and Queen Katherine, though innocent, has to go in order to get Elizabeth born. For this reason it is unnecessary to apply moral standards to King Henry: whether we think him resolute or merely ferocious, we cannot be sure if he turns the wheel of fortune or has simply become a part of its machinery. Certainly in the crucial event of the final scene, the birth of Elizabeth, there is a factor independent of his will, even though he takes the credit for it, as befits a king. In this final scene there is a "prophecy" by Cranmer about the future greatness of England under Elizabeth and her successors, which generically is a very masque-like scene, a panegyric of the sort that would have normally accompanied the presence of a reigning monarch in the audience.

The only thing is that this scene shows the final triumph of Cranmer and of Anne Boleyn, and the audience knows what soon happened to Anne, as well as to three of her successors, and eventually to Cranmer. It also knows that the reign of Elizabeth was preceded by that of Queen Katherine's daughter, whose existence Henry appears to have forgotten: "Never before This happy child did I get anything," he says. The parade of dignity and nobility, the exhibition of power and greatness controlled by a king who is not in the audience but confronting us on the stage, has few of the conventional elements of the masque, but it does leave us with a sense of transience, a world of "shadows, not substantial things," to quote another skilful masque writer, that soon disappears and gives way to what is in its future and the audience's present. Another episode in the play that suggests the masque is the dance of spirits around the dying Katherine, where there seems to be a glimpse of something transcending history. What impresses us most strongly about the play is the reversal of the ordinary standards of reality and illusion. Nothing could be more immediately real than the ups and downs of fortune in King Henry's court; nothing more illusory than a prophecy of a future three reigns away, or the sick fancies of a dying woman. But what the play presents is a sense of reality and illusion quite the opposite of this.

The Prologue insists on the seriousness of the play and the suppression of all buffoonery in it. Nothing of the very little that we know or can guess of Shakespeare's own political attitudes would lead us to believe that those attitudes were revolutionary or even liberal: there is no reason to suppose that he would have shrunk from Jonson's flattery of royalty if that had been part of his job. It is the integrity of the dramatic spectacle itself—and *Henry VIII* has, I think, far more integrity than it is usually given credit for having—that turns the whole solemn parade into a gigantic perversion of real social life, no less of one than Shelley's *Masque of Anarchy.* What Shakespeare was aware of as a dramatic craftsman, on the other hand, his sense of what the play needed, is sometimes shown by the incidents and characters he adds to his sources, and in *Henry VIII* this consists mainly of the two episodes, Queen Katherine's vision and Cranmer's prophecy, that have some standard features of the masque.

What emerges from a deeply serious, even tragic, play is an irony so corrosive that it has almost a comic dimension. The higher one is in social rank, the more one becomes bound to a formalized upper-class ritual. With a ruthless king as master of ceremonies, this ritual becomes a kind of sinister sacrificial dance, in which the most conspicuous figure becomes the designated next victim. In *The Two Noble Kinsmen* the sense of ritual compulsion is carried a step further. This play begins with the ritual of Theseus' wedding, and Theseus himself is possessed by the anxiety of ritual:

> Forward to th' temple, leave not out a jot
> O' th' sacred ceremony.

There are two similar commands later in the same scene. The ritual, however, is interrupted by a counter-ritual: three queens in black, one kneeling in front of each of the three chief figures, urge Theseus to war instead of love. The theme of death taking precedence over marriage is repeated in the climax of the play, when Arcite wins the battle with Palamon but dies. And just as death takes precedence of marriage, so a destructive and enslaving passion destroys the freedom of friendship. This is true not only of Palamon and Arcite, but of Emily. Emily's emotional life revolves around an early friendship with another woman: she has no interest in marriage, much less in marriage to the survivor of a fight to the death over her, but the rigid class code leaves her no choice. The source of the play is Chaucer's *Knight's Tale*, and Chaucer also has a clear sense of the compulsive and mechanical quality of these deadly ritual games. But *The Two Noble Kinsmen* exhibits a kind of sleepwalking commitment to them that seems almost Aztec, as in the emphasis on the fact that all those who have volunteered to assist Palamon and Arcite will lose their lives if their principal does. The action of the play is dominated by Venus, who is not Homer's laughter-loving Aphrodite but a goddess as menacing as the Indian Kali, flanked by her lover Mars, the god of war, and her child Cupid, the Eros who is fulfilled only by Thanatos or death.

In two of the earlier comedies that most closely resemble masques, *Love's Labour's Lost* and *A Midsummer Night's Dream*, there is a burlesque interlude that corresponds to the antimasque: the pageant of worthies in the former and Peter Quince's play in the latter. In both plays, however, the effect of the burlesque is not to bring out the superior dignity of the upper-class figures, but to throw an ironic light on their lack of self-knowledge. The gentlemen in *Love's Labour's Lost* are "worthies" who have dedicated themselves to a heroic cause which they abandon at the first distracting stimulus; Theseus in *A Midsummer Night's Dream* has had his own will and his conception of his duty quietly overruled by fairies in whose existence he does not believe. A much grimmer and starker burlesque appears in *The Two Noble Kinsmen*, in the form of a morris dance, an actual antimasque imported from a masque of Beaumont's, where the leading figure is a madwoman, "the jailer's daughter." This is a girl who fell in love with Palamon when he was her father's prisoner and set him free. It is the only "natural," spontaneous and apparently free-willed action in the play, and a totally disastrous one for her: her humiliation is so complete that she does not even have a name. After looking at this Venus-ruled play, we can perhaps understand why the action of *The Tempest*, which goes in the opposite direction, should culminate in a masque in which, although it is a wedding masque, one of the main themes is the exclusion of Venus.

I spoke of *Troilus and Cressida* as Shakespeare's closest approach to the dialectical and processional structure of Old Comedy. This again shows us the Trojans as victims of the heroic ritual code to which they have bound themselves. In such a situation someone more "realistic," like the ruthless Achilles or the wily Ulysses, comes out on top. In *The Two Noble Kinsmen* there is nothing corresponding to the Greeks of the earlier play, and in *Henry VIII* nothing corresponding to the Trojans, but the two plays taken together illustrate different aspects of the self-imprisoning human will to live in a world of illusion and call it reality. In the four better-known romances the movement of the action is more conventionally comic, but it is a movement towards a separating of the two orders of reality and illusion, the orders which for Wilson Knight are symbolized by music and the tempest. This takes us back to masque cosmology, as music and tempest are the two poles of the chain of being, the tempest the chaos at the bottom of existence and music the order and harmony imposed from above.

I spoke of *The Two Noble Kinsmen* as a play dominated by Venus: in the comic romances the god or goddess who acts as a providence for the action corresponds to the figure in the audience of the masque for whom the action takes place. Thus *Pericles* is the play of Diana, *Cymbeline* of Jupiter, *The Winter's Tale* of Apollo. The providence of *The Tempest* is a human magician, but his magic creates a wedding masque in which Juno appears, Juno being especially the patron of marriage, as in Jonson's *Hymenaei.* These deities are, so to speak, on the opposite side of the stage from the audience, but in the epilogue to *The Tempest* there is a strong hint that the magic and illusion of the play is in large part the creation of the audience. The audience has to release Prospero just as Prospero has to release Ariel, and for the same reason: he has been working for them, and now he wants his liberty. Similarly the gods who direct the action of *Pericles, Cymbeline,* and *The Winter's Tale* to a serene conclusion are working for the audience who recognize this conclusion as "right."

In the fine craftsmanship of Ben Jonson's verse there is something almost plastic, something that makes his own metaphor appropriate when he speaks of "the well joining, cementing, and coagmentation of words; when as it is smooth, gentle, and sweet, like a table upon which you may run your finger without rubs, and your nail cannot find a joint." Such solidity of technical skill goes with the directing of the masque towards the central figure in the audience: all the illusion points to the waking and conscious reality in the recognition of that figure. But Shakespeare's verse is continually approaching the boundaries of conscious verbal expression, the area where conventional language begins to merge into the rhythms and sounds of a realm of experience we know nothing about, though magicians may claim some knowledge of it. This is the kind of verbal music that takes us beyond drama, with its antithesis of actors and spectators, beyond masque, where the actors sometimes rejoin the spectators, into a world where the distinction of actor and spectator no longer holds, where reality is what the word itself creates, and, after creating, sees to be good.

In New Comedy the normal action is the victory of a younger generation and its erotic ambitions over the older people who block them. Older people block younger ones, normally, because they want to keep on possessing them, and they want to possess them because the illusion of possession is the only way of concealing from themselves the fact that they are possessed. When they are baffled or reconciled we have a sense of rebirth, as the palsied grip of the elders on the comic society is relaxed and new energies take over. This New Comedy structure is incorporated into the romances: Imogen marries Posthumus and Perdita Florizel despite parental opposition, and Marina and Miranda are also joined with their lovers. There is also a cyclical pattern of renewal as the "winter's tale" of Leontes' jealousy gives place to a new spring, or as Imogen (whose story is closely related to another "winter's tale," the Snow-White story familiar from Grimm) waits out her winter until her stepmother dies and her obsessed father and, later, her lover can be brought to see the light. But the main theme in all the romances is the reintegrating of the older generation, Pericles with Thaisa, Cymbeline with Caesar, Leontes with Hermione, Prospero with the King of Naples and his own Milan inheritance. It is a fully mature life that becomes transformed, and such a theme is symbolically connected not with rebirth but with resurrection, which in a sense is the opposite of rebirth, a vertical thrust upward from death to a life which is no longer subject to cyclical rotation. Thaisa and Hermione are in effect raised from the dead, a power Prospero also claims, and the prayers said by Leontes over Hermione's grave are paralleled in the great song over the grave of "Fidele" in *Cymbeline* and in the false epitaph set up for Marina in *Pericles.*

This theme of illusory death and genuine resurrection is parallel to what we described in connection with the vertical movement up the *axis mundi* or chain of being in the masque. Changing a person into a statue would be an image of metamorphosis, or descent to a lower state of being; the "statuas moving" that Bacon mentions as frequent in masques, and which we found in Campion's *Lords' Masque*, is an image of restored identity. The crisis of *The Winter's Tale* is the changing of the alleged "statue" of Hermione into the real Hermione; a similar image of resurrection is employed when Pericles is roused from his stupor by Marina, and when Imogen recovers from the narcotic drug. We also noticed that in the masque what is higher on the chain of being is often represented by what is inside the antimasque curtain. Without going into the complicated question of the Elizabethan inner stage, we notice how frequently the "higher" place in the romances is represented by an inner one: the cave of Belarius in *Cymbeline*, Paulina's chapel in *The Winter's Tale*, Prospero's cell in *The Tempest*.

Music is the symbol of the higher or paradisal world for many reasons. It represents the original order and harmony that are being regained, as in the traditional music of the spheres. Its rhythm, again, symbolizes the higher quality of time in the regained world, a world where time is an expression of inward energy and not of objective fatality. This aspect of renewed time is often represented by the dance, as in Sir John Davies' poem *Orchestra*, and though Jonson spoke contemptuously of the "concupiscence of jigs" in Shakespeare's romances, the dances are there for structurally much the same reason that they are in Jonson's masques. The text is emphatic that music plays the decisive role in bringing Thaisa and Hermione to life, and supernatural harmonies surround Belarius and Prospero. There is also a different function of music, represented by the songs of the rascally Autolycus and the mischievous Ariel, in which it has a hypnotic effect, riveting the attention but putting the consciousness to sleep. Here it is working in the opposite direction of charm or paralyzing of action. We may compare the aubade "Hark, hark, the lark," sung to Imogen, after she has spent a night with Iachimo in her room, by order of the degenerate Cloten, whose obscene comments on the lovely song form one of the most extraordinary passages of bitonal counterpoint to be found even in Shakespeare. We take the song to be appropriate to the innocence of Imogen and her remoteness from the kind of thing represented by Iachimo on the one hand and Cloten on the other, but Cloten intends the song to be an aphrodisiac stimulant propelling her in his direction.

The fact that music is found on both sides of the polarizing action reminds us that the obvious genre in which to continue these romance and masque features is the opera, especially such an opera as *The Magic Flute,* with its fairy-tale setting (in what Gurdjieff would call "pre-sand Egypt") and its polarizing action, in which hero and heroine are pulled upwards from a dark realm to a light one. It is a rare soprano who can bring out the curiously inhuman quality of the Queen of Night's first great aria, which sounds as though written for a flute solo rather than a voice. The reason is that the Queen of Night is a magic flute too, and she has her own kind of music, though a kind in harmony with the songs of sirens, not the music of the spheres. There are many similar contrasts in Wagner and elsewhere, but they would take us too far afield.

The romance differs from comedy in that the concluding scene of a comedy is intensely social. The emphasis is thrown on the reintegrated community; there are multiple marriages, and the blocking characters are reconciled or have been, like Shylock, previously excluded. In the four comic romances there are glimpses of something beyond this, something closer to the imagery of pastoral, a vision of a reconciliation of man with nature, in which the characters are individualized against nature, like Adam and Eve in the solitary society of Eden. In *The Winter's Tale* the sense of "great creating nature" as an integral part of what man's life ought to be comes to a focus in the sheep-shearing festival, a masque scene of which the dance of the twelve satyrs forms the antimasque. In *The Tempest* the corresponding focus is in the masque of Prospero, where we meet the goddesses of earth, sky and rainbow in a world from which the deluge of the tempest has receded, where the rainbow, as in the Biblical deluge story, is the sign that the curse has been lifted from the ground.

The virginity of Perdita and Miranda, which is central to both scenes, is a state traditionally associated both with innocence, the primal state of man, and with magic. It is a state not expected to last: both girls are eager for marriage. Prospero's fussing about preserving Miranda's virginity to the last moment is not morality but magic: all magic, like all music, depends on timing, and it must be the right time when Ariel is released, when the world of magical illusion is dissolved, and when Miranda enters her brave new world. Perdita's dislike of grafted plants is not a hereditary nervousness about bastards, but a sense of the virginity of nature, of nature as a virgin mother who needs no fathering art. Both masques are interrupted, one by Prospero's speaking and the other by the "whoobub," as Autolycus calls it, of Polixenes, churning up the illusions of the lower world. The interruption is a part of the sense of the transient quality of the masque, but that transience gives us an insight into what, perhaps, all dramatic and ritual spectacles are about. Humankind, as Eliot says, cannot bear very much reality: what it can bear, if it is skilfully enough prepared for it, is an instant of illusion which is the gateway to reality.

Spengler Revisited

In July, 1918, when the German armies were on the point of collapse, a book appeared called *Der Untergang des Abendlandes,* by someone called Oswald Spengler. I use that phrase because Spengler then was nobody in particular, an *Oberlehrer* or *Gymnasium* teacher who had thrown up his job in 1910 in order to write, whose health was so bad he was never called up for military service even in the warm-body months of 1918, and who was so poor he could hardly buy enough food or clothing, much less books. Anonymity was a serious handicap in a country where scholars were ranked in a quasi-military hierarchy, and Spengler's book was refused by many publishers before being brought out in a small edition. Within a year it was one of the most widely read and discussed books in Europe, and Spengler began to revise and expand it. He was decoyed into other projects before he completed his masterwork, but finally did complete it with a second volume, as long and detailed as the first. The second volume, however, adds relatively little to the essential argument, though it provides more documentation. In 1926 an English translation of the first volume by C. F. Atkinson, called *The Decline of the West,* was published by Alfred A. Knopf, the second volume appearing in 1928. It is an admirable translation, with many helpful footnotes added by the translator. In English there is an excellent study of Spengler by H. Stuart Hughes (1952). It is a short book, but even so it takes in a much wider sweep of argument than I can take here: I am concerned only with *The Decline of the West* as a "revisited classic."

The philosophical framework of Spengler's argument is a Romantic one, derived ultimately from Fichte's adaptation of Kant. The objective world, the world that we know and perceive, the phenomenal world, is essentially a spatial world: it is the domain of Nature explored by science and mathematics, and so far as it is so explored, it is a mechanical world, for when living things are seen objectively they are seen as mechanisms. Over against this is the world of time, organism, life and history. The essential reality of this world eludes the reasoner and experimenter: it is to be attained rather by feeling, intuition, imaginative insight, and, above all, by symbolism. The time in which this reality exists is a quite different time from the mechanical or clock time of science, which is really a dimension of space. It follows that methods adequate for the study of nature are not adequate for the study of history. The true method of studying living forms, Spengler says, is by analogy, and his whole procedure is explicitly and avowedly analogical. The problem is to determine what analogies in history are purely accidental, and which ones point to the real shape of history itself. Thanks to such works as Bernard Lonergan's *Insight* (1957), we know rather more about the positive role of analogy in constructive thought than was generally known in 1918, and it is no longer possible to dismiss Spengler contemptuously as "mystical" or "irrational" merely because his method is analogical. He may be, but for other reasons.

Everything that is alive shows an organic rhythm, moving through stages of birth, growth, maturity, decline and eventual death. If this happens to all individual men without exception, there is surely no inherent improbability in supposing that the same organic rhythm extends to larger human units of life. In Spengler's day, philosophy was still largely dominated by the Cartesian model of the individual perceiver completely detached from his social context. But this is an unreal abstraction, however useful as a heuristic principle; man also perceives as a representative of a larger social unit. The next step is to identify that unit. Spengler finds that it is not the nation, which is too shifting and fluctuating to be a unit, not the race (though he wobbles on this point, for reasons to be examined presently), not the class, which is a source mainly of limitation and prejudice, not the continent, but the culture. The culture to which we belong is the "Western" culture, with its roots in Western Europe, though now extended to the Americas and Australia.

This culture has gone through four main stages, which Spengler symbolizes by the seasons of the year. It had its "spring" in medieval times, and the features of such a cultural spring are a warrior aristocracy, a priesthood, a peasantry bound to the soil, a limited urban development, anonymous and impersonal art, mainly in the service of the priests and the fighters (churches and castles), and intense spiritual aspiration. It reached its "summer" with the Renaissance, consolidating in city-states, princes surrounded by courtiers, a growing merchant class, and a high development of the arts in which names and personalities become important. Its "autumn" took place in the eighteenth century, when it began to exhaust its inner possibilities, of music in Mozart and Beethoven, of literature in Goethe, of philosophy in Kant. Then it moved into its "winter" phase, which Spengler calls a "civilization" as distinct from a culture. Here its accomplishments in the arts and philosophy are either a further exhaustion of possibilities or an inorganic repetition of what has been done. Its distinctive energies are now technological. It goes in for great engineering feats, for annihilation wars and dictatorships; its population shifts from the countryside into huge amorphous cities which produce a new kind of mass man. The first significant representative of this winter civilization was Napoleon the world-conqueror; Bismarck and Cecil Rhodes the empire-builder are examples of a type of force-man who will increase through the next centuries.

Before this culture we had the Classical culture, which exemplifies the pattern for us more completely, as it completed its winter phase. Classical culture had its "spring" with the Homeric aristocracy, its "summer" with the Greek city-states, and its "autumn" with Periclean Athens and the Peloponnesian War. Plato and Aristotle, corresponding to Goethe and Kant, exhausted the inner organic possibilities of Classical philosophy, and Alexander the world-conqueror corresponds to Napoleon. The break we express by the phrase "Greek and Roman" is now occurring for us; we are now about where Classical culture was at the time of the Punic Wars, with the world-states of the future fighting it out for supremacy. Of these world-states, only the Prussian tradition that runs through Bismarck seems really to have grasped the facts of the contemporary world, and to have embarked on the "self-determination" which Spengler sees as essential to a state in the winter phase of its culture. Although the theme is very muted in *The Decline of the West,* Spengler seems to have a hope—he regards it as a hope—that Germany may yet become the Rome of the future.

In addition to these two cultures, there is a "Magian" one, which comes in between the Classical and the Western. This culture is Arabian, Syrian, Jewish, Byzantine and eastern Levantine generally: it had its "spring" in the time of Jesus, its Baroque expansion in the age of Mohammed, and it began to exhaust its possibilities in what we should call the later Middle Ages. Spengler also identifies an Egyptian, a Chinese, and an Indian culture, all of which have lasted the same length of time and gone through the same phases. A new culture, Spengler says, is growing up in Russia now, and is still (1918) in its springtime phase. When a new culture, however, grows up within the confines or influence of an older one, it is subject to what Spengler calls a "pseudomorphosis," having its genuine shape twisted and deformed by the prestige of its senior. Thus although the "Magian" culture practically took over the Roman Empire, even eventually shifting its center to Byzantium, still the domination of the Classical culture forced it to express itself in many ways that were alien to it. The same thing is happening in Russia now, where the prestige of an aging culture, as Russia's adoption of Marxism shows, is squeezing the indigenous life out of the younger development.

Such cultures differ profoundly from one another, so profoundly that no mind in a Western culture can really understand what is going on in a Classical or Egyptian or Chinese mind. The differences can only be expressed by some kind of central symbol. The Greek is a purely natural man, in Spengler's sense of the word "nature": he cared nothing for past or future, had no history although he invented it for certain occasions, produced his arts without taking thought for the morrow, and lived in the pure present, the symbol of which for Spengler is the Doric column. Spengler suggests primary symbols for most of the other cultures: the garden for the Chinese, who "wanders" in his world; the straight way for the Egyptian, who was as obsessed by past and future life as the Greek was careless of them; the cavern for Magian culture, expressed architecturally as the mosque—the Pantheon in Rome being, Spengler says, the first mosque. As Yeats remarks in his *Vision,* taking his cue from Ezra Pound, Spengler probably got his cavern symbol from Frobenius. The new Russian culture is best symbolized as a flat plane: it expresses a "denial of height" in both its architecture and its Communism. The central symbol for the Western, or, as Spengler usually calls it, the "Faustian" culture seems to be that of a center with radiating points. Faustian culture is strongly historical in sense, with a drive into infinite distance that makes it unique among other cultures. The central art of Faustian man is contrapuntal music; Classical culture expressed its sense of the pure present in its sculpture. The approaches of the two cultures even to mathematics are quite different. Classical man thinks of a number as a thing, a magnitude; Western man thinks of it as a relation to other numbers.

This morphological view of history, which sees history as a plurality of cultural developments, is, Spengler claims, an immense improvement on the ordinary "linear" one which divides history into ancient, medieval, and modern periods. Here Spengler seems to me to be on very solid ground, at least to the extent that linear history is really, at bottom, a vulgar and complacent assumption that we represent the inner purpose of all human history. The Hebrews gave us our religion, the Greeks our philosophy, the Romans our law, and these contributions to our welfare descended from the Middle Ages to us. The Chinese and

Indians had little to do with producing us; they only produced more Chinese and Indians, so they don't really belong to history. "Better fifty years of Europe than a cycle of Cathay," as the man says in Tennyson. Hegel has been often and most unfairly ridiculed for advocating a view of history which made the Prussian state of his day its supreme achievement. But whenever we adopt this linear view, especially in its progressive form, which asserts that the later we come in time the better we are, we do far worse than Hegel. The linear view of history is intellectually dead, and Spengler has had a by no means ignoble role in assisting at its demise.

Spengler's view of history includes, however, a rather similar distinction between human life with history and human life without it. If we study the history of one of the great cultures, we find that institutions evolve, classes rise, and conquests expand in what seems a logical, but is really an organic, way. But if we try to write a history of Patagonians or Zulus or Mongols, we can produce only a series of events or incidents. These people live and die and reproduce; they trade and think and fight as we do; they make poems and pots and buildings. But their stories are chronicles or annals, not coherent histories. Lapland in the eighteenth century is much like Lapland in the thirteenth: we do not feel, as we feel when we compare eighteenth-century with thirteenth-century England, that it is five centuries *older*. Similarly, after a culture has completely exhausted itself, it passes out of "history." There are, therefore, two forms of human life: a primitive existence with the maximum of continuity and the minimum of change, and life within a growing or declining culture, which is history properly speaking.

A parallel distinction reappears within the cultural developments themselves. People have constantly been fascinated by the degree of accident in history, by the fact that, as Pascal says, history would have been quite different if Cleopatra's nose had been longer. Spengler distinguishes what he calls destiny from incident. The incidents of a man's life will depend on the job he takes, the woman he marries, the town he decides to live in, and these are often determined by sheer accident. But nothing will alter the fact that it will be his life. Cultures, too, have their real lives as well as the incidents those lives bring to the surface. Spengler does not mention Cleopatra's nose, but he does say that if Mark Antony had won the battle of Actium the shape of Magian culture would have been much easier to recognize. The incidents of Western history would have been quite different if Harold had won at Hastings or Napoleon at the Nile, but the same kind of history would have appeared in other forms. A modern reader would doubtless prefer some other word to "destiny," but the distinction itself is valid, granted Spengler's premises. In what a culture produces, whether it is art, philosophy, military strategy, or political and economic developments, there are no accidents: everything a culture produces is equally a symbol of that culture.

Certain stock responses to Spengler may be set aside at once. In the first place, his view of history is not a cyclical view, even if he does use the names of the four seasons to describe its main phases. A cyclical theory would see a mechanical principle, like the one symbolized by Yeats's double gyre, as controlling the life of organisms, and for Spengler the organism is supreme: there is no superorganic mechanism. Brooks Adams's *The Law of Civilization and Decay* (1895), which appears to have wrought such disaster in the impressionable mind of Ezra Pound, does give us a rather crude cyclical theory of history as an alternating series of movements of aggressiveness and usury, with apparently some preference for the former. Yeats's *Vision*, as just implied, is also cyclical, because it is astrological, and therefore sees history as following the mechanical rhythms of nature rather than the organic ones. It seems to me that Spengler's distinction between primitive and historical existence is the real basis of Yeats's distinction between "primary" cultures and the "antithetical" ones that rise out of them, but the spirits who supplied Yeats with his vision did not know much history.

In a way Spengler does give an illusion of a cyclical view: he knows very little about Chinese and Indian civilizations, and relegates the possibility of other such developments in Babylonia or pre-Columbian America to bare mentions. Fair enough: nobody expects omniscience. But this leaves us with a series of five that do run in sequence: the Egyptian, the Classical, the Magian, the Western, and the Russian. This sequence may have its importance, as I shall suggest later, but for Spengler himself cultures grow up irregularly, like dandelions. There was no inevitability that a new Russian culture would appear in the decline of a Western one, nor is there any carryover of contrasting characteristics from one to the other (except in the negative and distorting form of "pseudomorphosis"), such as a genuinely cyclical theory would postulate.

Spengler's analogical method of course rests, not only on the analogies among the cultures themselves, but on a further analogy between a culture and an organism. It is no good saying that a culture is not an organism, and that therefore we can throw out his whole argument. The question whether a culture "is" an organism or not belongs to what I call the fallacy of the unnecessary essence. It is an insoluble problem, and insoluble problems are insoluble because they have been wrongly formulated. The question is not whether a culture is an organism, but whether it behaves enough like one to be studied on an organic model. "Let the words youth, growth, maturity, decay . . . be taken at last as objective descriptions of organic states," Spengler says. Spengler's massed evidence for these characteristics in a variety of cultures seems to me impressive enough to take seriously. It is no good either denouncing him on the ground that his attitude is "fatalistic" or "pessimistic," and that one ought not to be those things. It is not fatalism to say that one grows older every year; it is not pessimism to say that whatever is alive will eventually die. Or if it is, it doesn't matter.

Again, I am not much worried about the "contradictions" or "ambiguities," which can probably be found by job-lots in Spengler's work. Anybody can find contradictions in any long and complex argument. Most of them are verbal only, and disappear with a little application to the real structure of the argument itself. Most of the rest arise from the fact that the reader's point of view differs from that of the writer, and he is apt to project these differences into the book as inconsistencies within it. There may remain a number of genuine contradictions which really do erode the author's own case, and I think there are some in Spengler. But for a book of the kind he wrote the general principle holds that if one is in broad sympathy with what he is trying to do, no errors or contradictions or exaggerations seem fatal to the general aim; if one is not in sympathy with it, everything, however correct in itself, dissolves into chaos.

Spengler's book is not a work of history; it is a work of historical popularization. It outlines one of the mythical shapes in which history reaches everybody except professional historians. Spengler would not care for the term popularization: he is proud of the length and difficulty of his work, speaks with contempt of the popular; and of his efforts to popularize his own thesis, such as *Prussianism and Socialism* (1919) or *Man and Technics* (1931), the less said the better. Nevertheless, his book is addressed to the world at large, and historians are the last people who should be influenced by it. What Spengler has produced is a vision of history which is very close to being a work of literature—close enough, at least, for me to feel some appropriateness in examining it as a literary critic. If *The Decline of the West* were nothing else, it would still be one of the world's great Romantic poems. There are limits to this, of course: Spengler had no intention of producing a work of *pure* imagination, nor did he do so. A work of literature, as such, cannot be argued about or refuted, and Spengler's book has been constantly and utterly refuted ever since it appeared. But it won't go away, because in sixty years there has been no alternative vision of the data it contemplates.

What seems to me most impressive about Spengler is the fact that everybody does accept his main thesis in practice, whatever they think or say they accept. Everybody thinks in terms of a "Western" culture to which Europeans and Americans belong; everybody thinks of that culture as old, not young; everybody realizes that its most striking parallels are with the Roman period of Classical culture; everybody realizes that some crucial change in our way of life took place around Napoleon's time. At that I am not counting the people who have a sentimental admiration for medieval culture because it represents our own lost youth, or the people who cannot listen with pleasure to any music later than Mozart or Beethoven, or the people who regard the nineteenth century as a degenerate horror, or the Marxists who talk about the decadence of bourgeois culture, or the alarmists who talk about a return to a new Dark Ages, or the Hellenists who regard Latin literature as a second-hand imitation of Greek literature. All these have a more or less muddled version of Spengler's vision as their basis. The decline, or aging, of the West is as much a part of our mental outlook today as the electron or the dinosaur, and in that sense we are all Spenglerians.

Thus T. S. Eliot's *The Waste Land*, published in 1922, was written without reference to Spengler, an author of whom Eliot would not be likely to take an exalted view. But look at the imagery of the poem:

spring	summer	autumn	winter
morning	noon	evening	night
youth	maturity	age	death
spring rain	river Thames	estuary	sea
Middle Ages	Elizabethans	18th century	20th century

The medieval references, it is true, come mainly through Wagner, and the eighteenth-century section was cut out on the advice of Pound, but the Spenglerian analogy is there in full force. The parallels with Classical culture are also there, even to the explicit allusion to the Punic Wars in the reference to the "ships at Mylae." W. H. Auden's "The Fall of Rome," and much of the imagery of *For the Time Being* are unintelligible without some comprehension, however slight, of Spengler's thesis. Similarly with many poems of Yeats and Pound, where the influence of Spengler is more conscious, especially in Yeats. James Thurber tells us of a man who read somewhere that if one did not acquire sexual knowledge from one's parents one got it out of the gutter, so, having learned nothing from his parents, he undertook an exhaustive analysis of the gutters of several American cities. In other areas we can be more fortunate. If we do not acquire our knowledge of Spengler's vision from Spengler we have to get it out of the air, but get it we will; we have no choice in the matter.

For students of English literature, at least, the most famous attack on Spengler occurs in Wyndham Lewis's *Time and Western Man*, as part of his general onslaught on the "time philosophy." And a most instructive attack it is. In the first place, we notice that Lewis has no alternative philosophy. He makes vague remarks about attaching more importance to space and painting and less to time and music, and says such things as "I am for the physical world." But his book is actually a quite lucid, often brilliant, example of the very procedure he proposes to attack. He shows how twentieth-century philosophy, literature, politics, popular entertainment, music and ballet, and half a dozen other social phenomena all form a single interwoven texture of "time philosophy," and are all interchangeable symbols of it. We are thus not surprised to find that Lewis's targets of attack are formative influences on his other work, as Joyce influenced his fiction and Bergson his theory of satire. And as *Time and Western Man* is really a Spenglerian book, doing essentially the kind of thing Spengler would do, including taking a hostile and polemical tone toward most contemporary culture, we are not surprised either to find that Lewis seldom comes to grips with Spengler's actual arguments. He does make some effective points, such as showing how a *Zeitgeist* patter can rationalize irresponsible political leadership by explaining that history says it's "time" for another war. But this would apply to a lot of people besides Spengler. What Lewis mainly attacks and ridicules are Spengler's sound effects.

It is true that Spengler's sound effects are sometimes hard to take, and the reason for their existence brings us to a problem that the literary critic is constantly having to face. I have elsewhere tried to show that it is intellectually dishonest to call a man's work reactionary, whatever his personal attitudes may have been, because it is the use made of it by others that will determine whether it will be reactionary or not. The pseudo-critic is constantly looking for some feature of a writer's attitude, inside or outside his books, that will enable him to plaster some ready-made label on his author. Genuine criticism is a much more difficult and delicate operation, especially in literature, where a man may be a great poet and still be little better than an idiot in many of his personal attitudes.

In a large number, at least, of important writers we find an imagination which makes them important, and something else, call it an ego, which represents the personality trying to *say* something, to assert and argue and impress. A great deal of criticism revolves around the problem of trying to separate these two elements. We have Eliot the poet and Eliot the snob; Pound the poet and Pound the crank; Yeats the poet and Yeats the poseur; Lawrence the poet and Lawrence the hysteric. Further back, Milton, Pope, Blake, Shelley, Whitman, all present aspects of personality so distasteful to some critics that they cannot really deal critically with their poetry at all. For somebody on the periphery of literature, like Spengler, the task of separation is still more difficult, and requires even more patience. It does a writer no service to pretend that the things which obstruct his imagination are not there, or, if there, can be rationalized or explained away. In my opinion Spengler has a permanent place in twentieth-century thought, but so far as his reputation is concerned, he was often his own worst enemy, and a stupid and confused Spengler is continually getting in the way of the genuine prophet and visionary.

We may suspect, perhaps, some illegitimate motivation in Spengler's writing, some desire to win the war on the intellectual front after being left out of the army. It would be easy to make too much of this, but he does say in the preface to the revised edition that he has produced what he is "proud to call *a German philosophy*" (italics original), although the real thesis of his book is that there are no German philosophies, only Western ones. In any case, he belonged all his life to the far right of the German political spectrum, and carried a load of the dismal *Völkisch* imbecilities that played so important a part in bringing Hitler to power. Hitler in fact represents something of a nemesis for Spengler the prophet, even though Spengler died in 1936, before Hitler had got really started on his lemming march. Unless he has unusual sources of information, a prophet is well advised to stick to analyzing the present instead of foretelling the future.

Spengler wanted and expected a German leader in the Bismarckian and Prussian military tradition, and he doubted whether this screaming *lumpen-Künstler* was it. He greeted the Nazis in a book called in English *The Hour of Decision* (1933), which the Nazis, when they got around to reading it, banned from circulation. But his general political attitude was sufficiently close to Nazism to enable him to die in his bed.

These personal attitudes account for many of the more unattractive elements in his rhetoric, which has all the faults of a prophetic style: harsh, dogmatic, prejudiced, certain that history will do exactly what he says, determined to rub his reader's nose into all the toughness and grimness of his outlook. He has little humor, though plenty of savage and sardonic wit, and a fine gift for gloomy eloquence. He is fond of murky biological language, like calling man a "splendid beast of prey," and much of his imagery is Halloween imagery, full of woo-woo noises and shivery Wagnerian whinnies about the "dark" goings-on of nature and destiny. Thus:

> With the formed state, high history also lays itself down weary to sleep. Man becomes a plant again, adhering to the soil, dumb and enduring. The timeless village and the "eternal" peasant reappear, begetting children and burying seed in Mother Earth. . . . There, in the souls, world-peace, the peace of God, the bliss of grey-haired monks and hermits, is become actual—and there alone. It has awakened that depth in the endurance of suffering which the historical man in the thousand years of his development has never known. Only with the end of grand History does holy, still Being reappear. It is a drama noble in its aimlessness, noble and aimless as the course of the stars, the rotation of the earth, and alternance of land and sea, of ice and virgin forest upon its face. We may marvel at it or we may lament it—but it is there.

It may not be everybody's poetry, but it is genuine enough of its kind. But occasionally we come across elements connected with this kind of rhetoric that are more objectionable. For example, Spengler knows that his argument really has nothing to do with the conception of "race," and in *The Hour of Decision* he makes it clear—well, fairly clear—that he regards the Nazi attitude to race as suicidal frenzy. But he *cannot* give up the notion that Jews are a separate entity: if he did, one of the most dearly cherished *Völkisch* prejudices would go down the drain:

> Spinoza, a Jew and therefore, spiritually, a member of the Magian Culture, could not absorb the Faustian force-concept at all, and it has no place in his system. And it is an astounding proof of the secret power of root-ideas that Heinrich Hertz, the only Jew amongst the great physicists of the recent past, was also the only one of them who tried to resolve the dilemma of mechanics by eliminating the idea of force.

According to Spengler's own thesis, a man who spends his life in seventeenth-century Holland belongs to the Western Baroque, whatever his religious or racial affinities. Most of Spinoza's contemporaries called themselves Christians, which is equally a "Magian" religion according to Spengler. But of course one never knows when such a prejudice will come in handy. "It is something fundamental in the essence of the Magian soul that leads the Jew, as entrepreneur and engineer, to stand aside from the creation proper of machines and devote himself to the business side of their production." This remark follows closely on a critique of Marx. As the Nazis said, capitalism and communism are both Jewish inventions. The biological function of women is also a fruitful topic for dark symbolization:

> Endless Becoming is comprehended in the idea of Motherhood. Woman as Mother *is* Time and *is* Destiny. Just as the mysterious act of depth-experience fashions, out of sensation, extension and world, so through motherhood the bodily man is made an individual member of this world, in which thereupon he *has* a Destiny. All symbols of Time and Distance are also symbols of maternity. *Care* is the root-feeling of future, and all care is motherly.

It is little surprise to learn that Ibsen's Nora "is the very type of the provincial derailed by reading." That is, if Nora had really responded to the *Zeitgeist,* and understood that she *was* Time and

Destiny, she would have done nothing so unfeminine as read books, but would have remained illiterate, pregnant, and absorbed in her doll-house.

There is also the unnecessary value judgment implied in the word "decline" itself. Strictly speaking, according to Spengler Western art is not getting any better or worse as it changes from medieval to Renaissance to Baroque conventions; it is simply growing older. But Spengler wants it to decline and exhaust its possibilities, because he wants his contemporaries, at least the German ones, to devote themselves to the things required by their cultural age, which for him are technological, national socialist, and military:

> I would sooner have the fine mind-begotten forms of a fast steamer, a steel structure, a precision-lathe, the subtlety and elegance of many chemical and optical processes, than all the pickings and stealings of present-day "arts and crafts," architecture and painting included. I prefer one Roman aqueduct to all Roman temples and statues. . . .

The Romans who built aqueducts and carried out huge massacres and purges also produced Lucretius, Virgil, Ovid, Horace and Catullus. Not one of these names appears in Spengler's indexes (except Horace by courtesy of the translator). He would say, with the Hellenists mentioned above, that Latin poetry was an inorganic repetition of Greek poetry, but it wasn't. But, of course, for him as for others the word "decline" is an easy way of dismissing anything in the contemporary arts that one finds puzzling or disturbing. When Spengler's book was published, the fashionable myth was the myth of progress, and Spengler's evidence that technological advance could just as easily be seen as a hardening of the cultural arteries was useful as a counterweight. But its usefulness, like so many other things in history, has exhausted its possibilities now that this aspect of technology is obvious to everybody.

After all this has been said, and a great deal more that could be said taken for granted, it is still true that very few books, in my experience, have anything like Spengler's power to expand and exhilarate the mind. The boldness of his leaping imagination, the kaleidoscopic patterns that facts make when he throws them together, the sense of the whole of human thought and culture spread out in front of one, the feeling that the blinkers of time and space have been removed from one's inward eyes when Greek sculptors are treated as the "contemporaries" of Western composers, all make up an experience not easily duplicated. I first encountered him as an undergraduate, and I think this is the best time to read him, because his perspective is long range and presbyopic, and his specific judgments all too often wrong headed. Some of his comparative passages, such as his juxtaposing of colors in Western painting with tonal effects in Western music, read almost like free association. Any number of critics could call these comparisons absurd or mystical balderdash. But Spengler has the power to challenge the reader's imagination, as critics of that type usually have not, and he will probably survive them all even if all of them are right.

The best-known philosophy of history after Spengler, at least in English, is that of Arnold Toynbee, whose *Study of History* began appearing while Spengler was still alive. Toynbee has twenty-one cultures to Spengler's seven or eight, and twenty of them follow, more or less, Spengler's organic scheme of youth, maturity, decline (accompanied by a "time of troubles") and dissolution. But the twenty-first is Toynbee's own Western culture, and that one has just got to be different: to assume that it will go the way of the others would be "fatalism," which is what he professes to object to in Spengler. So he develops a "challenge and response" theory which enables him to use a mechanical metaphor instead of an organic one at the stage corresponding to "decline," and talk of "breakdown" instead. But the sequence of genesis, growth, breakdown and disintegration in Toynbee seems more jumbled than Spengler's consistently organic model. He begins his discussion of the causes of "breakdown," at the beginning of Volume Four, with a critique of Spengler which has all the air of a dodged issue. He says that it is too early to say whether Western culture has come to its "time of troubles" yet, which is quite a statement to make in 1939; he says Spengler is a "fatalist," which as we have seen is irrelevant, and he says that Spengler treats a metaphor as though it were a fact. But every historical overview of this kind, including Toynbee's, is and has to be metaphorical. When we look at Toynbee's own table of contents we find "nemesis of creativity," "schism and palingenesis," "withdrawal and return," and if those are not metaphors I don't know the meaning of the word. He also seems to feel that ignoring Spengler's distinction between destiny and incident will give more sense of freedom to man by putting more emphasis on the accidental factors of history. There is of course a great deal that is of value and interest in Toynbee's books, but as a Spenglerian revisionist he seems to me to be something of a bust. Except for one thing.

That one thing is his account of the passing of Classical into Western culture. He says that when a culture dies it forms an internal and an external proletariat. The late Roman Empire had its internal proletariat in the bread-and-circus mobs of Rome and the other big cities, and its external proletariat in the Goths and Vandals breaking through the periphery of the Empire. Out of these two forms of proletariat there emerged a "universal Church," which acted as the tomb of the old culture and the womb of the new one. Spengler also speaks of a "second religiousness" which enters a culture in its final stages: it seems to be one of his most useful and suggestive ideas. But he thinks of Toynbee's internal proletariat simply as a rabble: "The mass is the end, the radical nullity," he says. He overlooks both the connection of primitive Christianity with the proletariat and its extraordinary power of organization. It seems to me that Toynbee gives a more rational explanation of the historical role of Christianity in this period than Spengler gives. Toynbee ignores Spengler's "Magian" intermediate culture, but his own view does not necessarily do away with it: it merely points to something else that was also happening, to different aspects of what was happening, and to a process which would also account for the "cavern" imagery that Spengler associates with Byzantine culture. It also provides a means of explaining something very important that Spengler leaves out.

This is the curious fascination of Western culture with the idea of making itself into a reborn Classical culture. In its "spring" period its poets devoted great energies to recreating the visions of Virgil and Ovid; in its political life, it revolved around the conception of a reborn Augustus, a Christianized Roman Emperor. Why is the central mythical figure of English literature King Arthur, who has so vague and hazy a historical existence? At best he was merely a local British leader making a temporary rally against the Saxons, who of course won in the end. Why not make more of, say, Alfred, who really was a great man, and whose historical existence is not open to doubt? When we read in Geoffrey of Monmouth that Arthur conquered the armies of Rome, and remember that his colleague in romance was Charlemagne, we get a clue: he is a prototype of the reborn Christian Caesar, the Holy Roman Emperor. This symbolism of recreating Classical culture reaches its climax with the Renaissance, a word which means the "rebirth" of Classicism. It is highly significant that Spengler is rather silly about the Renaissance, which he treats as an un-German interruption of the development of German Gothic into German Baroque. He also seems unaware of the extent to which the same idea dominated, to or past the verge of obsession, a long series of German writers, from Winckelmann through Hölderlin to Nietzsche and George, the last two of whom Spengler certainly knew well. Of course Toynbee's death and rebirth pattern does introduce a more cyclical element into history than Spengler admits. Vico is often regarded as a precursor of Spengler, though I see no evidence that Spengler had read him, but Toynbee brings us much closer to what Vico means by the *ricorso* than anything in Spengler.

If one culture can recreate another one in this way, we have to abandon what seems to me in any case a profoundly unacceptable element in Spengler's argument: his insistence that every culture is a windowless monad, and cannot be genuinely influenced by another culture. "To the true Russian the basic proposition of Darwinism is as devoid of meaning as that of Copernicus is to a true Arab." This remark may be a curious anticipation of the Lysenko business in Stalinist Russia, but on the whole such observations are clearly nonsense: there are a lot of Arabs who know that the earth goes round the sun, and they are not bogus ones. In fact science, in general, is the great obstacle to Spengler's cultural solipsism. Granted that different cultures will construct different scientific world-pictures, there is an obviously translatable quality in science, which makes its principles quite as comprehensible to Chinese or Indians as to Germans or Americans. Such science might even develop a world view on a supercultural scale. We notice that Spengler casts some uneasy glances at what he calls "the ruthlessly cynical hypothesis of the Relativity theory." He tries to see it, of course, as "exhausting the possibilities" of Western science, but he seems to be not quite sure that its view of time will be content to confine itself to the world of measurement and stay out of his dark existential territory.

Apart from this, however, perhaps the fact that Western culture has spread over the world means something more than simply the capacity for expansion which Spengler assigns to the Faustian spirit. If science is a universal structure of knowledge, it can help mankind to break out of culture-group barriers. Spengler of course thinks this is a pipe dream, and insists that the people of Asia and Africa have no interest in Western science or technology except as a means of destroying the West. But Marx is a far more effective prophet in the world today than Spengler, and the reason is that he emphasizes something uniform and global in the human situation. The factors which are the same throughout the world, such as the exploitation of labor, have always been, if not less important, at any rate less powerful in history than conflicts of civilizations. Now they are more important, and growing in power. The industrial revolution brings a new factor into the situation which cannot be wholly absorbed into a dialectic of separate "cultures," important as those have been. The question whether Western civilization will survive, decline or break down is out of date, for the world is trying to outgrow the conception of "a" civilization, and reach a different kind of perspective.

If the death-to-rebirth transition from Classical to Western culture happened once, something similar could happen again in our day, though the transition would be to something bigger than another culture. This would imply three major periods of human existence: the period of primitive societies, the period of the organic cultures, and a third period now beginning. Spengler, we saw, attacks and ridicules the three-period view of ancient, medieval and modern ages with, we said, a good deal of justification. But he also remarks that the notion of three ages has had a profound appeal to the Faustian consciousness, from Joachim of Floris in the thirteenth century onward. It is possible that what is now beginning to take shape is the real "Third Reich," of which the Nazis produced so hideous a parody.

The detail of Spengler's vision is all around us, in the restless wandering of great masses of people, in the violence and overcrowding of our almost unmanageable cities, in the strong ethical sense in some social areas, which Spengler compares with Buddhism in India and Stoicism in Rome, neutralized by dictatorships and police states in others, in the "second religiousness" of Oriental cults and the like, in the brutality and vacuousness of our standard forms of entertainment, in the physical self-indulgence paralleling the Roman cult of the bath, in the rapid series of vogues and fashions in the arts which distract us from their inner emptiness. It would be disastrous to pretend that these are not features of cultural aging. It would be still more disastrous to underestimate the powerful inertia in society that wants to "decline" still further, give up the freedom that demands responsibility, and drop out of history. What Spengler said would happen is happening, to a very considerable degree. But while Spengler is one of our genuine prophets, he is not our definitive prophet: other things are also happening, in areas that still invite our energies and loyalties and are not marked off with the words "too late."

Part Three

FOUR POETS

Agon and Logos

Milton intended *Paradise Lost* to be a Christian conquest of the Classical epic genre, and similarly *Samson Agonistes* is a Christian conquest of the Classical genre of dramatic tragedy. In Classical literature, as in Classical life and culture generally, there are, as Milton sees it, two elements. One is a development of natural human ability, or what we now call creative imagination, outside the Christian revelation, and therefore possessing, not the truth of that revelation, but an analogy of or parallel to that truth. Although the poetry of the Bible, according to *The Reason of Church Government,* is better as poetry than Classical poetry, the latter is a safer model for poets not sure of receiving the highest kind of inspiration. But Classical culture is not simply a human development, unfortunately: man without revelation cannot avoid accepting some demonic version, which means parody, of that revelation. Hence such forms as the Homeric epic and the Sophoclean tragedy are genuine models of style, decorum, and "ancient liberty"; at the same time they are also connected with something ultimately demonic, a pseudo-revelation from fallen angels. The use of Classical genres by a Christian poet should show in what respects they are humanly analogous to the forms of Christian revelation, and in what respects they are demonic parodies of them.

In *Paradise Regained*, a brief epic for which Milton mentions no Classical model, the sense of parody is at its sharpest. Christ can overcome the temptations of Satan because he can clearly see the demonic taproot of everything Satan offers. I have never understood why Christ's rejection of Classical culture in that poem should be such a puzzle to critics: it seems so obvious that in that context Christ has to reject every syllable of it. It does not mean that *Milton* is rejecting it: it is only because Christ does reject it that Milton can accept so much of it. The rejection of the English dramatic tradition in the Preface to *Samson Agonistes* is much harder to understand. The theme of *Paradise Regained* is, appropriately, a parody of a dragon-killing romance, or, more accurately, it presents the reality of which the dragon-killing romance is a parody. For Milton there is no strength except spiritual strength, and no conflict except mental conflict, hence the prophecy that the Messiah will defeat the serpent can only be fulfilled by a dramatic dialogue.

In *Paradise Lost* too, so far as we can think of it as an epic modelled on Homer and Virgil, the sense of parody is much sharper than the sense of analogy. The Classical epic is a poem of heroic action, of *klea andron*, brave deeds of men. Christianity has a completely opposed notion of what a hero is: a Christian hero is one who imitates or approximates the heroism of Christ, which consisted in suffering, endurance, and compassion. The sense of opposition doubtless greatly intensified in Milton's mind between his discussion of Christian heroism in *The Reason of Church Government* and the writing of *Paradise Lost.* In the latter poem, in any case, the conventional heroics of the Classical epic are mainly transferred to Satan and the other devils. There is, it is true, a great war in heaven in which the faithful angels perform prodigies of valor, but when on the third day the Son of God disposes of the entire rebel host single-handed, the sense of parody is strongly reinforced. The whole war in heaven is something of a joke to God, for whom any strength apart from his will does not exist. The same sense of the identity of strength and divine will, along with the unreality of any strength apart from it, recurs in *Comus,* where the elder brother explains how the

Lady's chastity is an invincible strength, and in the Samson story itself, where Samson kills a thousand Philistines "With what trivial weapon came to hand," the jawbone of an ass (142–3).

Paradise Lost, as I have said elsewhere, restates in Christian terms, reversing the pagan ones, not only what a hero is but what an act is. For Milton the only genuine act is an act performed according to the will of God. Adam's eating of the tree of knowledge was therefore not an act, but the pseudo-act of disobedience; the revolt of Satan was the parody-act of rebellion. The only genuine actions in *Paradise Lost* are those performed by the Son of God, the acts of creation and redemption. The same principle, applied to *Samson Agonistes,* will help to explain Milton's conception of tragic action. Nothing really happens anywhere except the accomplishing of the will of God. In the world of the angels above man this will can be clearly seen as a benign providence; in the world of animals below man it can be seen in a kind of reflecting mirror, as the automatic accuracy of instinct. As the working of God's will is relatively uncomplicated in these worlds, there is no possibility of anything like tragic action, as Milton conceives it, among either angels (faithful angels, of course) or animals.

In human life too it is still true that nothing really happens except the accomplishing of God's will, or what we call providence. But there—or here—the will of God is much harder to see, because it is concealed by the powerful current of pseudo-acts released by human passion and demonic instigation. God's providence can be seen by the human reason, but the reason, being normally a submerged and suppressed critic of a dictatorial passion, is seldom attended to. The three levels of reality are indicated by the Messenger when he says (1545–7):

> But providence or instinct of nature seems,
> Or reason, though disturb'd and scarse consulted,
> To have guided me aright, I know not how.

They also appear in one of the choral odes, where God is told that in relation to man he (670–3)

> Temper'st thy providence through his short course,
> Not evenly, as thou rul'st
> The Angelic orders, and inferiour creatures mute,
> Irrational and brute.

Human life sets up a kind of perpetual Saturnalia or inversion of the providential order, in which the wicked flourish and the good are persecuted or ridiculed. For the most part we have to wait for a judgment after the end of life, whether of an individual life or of human history itself, in order to see good vindicated and evil confounded. But every once in a while the wicked do meet with appalling disasters in a form which makes it clear to the eye of reason that the disaster is the consequence of previous folly or arrogance. The good, merely because they are good, are in for a rough time in human society: their normal fate is, at best, ridicule or neglect, at worst martyrdom. The good man, or prophet as he usually is, is an agent of a counter-counter-movement in human life, of God's will working against human evil, and his life may well be tragic in relation to that evil, which often claims him as its victim. Yet the good may occasionally be recognized as having been right even through the torrent of lies and illusions which is the normal course of history.

We have tragedy when it is possible for the human reason, in contemplating the fall of Belshazzar or the justification of Job, to catch a glimpse of the working of God's will in human life against the power of human passion or evil. Tragedy is thus, for Milton, the recognition of God's will by human reason in the form of justice or law. As justice or law is an equalizing or balancing principle, its emblem being the scales, the tragic vision has the equalizing effect that Aristotle calls catharsis. According to the explanation of catharsis given by Milton in his preface to *Samson Agonistes,* the consequences of human passion cannot be seen as tragic by human passion, but only by human reason, which casts passion out of itself by seeing a greater passion before it, on the principle of like curing like in homeopathic medicine. That is, in the soul passion normally dominates reason; in tragedy passion is externalized, in a position where only reason can recognize it;

the effect of catharsis is thus to revolutionize the soul, restoring reason to its ascendancy and casting out passion by passion.

There are, as is obvious, at least two levels of tragic action. The lower level, in which disaster appears to be the inevitable consequence of folly or wrongdoing, is what is expressed by the word nemesis in Greek tragedy. This kind of nemesis-tragedy has already happened to Samson before *Samson Agonistes* begins: it belongs to a play that Milton gave a title to but did not write, *Samson Hybristes.* In the play that we have, this nemesis action is the tragic action so far as it affects the Philistines. Samson himself goes through a redemption in which he is accepted once again as an agent of God's will and a champion of Israel. Hence, though he is inevitably involved in a tragic death, it is not a death to which the conception of nemesis is any longer relevant.

The tragedies of the Philistines and of Samson are, respectively, the elements of demonic parody and of analogy in the tragic action. What happens to the Philistines is the same kind of thing that happens to such figures as Ajax in Sophocles or Heracles in Euripides, where the causes of catastrophe are, ultimately, devils. Samson, on the other hand, is a human analogy of Christ, of whose death his death is a prototype. It follows that the central area of tragic action, for Milton, is the Old Testament, where the Christian reader or audience may see the higher kind of tragedy in its true perspective, as part of the analogy of the law.

This conception of two levels of tragic action, however, recurs in Greek tragedy, most explicitly at the end of the Oresteia. Here there is a nemesis movement represented by the Furies, who are not capable of distinguishing the elements of equity in a tragic situation, such as the amount and kind of provocation given by the victim, but are the unleashing of an essentially automatic force, the righting of a disturbed balance in nature. This nemesis movement is overruled by a legal decision in which gods and men are included, and which is the higher tragic vision of the whole action, ending in the acquittal of Orestes. Similarly in the two Oedipus plays of Sophocles. In the first one, *Oedipus Tyrannos,* Oedipus tears out his eyes in a kind of reflex revulsion of horror, without stopping to consider that his own unconsciousness of the guilt he has been involved in is a point of some ethical relevance. The action of *Oedipus Tyrannos* goes through a self-discovery which moves backwards in time and ends in blindness; *Samson Agonistes* goes in the opposite direction, through a progressive and forward-moving self-discovery away from blindness. It therefore runs parallel (to a very limited degree) with the action of the second Oedipus play, *Oedipus at Colonus.*

We first see Samson in the throes of nemesis, tormented by the mechanical furies of his own conscience. Christian ethics has always distinguished remorse from repentance *(metanoia)*, and although there is genuine repentance in Samson, the sterile brooding, the self-chewing which is what "remorse" literally means, is more prominent at first. Just as Samson's body is infested by vermin, so all the mental vermin engendered by the lord of flies (the devil Beelzebub, invoked by Harapha) are infesting his mind, producing there what at times suggests an allegorical reading on Milton's part of the torments of Prometheus (623–4):

> Thoughts, my Tormentors, arm'd with deadly stings
> Mangle my apprehensive tenderest parts.

Samson has been tempted and has lost, and the result of losing a temptation is demonic possession. The Chorus is puzzled by the fact that Samson is so much worse off than they are: there seems to be a kind of manic-depressive rhythm in nemesis which ensures that the bigger they are, the harder they fall. This is closely linked with the wheel-of-fortune rhythm in tragedy that so fascinated medieval writers (687–91):

> Nor only dost degrade them, or remit
> To life obscur'd, which were a fair dismission,
> But throw'st them lower then thou didst exalt them high—
> Unseemly falls in human eie,
> Too grievous for the trespass or omission.

The overtones of this last line would take us a long way—into the Book of Job, for example. But to the main point the answer, or part of the answer, is that those elected by God are capable of sin in a way that ordinary people, or what the Chorus calls the "common rout" (674), are not. This is *a fortiori* true of Adam in Eden, for whom the most trivial of trespasses, by ordinary human standards, was also the greatest possible sin. Yet even Adam could not fall as low as the devils, who fell from a greater height. The same principle applies in reverse to the Philistines. The divine vengeance on them extends primarily to their lords and priests: in the destruction of their temple "The vulgar only scap'd, which stood without" (1559). The wheel-of-fortune rhythm for them may be heard in the two off-stage noises, the shout of triumph and the death-groan, which we hear as the wheel turns a half-circle.

The nemesis of Samson takes the form of "captivity and loss of eyes," and the action of the play, we said, so far as it affects Samson, moves away from nemesis. Manoa has elaborate plans to free Samson from captivity, and he also expresses the hope that God will restore Samson's eyesight along with his strength. Much of this is only the facile hopefulness of a rather weak man, but it is true that symbolically Samson's freedom and vision are both restored. They are restored within the realities of his situation, which means that the process is full of tragic ironies, starting with the reversal of Manoa's picture of how the restoration might take place. But it does take place none the less. At the beginning of the play Samson is a slave in both external and internal bondage: besides being "at the mill with slaves," he is in a "Prison within a Prison," and is, as the Chorus says, "the Dungeon of thy self" (41, 153–6). Yet he asserts his spiritual freedom, negatively, by refusing to take part in a Philistine festival, and then positively by accepting the dispensation that God gives him to go, of which more later. At the temple itself he performs various feats in obedience to commands, but the crucial act he performs "of my own accord," as a free man. Similarly, although in his blindness he possesses an internal light, such as Milton claims for himself in the *Second Defence* and elsewhere, he is well aware that, as the Chorus says, it "puts forth no visual beam." But in his final enterprise he is, according to the Semichorus, "with inward eyes illuminated" (163, 1689).

In the Book of Judges Samson's final prayer is "let me die with the Philistines." Milton does not quote this directly, though it is the theme of Samson's speech to Manoa, but he does ascribe to Samson a most eloquent longing for death. This longing in itself is despair, but God transmutes it to a heroic achievement ending in death. God is thus acting in accordance with the same homeopathic principle, of casting out salt humors by salt and the like, which is part of the catharsis of tragedy. And in proportion as Samson is released from nemesis, the whole nemesis machinery is transferred to the Philistines. It is they who acquire the hybris or "spirit of frenzy" which is the normal condition of the Greek tragic hero. With the last line of the first Semichorus, "And with blindness internal struck" (1686), the transfer is completed.

The "spirit of frenzy" is associated with drunkenness, the "jocund and sublime" Philistines being a contrast in this respect to the water-drinking Samson. It is still morning, but, as Milton remarks in the Commonplace Book, people who are habitually drunk can get drunk without the aid of wine. This drunkenness however is a Dionysian drunkenness, an enthusiasm or possession by a god, or what they consider a god. The Bible says of Samson that his hair began to grow again when he was in the Philistine prison-house. There are few concessions to probability in folk tales, yet we may perhaps ask the question: once the Philistines had learned the secret of Samson's strength, why did they allow his hair to grow again? Two answers are suggested by Milton. One, the mill owners were making a good deal of money by exploiting his labor, "The work of many hands," as Samson calls it. Two, the Philistines really believed in the power of Dagon, and therefore believed that Samson's strength could be contained within limits convenient to them. It was this belief in particular that was their "spirit of frenzy."

The King James Bible says that Samson was commanded to make sport for the Philistines, and, as the schoolboy added, he brought down the house. The New English Bible makes it clear that what Samson had to do was fight, like a gladiator. The two translations are not inconsistent: elsewhere in the Old Testament (as Huizinga points out in *Homo Ludens*) to "play" or "make sport" can mean to fight to the death. But gladiatorial fighting would not have suited Milton's conception. Dramatically, Samson would not want to spoil his climax by killing individual Philistines. More important, Milton says more than once that when Samson had his genuine strength, no single person dared oppose him. Hence the behavior of Harapha. The model for Harapha's character is his son Goliath, and while Goliath is certainly a boaster—it was conventional for warriors of his type to begin battles with boasts—there is no indication that he is a coward. He expects King Saul to come out to meet him, the Saul who was said to be head and shoulders over every man in Israel, and when David turns up with his slingshot he is genuinely disappointed as well as contemptuous. During the colloquy with Harapha Samson suddenly asserts his role once again as a champion of Jehovah, and Harapha does not dare pursue the matter further. He may, of course, have been a coward all along, but it may be that something more than simple cowardice is breaking him down.

It is essential to Milton's dramatic purpose, then, that Samson in the temple is purely an entertainer, almost the buffoon, of a Philistine carnival, an *agonistes* in the sense of a performer or actor—hardly as a contestant in games, for he is not competing with anyone. At the same time he is a tragic hero, a defeated champion, and an *agonistes* in that sense, to his Danite followers. The action moves quickly through what Yeats would call a double gyre, as the tragedy becomes a triumph and the carnival a shambles. It is this aspect of Samson's situation in particular that makes him a dramatic prototype of Christ, for Christ is also a tragic hero to his followers as well as a mocked and ridiculed figure of a carnival to his enemies, and the same reversal of action occurs there.

In *Samson Agonistes* the reversal is expressed in a complex imagery of light and darkness. Milton knew too much Hebrew not to pick up the overtones of *shemesh*, the Hebrew word for sun, in

Samson's name, and perhaps he saw something of a solar-shaped myth in the story of the long-haired hero who fell into the dark prison of the west. The play opens at sunrise with Samson physically in the open air, but, like other titans, including Prometheus at the end of Aeschylus's play, he seems to be symbolically in a kind of subterranean prison or "interlunar cave," and the very rare classical allusions in the play link him with Atlas and Ixion. It is almost as though Samson, or a power guiding Samson, were moving under the world like the sun at night, back to the place of its rising. The action ends abruptly at noon, with the zenith of the Philistine triumph suddenly blown to pieces by the explosion of a dark hidden fire rising like the phoenix from its ashes. From the Israelite point of view, this means that the "total eclipse" Samson complains of has lifted and that although "he seems to hide his face," the true sun-god has unexpectedly returned.

Samson Agonistes is a real play, with a real plot and real characters, and it could be acted with success, I should think, in front of any audience ready to accept its conventions. Yet Milton said that it was not intended for the stage, a statement often connected with the prejudice against stage plays among extreme Puritans in England. The prejudice itself is not very interesting nor particularly relevant to Milton, but the traditions behind it are more so.

What Milton would call paganism is a religious development focussed on visual symbols. Polytheism is impossible without pictures or statues to distinguish one god from another. As a pagan society becomes more centralized, it converges on a capital city, such as Gaza is described as being, and the visual worship of gods is supplemented by various forms of spectacle, including a strong concentration on the supreme ruler or king as a visible symbol. Hebrew religion is founded on revelation, which means revelation through the ear. In the theophanies of the Old Testament, God speaks and man listens, but the status of what is visible is much more doubtful. Even where the vision is expressly said to be of God, the description is always of something or someone else, variously described as an angel, a spirit, or simply a man. Much of the vagueness in Milton's conception of the Holy Spirit is simply the result of his accepting literally the ambiguities in such passages. God is, in himself, invisible, and hence, as the first two commandments enjoin, no permanent image of him should ever be made. Thus in the story of the burning bush, the visual object, the burning bush itself, is there only to catch Moses' attention: what is significant is what is said. We are told that God spoke, but that the angel of the Lord appeared; that Moses had no trouble listening to God, but could not look at him.

The shift of metaphors from eye to ear, in other words, introduces into religion the conception of idolatry, and this in turn is the source of two characteristics which separate the Biblical tradition from the pagan one. These are the dialectical and the revolutionary. Polytheism, even when it takes the form, as it did with the Philistines, of concentrating on a single national deity, has the kind of tolerance that is the result of intellectual vagueness, because the conception "false god" is very difficult for it to assimilate. At the same time it is also conservative and authoritarian, because its religion is ultimately the authority of the state. The Philistines have both lords and priests, but it is clear that the lords have supreme power. The Bible was produced by a subject nation never lucky at the game of empire, and it looks forward to a future in which the great powers of the earth, along with their gods, will be overthrown. The visual metaphors are transferred to this future state: the "day of Jehovah" in Judaism, the second coming in Christianity, are occasions that will be openly visible to the faithful. Hence the objections of early Christians, including Tertullian and Lactantius, to the games and contests of the Roman circus, which, apart from their brutality, focussed attention on the power of the secular state and its heathen cults. It was essentially the visual stimulation in them that was dangerous, and the title of Tertullian's attack has a visual emphasis: *De Spectaculis.* Tertullian urges his readers to avoid all such entertainments and concentrate on the better spectacles afforded by Christianity, the future second coming of Christ and the Last Judgment. Milton refers to this passage in his Commonplace Book in a way which makes it quite clear that he has no use for the blinkered bigotry that lumped in the plays of Sophocles with gladiatorial fights as equally "stage shows." But of course the fundamental Christian emphases are also his.

The visual image is centripetal: it holds the body immobile in a pose of static obedience, and sets the sign of authority before it. The revelation by the Word is centrifugal: it is primarily a command, the starting-point of a course of action. In the Biblical view everything we can see is a creature of God, and a secondary repetition of the primary Word of God: "let there be light, and there was light." Adam was surrounded with a visible paradise, but what the forbidden tree primarily forbids is idolatry, the taking of the visible object to be the source of creative power, as Eve does when after her fall she bows in homage to the tree. Since the fall, paradise has been an invisible and embryonic inner state, to be brought into being by the revelation through the Word. The Word not only causes all images of gods to shrivel into nothingness, but continues to operate in society as an iconoclastic force, in other words a revolutionary force, demolishing everything to which man is tempted to offer false homage. To revert to the burning bush story, God there tells Moses that he is entering history, giving himself a Hebrew name and a specific and highly partisan politican role, the role of delivering an oppressed class from the constituted authority of their oppressors. Further, God defines himself existentially as "I am," not essentially as He Who is, so that there is no possibility of Hebrew religion ever depersonalizing its supreme God, as Classical religion tended to do in Stoicism and elsewhere.

As Christianity became a social institution, the Tertullian prejudice against visual stimulation relaxed somewhat, and in medieval Christianity there is again a strong emphasis on the visual symbols which are the normal sign of a secure and confident society. This emphasis on the visibility of the Church was followed in its turn, in some areas of Protestantism, by an iconoclastic reaction which condemned the use of images, the decoration of stained glass and sculpture, and the visual focus of the elevated host, and therefore, of course, revived the old condemnation of spectacles in theatres. Milton was no William Prynne, but he was a revolutionary iconoclast whose instinct, in attacking the government of Charles I, was to center his attack on the visual image of royalty, and on the dangers of that image as a potential source of idolatry. Hence he could hardly avoid reflecting some of the same anti-visual tendencies that were present in his cultural milieu.

In this world the essential conflict between good and evil takes the aural form of a conflict between the Word and the oracle, true and false rhetoric. Yet the ultimate object of all false rhetoric is a visual image commanding obedience to something other than God. Thus in *Paradise Regained* Jesus enters a desert, with no visual features to distract him, to engage in a mortal combat with the false word, the accuser. But Satan can only operate by summoning up a series of visual hallucinations. If Christ were to accept any one of these, he would instantly have become identified with it, according to the Psalmist's axiom about idols (Psalm 115): "They that make them are like unto them," which is echoed in *Paradise Lost* in the passage about the metamorphoses of the devils (X, 540–1):

> what they saw,
> They felt themselves now changing.

Samson Agonistes exhibits a parallel conflict between the Word of God within Samson, the ultimate source of his strength, and the temptations of the accuser, which take the form of a sequence of dialogues. The importance of this aspect of the conflict is one of the things that Samson's blindness symbolizes. Samson lives in a kind of seance-world of disembodied voices, between the mill with its slaves and the temple with its lords: as he says of the Chorus (176–7):

> I hear the sound of words; thir sense the air
> Dissolves unjointed e're it reach my ear.

Everyone who speaks to Samson, including Manoa and the Chorus, has something to add in the way of reproach, something to suggest distrust or uncertainty, something of Eliot's "loud lament of the disconsolate chimera" heard by the Word in the desert. Even Samson's hearing has to be mortified: he can only break from Dalila by, so to speak, putting out his ears. Greek tragedies of course also concentrate on dialogue and have catastrophes reported by messengers, but still a Greek play, with its masks and amphitheatre setting, is a very intense visual experience, as the etymology of the word theatre reminds us. The action of Milton's play, like that of the Book of Job, forms a kind of visual anti-play. In this respect it anticipates some of the techniques of a later dramatist who has also often been called a Puritan, Bernard Shaw. Superficially it seems like a discussion of past and future events without any action at all except what is offstage. More closely examined, the action is there all right, but it is a curious kind of internalized action: the important events are going on invisibly in Samson's mind.

Meanwhile, the Philistines are preparing their festival of Dagon. I have been calling the building that Samson destroys a temple, because that is symbolically what it is, a place for the celebration of the Dagon cult. But of course, it is also a theatre, as the Messenger calls it, a very un-Athenian theatre where the entertainment is like that of a Roman circus. The Philistine program committee, like so many of its kind, has not engaged its chief attraction until the last moment, which explains, if it does not excuse, the frantic mixture of bluster and promises in the Officer's message. So Samson is removed from an action of which his mind is the circumference to a theatre in which, blind and unable to stare back, he is the visual focus for the whole Philistine society, the gaze of Gaza, so to speak. But by that time he is once again an agent of God, and it is very dangerous for a Philistine society to make a visual focus out of that.

We remember that Tertullian urged his readers to withdraw from actual spectacles and feast their minds on the tremendous show promised in the Book of Revelation, when all their enemies would be seen burning in the lake of fire. In the famous passage about literary genres in *The Reason of Church Government* (*Yale* I, 812 ff.), the Scriptural model for tragedy is said to be the Book of

Revelation ("intermingling her solemn Scenes and Acts with a sevenfold *Chorus*"). Nothing could be less like the Book of Revelation than *Samson Agonistes,* and yet *Samson Agonistes,* with its seven great choral odes (it has seven characters also, counting the Chorus as one), has for its subject a prototype of the underside, so to speak, of the vision of the Book of Revelation. This is the aspect of it that comes to a climax in the elegy over the fall of Babylon in chapter eighteen. The identification there of the city of Babylon with the Great Whore who says "I am a queen, and no widow," and the emphasis on merchandise and shipping, perhaps indicates a larger significance for the role of Dalila and the elaborate ship imagery attached to her in *Samson Agonistes.* This larger significance is anticipated in *Paradise Lost,* with its comparison of the fallen Adam and Eve to Samson and "Philistean Dalila."

The visual emphasis that Milton distrusts as potential idolatry exists in time as well as space. In time it takes the form of an anxiety of continuity, which produces the doctrine of apostolic succession in the Church and the principle of hereditary succession in the state. The belief that all matrimonial contracts have to be treated as unbreakable is a by-product of the same anxiety. Apostolic succession replaces the spiritual succession of those called by God with the mechanical continuity of a human office; hereditary succession similarly destroys the divine principle of the leadership of the elect. The genuine king, like the genuine prophet, emerges when God calls him. The succession of leaders and prophets is discontinuous in human terms, and no human devices will safeguard it. Thus, according to the opening of the Gospel of Matthew, Jesus was legitimately descended from Abraham and David through his father Joseph, and yet Jesus was not the son of Joseph. Samson was one of a line of heroes called by God when his people turned again to God after a period of apostasy. The calling is represented by a very beautiful annunciation story in the Book of Judges, which ends with the angel returning to heaven in the fire on an altar. This image, twice referred to in *Samson Agonistes,* modulates into the image of the phoenix, the image of divine succession, a unique power of renewal through total self-sacrifice which cannot be programmed, so to speak, by any human institution.

One play that I often think of in connection with *Samson Agonistes* is Racine's *Athalie*, another great seventeenth-century tragedy on an Old Testament subject. The connection is largely one of contrast, *Athalie* being a spectacular play with crowds of characters: like Byron later, in a very different way, Racine thinks of the Old Testament not as the desert of the law but as a source of Oriental glamor. We notice too how *Athalie* turns on the issue of hereditary succession through the youthful prince Joash, who is in the Davidic line leading to Christ. In this, if in nothing else, Racine resembles Shakespeare, whose histories in particular so strongly emphasize the crucial importance of a clear line of succession. I suspect that the prominence of this theme in Shakespeare is one reason why Shakespeare has so little influence on the tragic drama of Milton.

The Biblical narrator remarks of the age of anarchy following Samson: "In those days there was no king in Israel; every man did that which was right in his own eyes." The Old Testament never quite makes up its mind whether hereditary kingship was a good thing for Israel or not, but still the glories of the reigns of David and Solomon are made much of, and it is easy for a Christian reader to see in these royal figures the prototypes of Christ as the world's only really legitimate monarch. Certainly the distinction between the person and the office, which Milton makes so much of in the regicide pamphlets, is derived from the Old Testament's attitude to kings. In *The Reason of Church Government* there is a long allegorical passage describing the king as an unfallen Samson, an image about his long hair being echoed in *Samson Agonistes.* The inference seems clear that Samson, so long as he was a leader chosen by God, was not merely a legitimate king but may at one time have had the power to set up the kingdom of God on earth, there being no limits to the divine strength which was the source of his. One of the remarks about Samson made by the Chorus brings out this larger dimension of his significance (173–5):

> But thee whose strength, while vertue was her mate,
> Might have subdu'd the Earth.
> Universally crown'd with highest praises.

However, Samson did not redeem the world: his achievement has to be paralleled and contrasted with that of Christ. *Paradise Lost* tells the story of how man lost the garden that was all about him, and of how he is enabled to regain this garden as an inner state. In *Paradise Regained,* Christ, by successfully resisting the temptation, symbolically transforms the desert he is in into the Garden of Eden again, as the poem's seventh line tells us. But the garden imagery is combined with that of the temple, the central image of the Jewish law that Christ both obeys and transcends in the action of the poem. Milton followed Luke's account of the temptation, where placing Jesus on the pinnacle of the temple is Satan's final act, accompanied by a quotation from Psalm 91:11–12, designed to suggest that if he falls off no harm will come to him. Christ remains motionless on the pinnacle, which means that the true temple of God passes into his own body, becoming a temple which can be raised again after it is destroyed, in contrast to Herod's temple below him, which was permanently destroyed a few years later. The two temples represent the two aspects of the law, which for Christianity is simultaneously abolished and fulfilled by the gospel.

Paradise Regained was a natural sequel to *Paradise Lost,* and one can see how, typologically, Milton was attracted to the story of Samson as the Old Testament counterpart of the same theme. As an Old Testament prototype of Christ, Samson, in destroying the demonic temple, illustrates the kind of thing that, according to Milton, man by himself can do in self-redemption. Man cannot transform himself into a superior being, or redeem himself; but he can express a willingness to be redeemed by knocking down the idols that surround him. What is achieved by this may be negative and iconoclastic, but it is by no means futile: it indicates the mental separation from nature that man has to make before he can be joined to God. In a sense it is really Samson who fulfils the prophecy in Psalm 91 quoted by Satan, for although he does fall under the temple and is crushed in the fall, his achievement, in its proper context, is providentially sustained.

If *Samson Agonistes* did not exist, we could say with some confidence that Milton could never have chosen Samson for a hero, because Samson is the only important Old Testament figure who simply will not fit into Milton's conception of the Old Testament. The statement remains essentially true even after we see how Milton has transmuted his hero. The stories about Samson in the Book of Judges are savage and primitive even for that very savage and primitive context. The Chorus does the best it can with Samson's chief and not very amiable virtue of total abstinence from wine, but it can only celebrate his feat of tearing up the gates of Gaza by suppressing the reason for his spending the night there. In nearly all the folk tales related to the Samson and Dalila motif, the part of Samson is played by an ogre or cannibal giant whom everyone is glad to be rid of, and the vicious and lethal practical jokes that Samson plays on the Philistines clearly roused a reserved admiration in Milton, even though he shared the bias of the Biblical narrative. Milton tells us that Samson, as he gropes for the pillars of the temple (1637–8)

> stood, as one who pray'd
> Or some great matter in his mind revolv'd.

We know from the Book of Judges that the subject of his meditations is a plea for private revenge, "only this once." This also has to be suppressed, as no catastrophe involving the will of God, for Milton, can take place without manifesting the axiom "Vengeance is mine," which belongs to a higher morality than the Biblical Samson can reach.

For Milton the Old Testament is the book of the law, and it is extraordinary to see how the wild berserker of the Book of Judges has been so tamed by Milton that he can find his way through a surprising amount of casuistry. The nicest legal points of the limits of civil obedience to a spiritually hostile power, of the obligations of a wife to a husband of a different nation and religion, of the relation of a deliberate action necessarily involving death to wilful suicide, of the distinction between command and constraint, are raised and debated with great skill in the play, most of them by Samson himself. Another set of associations of the Greek word *agon* is with law cases, where *agonistes* means advocate. This aspect of Samson connects with the legal metaphor in the Bible by which the conception of a redeemer developed out of words meaning an ally in a lawsuit or trial.

Samson has to work his way from bondage to liberty through the law, and hence to some extent he recapitulates Milton's own program for the people of England. Questions of religious, domestic, and civil liberty are the main issues raised in his colloquies with Manoa, Dalila, and the Philistine Officer. From the beginning Samson is marked out in contrast to his followers who prefer "Bondage with ease to strenuous liberty." In worldly terms it is the maddest paradox that Samson, being worked to death as a slave in a Philistine mill, is actually closer to freedom than he would be living at ease in retirement at home, but as God conceives of liberty this is none the less true. Thus Manoa's proposal, made out of the most genuine love for Samson, is still a very subtle and dangerous temptation, as is more obvious when it is repeated, in a more sinister context, by Dalila. Dalila, of course, represents the threat to domestic liberty in its crucial form of marriage to an idolater. The Bible does not call Dalila Samson's wife, but in Milton she must be a wife to absorb his divorce arguments. The Officer's summons brings the whole dialectic of liberty in an ungodly world into a dramatic focus. So far as the Philistines are Samson's secular overlords, they have a right to his obedience; so far as he is being ordered to join in an act of worship to Dagon, they have none. Samson decides that what he is being summoned to is a religious event, and refuses to take part in it.

In *Paradise Regained*, after Christ has refused all of Satan's temptations, Satan sets him on the pinnacle of the temple, where he remains miraculously poised. Miraculously, because he has done all he can; what he has done has been accepted by the Father, and the Father moves in to sustain him at the crucial point. On a smaller scale, the Lady in *Comus*, still paralyzed after repudiating Comus, is miraculously saved by Sabrina, according to the promise of the last two lines of the masque:

> Or, if Vertue feeble were,
> Heav'n it self would stoop to her.

Samson has also done what he can and has also come to the end of his own will. As noted previously, during the encounter with Harapha Samson reasserts himself as a champion of Jehovah, and Harapha slinks off, perhaps because he was a coward anyway, but more likely because Samson's claim has been accepted. Samson is, like Jesus in *Paradise Regained,* a man under the law, to an exceptional degree because of his Nazirite vow. The nearest that any Old Testament character can get to the freedom of the gospel is a dispensation, when God transcends his own law, and moves his elect to do the same. Samson's first marriage to the woman of Timnah was such a dispensation. We are not told, either by Milton or the Bible, that his marriage to Dalila was one too, but if it were, the dispensation to Samson parallels the dispensation to Hosea, made for very different purposes, who was ordered first to marry a "wife of whoredoms" and then to "go again" and love an adulteress. The fact that God has fully accepted Samson once again is marked by another dispensation, when God's will takes over Samson's will and changes his mind about going to the festival. Of course, this moment also makes it certain that Samson will die, just as the moment of Christ's triumph over Satan in *Paradise Regained* makes the Crucifixion certain. Hence it is not only the crisis of the action, but the peripeteia or turning point of the tragedy. Samson says (1372–9):

> If I obey them,
> I do it freely, venturing to displease
> God for the fear of Man, and Man prefer,
> Set God behind; which, in his jealousie
> Shall never, unrepented, find forgiveness.
> Yet that he may dispense with me, or thee,
> Present in temples at idolatrous rites
> For some important cause, thou need'st not doubt.

The word "yet" may well be the most precisely marked peripeteia in the whole range of drama.

A second major change that Milton makes in Samson's character is in his relation to society. In heroic literature there is often a narrative tension, and sometimes a moral tension as well, between the themes of war and of quest. There is, let us say, a central war going on which it is the duty of heroes to engage in, but the crucial hero, whose presence is necessary for success, has withdrawn from the action or is on some private venture of his own. The role of Achilles in the *Iliad* comes readily to mind: much closer to the general tone of the Samson stories in the Bible is the situation in Ariosto. Here the heroes who are supposed to be fighting in a crusade, defending Paris against the infidels, keep wandering off and rescuing attractive heroines in remote quarters of the earth, and the climactic action, reminding the modern reader of the American crusade against Communism, is a trip to the moon to recollect some scattered heroic wits. In *Paradise Regained* the crusade and the lonely quest are united in the person of Christ, because for Milton Christ is the only figure in history in whom they could have been united.

Samson in the Bible is a pure quest figure: he lounges about the Philistine countryside killing and destroying and burning crops and sleeping with their women, but with no hint of any organization behind him. The final sentence in the Book of Judges, "He judged Israel twenty years," comes as a considerable shock: *that* Samson has never shown the slightest capacity to judge anything, much less lead a nation. But in Milton all Samson's exploits are carefully integrated into a consistent crusade for God's people against God's enemies. To the Chorus's reproach, "Yet *Israel* still serves with all his Sons," Samson responds, "That fault I take not on me" (240–1), and goes on to show that the failure of his people to follow him was as crucial as his own failure. The same awareness of his social surroundings comes out even in details. When the timid Chorus expresses uneasiness after Harapha's departure, and again after the first exit of the Officer, Samson quiets their fears very unobtrusively, but in a way which shows the born leader under all the rags and filth and chains.

Samson's role as leader makes clear many things about *Samson*

Agonistes, beginning with its date, which some people have tried to put earlier than 1660. The death of Samson, though tragic, points to a world above tragedy; the destruction of the Gaza aristocracy, though tragic, or at least "sad," as Manoa says, points to a world below it. In between is the tragic failure of Israel to live up to its role as God's people. In many tragedies there is a non-tragic point of escape indicated in the action, a moment of opportunity, of taking the tide of fortune at the flood, and the missing of this point is part of the parabola shape of tragedy, the point from which the "catastrophe," which means the downward turn, begins. Near the end of the play Manoa says that Samson (1714–16)

> to *Israel*
> Honour hath left and freedom, let but them
> Find courage to lay hold on this occasion.

But the Bible tells us that in a few years the Philistines were stronger than ever. As they occupied territory assigned to Dan in the conquest of Canaan, Dan moved out and went north. In the Book of Judges, the account of Samson is immediately followed by another story about the Danites in which, after appearing in a most contemptible light as idolaters, thieves, and murderers, they vanish from history. In Jacob's prophecy of the twelve tribes at the end of Genesis, Dan is described as a treacherous "serpent in the way," and in the list of the twelve tribes in the Book of Revelation the name of Dan is omitted. For Milton this would practically mean being erased from the book of life.

The tragedy of Israel, and of Dan in particular, is an allegory of the tragedy of the English people, choosing a "captain back for Egypt," as Milton says in the *Ready and Easy Way*, and deliberately renouncing their great destiny. The self-identification of the blind Milton, living in retirement after the Restoration, with the blind Samson is impossible to miss: it is there in the complaints about poverty and disease, its furthest reach being perhaps the curious parenthesis about fair-weather friends: "Of the most I would be understood" (190–1). But there may be some identification also with the hopeful and bitterly disappointed Manoa, if we think of the great image in *Areopagitica:* "Methinks I see in my mind a noble and puissant nation rousing herself like a strong man after sleep, and shaking her invincible locks." This is precisely Manoa's picture of Samson miraculously restored to his strength as though the blinding and captivity had been only a bad dream. In *Samson Agonistes* we are somberly reminded not only of the original story of Samson, but of the fact that it was so brief and so ineffectual an episode in the history of Israel. Within a generation after the death of Dan's great champion, Dan had effectively ceased to exist as a tribe. No once favored group of people, whether Danites in Israel or Puritans in England, is likely to get a second chance to renounce its destiny.

In the criticism of Shakespeare we notice how much of what is written really amounts to a rationalizing of the acting. What is said about characters, repetition of imagery, or the mood and emotional tone of the play, is very often potentially a set of suggestions for some producer or group of actors to consider for a possible performance. The ontological status of such criticism is a matter of some interest, especially to those who believe that there is such a subject as hermeneutics. For *Samson Agonistes* the critical situation is considerably altered by the presence of a chorus. A chorus in the play is primarily a stylizing of the audience. The Danites in *Samson Agonistes,* like Job's friends, represent a kind of moral norm. They are on the right side and are carried along by the action to genuine profundity and eloquence at the end, but, like so many of Jesus' disciples, they never fully understand the meaning of the events they are involved in. They function as eyes for Samson, but they do not see what he sees. Some of the verse given them to speak seems to me to be doggerel, or, if that is too violent a word, an indication that the highest kind of spiritual insight is not being expressed.

From the point of view of the Chorus, the action of the play is a melodrama with Jehovah as hero and Dagon as villain. Jehovah is the true God: somehow or other the Philistines ought to know this; somehow or other they ought to accept, as a valid argument, Samson's explanation of his attack on them (1211–13):

> I was no private, but a person raised
> With strength sufficient, and command from Heav'n,
> To free my Countrey.

Samson's act is cited by Milton in his *First Defence* as a precedent for the Parliamentary revolution. When God himself is a partisan actor in history, it is not difficult to hear in the background the tedious self-righteous cry: whatever we do is right because we're we, and they, after all, are only they.

Against this is the creative imagination of the poet working out his play, and giving to every aspect of that play its own realization. It is particularly in the last speech of Dalila that we can understand how Milton is a true poet, and of Dalila's party without knowing it, at least as long as he is speaking with her voice. The Chorus says smugly, "A manifest Serpent by her sting" (997), but we are bound to have some dramatic sympathy, if not moral sympathy, with Dalila in her desperate attempt to restore her self-respect, after Samson's bitter and contemptuous rejection of her, by building up a fantasy about her future fame. However we see her, we can understand that she sees herself as a kind of Antigone, damned whether she does or doesn't. When she designs a memorial for herself in language anticipating Manoa's design for Samson's tomb, we concur in the imaginative symmetry, just as we do in *Paradise Lost* when Moloch persuades Solomon to build him a temple opposite Zion. When she compares herself to Jael, we can agree that Jael's act was also treacherous, if less cold-blooded than hers. Above all, when she appeals to Fame to justify her, we can see, at least for the moment, that although Fame seems the most arbitrary and whimsical of all gods, still there is a rough justice in his (or her) dispositions, and that he averages out to a more fair-minded god than a jealous Jehovah.

Then we come back with a shock to realize how much of Milton himself is standing in the *choros geronton,* agreeing with them that God's ways are just and justifiable. For most modern readers, I should think, Milton's creative imagination is always right and his justifying apparatus always wrong: the imagination is that of a poet who is for all time; the apparatus comes from seventeenth-century anxieties which, at least on their political side, were as dead as mutton even before *Samson Agonistes* was written, to say nothing of three centuries later. Yet the imagination would probably never have conceived a line without the driving force of the anxieties. What is our final role as readers? Do we simply try to deliver the immortal poet from the "prison within prison" of the anxieties of his age and class, or can we find a place for them too in our response?

The answer begins with the fact that we have our own anxieties too, and that they are unlikely to meet the test of time any better than his. The task of criticism is neither to leave such a work as *Samson Agonistes* sitting in the seventeenth century, ignoring all the reasons for its appeal to us, nor to annex it to our own age, ignoring its original assumptions. The two points of 1671 and 1971 form the base of a triangle of which *Samson Agonistes* itself is the apex, in a world above both, though related to both.

Milton describes the action of *Paradise Lost,* at the beginning, as "this great argument," and the action of *Samson Agonistes,* at the end, as "this great event." The question whether Christianity and tragedy are compatible has often been raised; the real question, however, is not that, but the relation of tragedy to a revolutionary attitude. I have tried to indicate very briefly the revolutionary qualities of the Biblical tradition which were followed so closely by Milton: its conception of God as having a historical role in delivering a subject nation from its overlords; its iconoclasm; its insistence on right belief, and its utter repudiation of all gods except its own. *Paradise Regained* and *Samson Agonistes* are both, in different ways, set within the human situation, and they therefore express the central revolutionary attitude, in both religious and social context, that Milton held and expressed in his prose writings.

The revolutionary mind does not reject tragedy, but it prefers to think of it as explicable, as something with a cause, and therefore, if possible, a cure. It is apt to get impatient with the contemplating of a tragic situation as an ultimate mystery at the heart of things. *Paradise Lost* is among other things an attempt to account for the origin of tragedy: it deals, rather more coherently than Nietzsche was later to do, with the birth of tragedy from the spirit of music. In the third book, however, Milton shifts the scene to the angelic order, above tragedy, where God explains the human situation from that perspective. Here Milton deserts the revolutionary point of view of his own religion, which means that, not being an angel, he is compelled to adopt the rival perspective of the pagan world. The model for the God of Book Three is Zeus in the *Odyssey:* nowhere in the Bible does God speak in such a tone. Still, the effort to gain a larger perspective on tragedy in *Paradise Lost* is deeply significant.

The supreme Greek god, from Homer to the Stoics, is, we said, an essential God, He Who is; the God of the burning bush is an existential I am. We may perhaps suggest, however simplistic it may sound, that when God is conceived as essential, tragedy becomes existential, and vice versa. In Greek literature tragedy is inherent in the human situation, and it is that partly because in the long run the gods can shrug it off and detach themselves from it. For Milton, no tragic action can take place without the will of God being directly involved, and therefore tragedy, for Milton, is ultimately explicable in terms of God's revelation. Writers who elude this antithesis, notably Shakespeare, cannot have a decisive influence on Milton's tragic form: Shakespeare's tragedies are not religious in so specific a sense.

So when the Chorus describes itself at the end of the play as being equipped (1755–6)

> with new acquist
> Of true experience from this great event

it is possible that, once again, the Chorus does not fully understand what it is saying. It is seeing the death of Samson much as a Greek audience might see the end of *Oedipus at Colonus,* as a deep and awful mystery, something to be contemplated as a vision. It sees the hand of God in it, of course, but in a way that deepens the sense of mystery. The Danites see only as far as the old dispensation allows them to see. For Milton, and ideally for us, the words "new" and "true" carry a heavier weight of meaning: true experience is something that leads to renewed action, as the experience of losing Lycidas led his friend "Tomorrow to fresh woods, and pastures new." As the blinded Samson says to the sighted Harapha, in a line with a dozen kinds of irony in it: "The way to know were not to see but taste" (1091). Like the Chorus, we are led to "calm of mind, all passion spent," but we are not necessarily old and tired and blinkered by the law. When catharsis dissipates, for an instant, the clouds of passions and prejudice and anxiety and special pleading, some of us may also catch a glimpse of a boundless energy which, however destructive to social establishments, is always there, always confronting us, and always the same, and yet has always the power to create all things anew.

Blake's Reading of the Book of Job

For all the discussion that there has been over Blake's illustrations to the Book of Job, much of the best of it contributed by the subject of this *Festschrift,* there is perhaps still room for more consideration of how Blake read the book. Everyone realizes that Blake re-created the book in his engravings, and was not simply illustrating it. At the same time he appears to be following it with considerable fidelity, and his attitude toward it, in striking contrast to his attitude toward the original of the other great work of his last period, the illustrations to Dante's *Commedia,* seems to be on the whole an attitude of critical acceptance. He remarked, apropos of Homer, that "Every Poem must necessarily be a perfect Unity," but that the *Iliad* is not "peculiarly so," which implies that the perfect unity is potential in the poem itself, and is really achieved by the reader. The sense of unity that one feels about the Job engravings, considered as a series, indicates that Blake extracted a corresponding unity out of his text.

This fact is more complicated than it looks, because despite the Book of Job's formidable literary reputation, it is not easy to see how its argument makes a sense congenial to Blake. It begins with the astonishing scenes of Satan in the court of God, where Satan has the role, always central to his nature for Blake, of the accuser of mankind. He suggests that God has set things up in such a way that he can't lose: if he rewards obedience, he gives man so powerful a motive for being obedient that the service of God becomes a conditioned reflex. He may be raising the issue of man's free will, but not in a way that could ever help man to become free. Later in the poem, Job's three friends keep revolving around the central pseudo-problem of the righteousness of God's ways. Those who do well will be rewarded and those who do evil will be punished; therefore it must be a crime to be unfortunate. If it were not, God would not be a just God. The suppressed premise here is that God administers both the human moral law and the physical natural law, but it never occurs to them to doubt this. Blake doubts it, however: it is the basis of what he repudiates as natural religion.

The friends' view of providence is easily refuted by experience, but when it is, they can give two possible answers. One is to say that God's ways are inscrutable, although they seem to the unprejudiced reader to be merely insane on such premises. The other is to assume that God's providence will manifest itself in another world, from which no evidence ever leaks out. If it appears that "honesty is the best policy" is nonsense, the argument shifts to "maybe it doesn't seem so now, but you just wait."

The arguments of the three friends reach a deadlock, and Elihu takes over, to overwhelm Job with the eloquence of what he has to say "on God's behalf" (36:2), but although his eloquence is genuine enough, he is concerned mostly with restating the earlier arguments. When God himself answers Job out of the whirlwind and asks "Who is this that darkeneth counsel by words without knowledge?" (38:2), apparently meaning Elihu, we expect the definitive revelation to which the whole drama seems to have been leading up. But we feel uncomfortable about the way in which God triumphantly displays a number of trump cards that seem to belong to a different game. He asks Job a series of rhetorical questions which have a hectoring and bullying sound to them. Were you around when I made the world, or do you understand all about how it was made? No? Well, then, why are you raising doubts about my administrative competence? This is followed by poems on the two beasts behemoth and leviathan—remarkable poems, but we wonder about their relevance to Job's boils and murdered children. Job replies meekly that he has "uttered that I understood not; things too wonderful for me which I knew not . . . wherefore I abhor myself, and repent in dust and ashes" (42:3–6). God then appears to say, in effect, "Well, that's better," and forthwith restores Job to prosperity. Job's friends and their natural religion, apparently, have really been right all along, even though they are said not to be. Somehow it does not sound like the kind of argument that Blake would regard with much favor.

The Book of Job is technically a comedy by virtue of Job's restoration in the last few verses, but the comic conclusion seems so wrenched and arbitrary that it is hard to think of it as anything but a wantonly spoiled tragedy. In all the gropings that Job and the three friends and Elihu all make after some explanation for Job's plight, one explanation that they never speculate about is the one that has already been given to the reader. It never occurs to them that God might have deliberately exposed Job to such an ordeal in order to win a wager with Satan. They are all, including Job himself, far too pious and sincere for such a notion ever to occur to them. The prologue in heaven hangs sardonically over the whole debate, and we wait for God to reveal to Job something of what the reader knows. But not a word is said about Satan at the end of the action, and Job learns nothing about the original compact. The simplest answer is to suppose that the Book of Job, begun by a colossal poetic genius, fell into the hands of a superstitious editor whose attitude was a cruder version of that of Job's friends, and who twisted one of the world's profoundest poems into an obscurantist tirade against the use of the questioning intelligence. Something like this could have happened: there are signs of nervous editing, as in so many parts of the Bible, and it is impossible to say how far expurgation has gone. But such a hypothesis is of no use to us: the version we have is the only one that has influenced later literature and religion, and the only one that Blake read. He must have read it, however, in a way very different from the summary of it just given.

First of all, the comic conclusion, the restoring of Job to prosperity, would not have seemed arbitrary to Blake, but inevitable. The Bible as a whole takes the form of a U-shaped narrative in which Adam loses his garden and is led back, at the end of time, to a restored garden which is also a city. This means, according to Milton, that he loses paradise as a physical environment and regains it as an inner state of mind. The latter, Michael tells Adam in *Paradise Lost,* is "happier far" than the original Eden. Blake would have seen the story of Job as an epitome of the Biblical narrative, in which the final restoration provides a greater happiness than the original state. As Blake sees the story, Job begins in the state of Beulah, the pastoral repose of Plate 1, and ends in the apocalyptic state of Eden (in Blake's sense of the term) of Plate 21. The contrasts are obvious and have often been noted: the musical instruments have been taken down from the trees in the later plate, suggesting, by way of Psalm 137, that even the original state still had something of alienation and exile about it; the sheep have wakened up, and, in contrast to the first plate, the sun is rising and the moon setting. The sacrificial altar common to the foreground of both plates contains significant inscriptions about the importance of outgrowing the literal and ritual aspects of religion which sacrifice represents. The genuine form of sacrifice, self-sacrifice, or what Blake calls the annihilation of the Selfhood, is the real subject of Plate 18.

Job is one of the "wisdom" books, and the primitive conception of wisdom, still clearly visible in the Old Testament, is that of following the tried and tested ways, the ways sanctioned by custom and tradition. This means that wisdom is primarily an attribute of advanced age, when one has had most experience in being conservative. In the Book of Proverbs and elsewhere there is a strong emphasis on bringing up young people in the ways of their seniors, and on being prompt to punish them if they diverge. There are three stages of a conflict of age and youth in the Job plates: the relation of the God of the opening plates to an obviously much younger Satan; the relation of the three friends to the youthful Elihu; and the relation of the God of the closing plates (Jehovah, more or less) to Jesus.

The God of Plates 2 and 5 is the weak, sick *dieu fainéant* who is the God projected by Job himself into the natural order. As long as a virtuous moral life can be associated with a comfortable physical one, such a deity may seem providential and benignant. But when the crunch comes he turns into Satan, the author of evil and disaster. This fact is not realized by Job, his three friends, or Elihu, all of whom try to work out some explanation of Job's plight in terms of God alone. But for Blake the God of the opening plates resigns his power to Satan in the same way that God the Father transfers power to his Son in *Paradise Lost*, and similarly demonstrates by doing so the essential link between their natures. Many years earlier Blake had remarked that "in the Book of Job, Milton's Messiah is call'd Satan."

The identity of the God of Plate 2 with Satan is clear in the nightmare of Plate 11, where at the bottom of the plate Paul's description of the Antichrist is quoted. The Antichrist is notable for his superficial resemblance to Christ, and similarly, all gods portrayed as old men in the sky are variants of the Satan whom Paul, again, calls the prince of the power of the air. Over the head of God in Plate 2 is the inscription *Malak Yahweh*, along with the translation "The Angel of the Divine Presence." This recalls the passage in *A Vision of the Last Judgment* in which Blake speaks of "That Angel of the Divine presence mention'd in Exodus, xiv c., 19 v. & in other places; this Angel is frequently call'd by the Name of Jehovah Elohim, The 'I am' of the Oaks of Albion." Apparently Blake means that the existential reality or "I am" of God is identical with the human imagination, but when it gets projected into the outer world of nature it is perverted into something evil. Laocoon, strangled by the serpents of reasoning, is also identified by Blake with the perverted form of this Angel. In Plate 2 the primary Biblical reference may be to Numbers 22:22, where the *Malak Yahweh* blocks the path of Balaam as his "Satan," or adversary. The verse in Exodus that Blake refers to reads: "And the angel of God, which went before the camp of Israel, removed and went behind them; and the pillar of the cloud went from before their face, and stood behind them." The two tendencies in man to be "idolatrous to his own shadow" and yet continually to recover his own creative powers alternate like the pillar of cloud and the pillar of fire in the Exodus story. When the Angel comes the other way, from the outer world into the human consciousness, it makes possible, for Israel, the great revolutionary feat of escaping from Egypt and achieving its own identity.

The design on Plate 5 takes the form of a vortex or gyre in which an imaginary God turns into a real devil, the order of nature which everything genuine and creative in human life has to fight against. The fall of Job repeats the fall of Adam, and its cause is the same: the pseudo-knowledge of good and evil which first tries to separate them, and ends by realizing that in such knowledge evil is the rule and good an accidental and precarious exception. This vortex is again reversed in Plate 13, where it becomes the "whirlwind" out of which God answers Job. We remember the vortex in *Milton* which takes Milton from "Heaven" to earth, earth being the place where "Heaven" has to be realized. Milton enters Blake's left foot, but ordinarily, when the projected God reverses his movement and becomes the real one, the Word of human imagination, what he enters is the ear, which is also a kind of vortex, called "labyrinthine" in *Jerusalem*, and described in *The Book of Thel*, in a very different context, as a "whirlpool fierce to draw creations in." But the God of the whirlwind in Plate 13 has to be clarified a good deal before he becomes the genuine human imagination: this process is completed in Plate 17 with the significant caption from Job 42:5: "I have heard of thee by the hearing of the ear; but now mine eye seeth thee." The only New Testament reference to Job, "Ye have heard of the patience of Job, and have seen the end of the Lord" (James 5:11), quoted by Blake on Plate 7, repeats this progress from ear to eye. For Blake, no one can "see" God until God becomes a human being, and even then he is not so much what we see as what we see with. Some Renaissance mythographers saw in the story of Narcissus, who exchanged his identity for that of his objective reflection in water, a counterpart to the Biblical story of the fall of Adam, and Blake, describing the fall of Albion in *Jerusalem* in imagery closely related to the Book of Job, also speaks of Albion as becoming "idolatrous to his own shadow." The recovery by Job of his own imagination is Narcissus coming in the opposite direction, the reflected shadow becoming his own substance.

The fact that Blake saw in the story of Job a microcosm of the entire Biblical story is the reason for the two major changes that he makes from what is in the text: the role of Job's wife and the character of the three friends. In the text Job's wife is a Dalila figure, a temptress who suggests that Job renounce his integrity, and this is how Blake depicted her in earlier illustrations of the book. In *Jerusalem* Albion's wife, "Brittannia," is a very shadowy, not to say unnecessary, character: the main theme is the restoration to Albion of his daughter Jerusalem. This emphasis on the restored daughter (apart from the link with *King Lear,* whose three daughters are also Albion's) was derived from a parallel emphasis in the Book of Job, as illustrated here in Plate 20. But still, when the Book of Job is thought of as a miniature Bible, Job occupies the place of Adam or Israel or, again, Albion, the symbolic figure of humanity, and Job's wife thus becomes the Eve or Rachel who must form a part of his redemption.

Similarly, the three friends are almost wholly demonic in Blake's illustrations, and are assimilated to the threefold accuser figure who runs through all Blake's work from the early "Accusers of Theft, Adultery and Murder" to Hand in *Jerusalem,* and who are, or is, identified with the three accusers of Socrates (*Jerusalem* 93) and, probably, the three witnesses against Faithful in *The Pilgrim's Progress.* The three friends have been constantly ridiculed, from the Book of Job itself on, as "miserable comforters," and yet it is said of them, in a verse quoted on Plate 8, that "they sat down with him upon the ground seven days and seven nights, and none spake a word unto him: for they saw that his grief was very great" (2:13). Seven days of silent sympathy from friends who are at least not fair-weather friends, and have nothing to gain from visiting Job in his destitution, may deserve some sympathy in its turn. But when we think of Job as continuously martyred humanity, it is hardly possible to see in the friends anything but representatives of the continuous social anxiety, the Theotormon complex, so to speak, that makes human misery constant by trying to rationalize and explain it away in every crisis. We may note that a still later treatment of the Job story, MacLeish's *J.B.*, follows Blake both in favoring the wife and in denigrating the friends.

The friends, in any case, try to remain loyal to the *dieu fainéant* of the opening plates, the God of natural religion. Nature for Blake is the state of experience, indifferent to human values, exhibiting no sense of design or purpose beyond an automatic and mechanical one, and caring nothing for the individual. Job suffers not because of anything he has done but because he is in the world of Satan or Nature, like the rest of us. Satan achieved his power through God's "permission," or, to come closer to Blake, through the inevitable collapse of all efforts to unite the vision of innocence, of the world as created and protected, with the contrary vision of experience. Such efforts, we said, look plausible only to those who happen to be both "good" and prosperous. But the prosperity is a matter of luck, and Job's sufferings illustrate a principle often referred to elsewhere in Blake, that if we stay in Beulah it will sooner or later turn into "Ulro," that is, "meer Nature or hell," as Blake calls it in his notes to Swedenborg. The God of Plates 1 to 5 sooner or later turns into what Blake calls the ghost of the priest and king, the conception that rationalizes tyranny.

And just as the senile God of Plate 5 is pushed out of the way by a viciously destructive and younger Satan, so the harangues of the three friends give place to the monologue of the young Elihu, who begins with a perfunctory apology for withholding his wisdom for so long while the old men drivelled. Elihu consolidates the confused and variable notions of natural religion that the three friends propound into a closed system of fatalism. He is shown in Plate 12 pointing upwards with his left or sinister hand to a sky with twelve stars in it, representing the cycle of the Zodiac. Like all his kind, he insists on the grandeur of nature and the littleness of mankind: "Look upon the heavens and behold the clouds which are higher than thou" (cf. Job 35:5). If we have been reading the Book of Job along with Blake, we have already been told that wisdom is not there, or anywhere else in nature: "The depth saith [Wisdom] is not in me: and the sea saith, It is not with me" (28:14). Elihu has thus much the same role as that of Newton in *Europe:* he is a spokesman of natural religion so fully articulate that he overreaches himself and blows his whole system, in more than one sense, sky-high. He is a negative agent of Job's emancipation, as Newton is for Blake's time. The words in Plate 12 just quoted are attached to the figure of a sleeping old man at the bottom of creation, whose dreams rise up from his head into the stars. This figure is Blake's Albion, and the design recurs in the account of Albion's fall in *Jerusalem* 19.

The third and decisive conflict of age and youth forms the resolution of the sequence, when God as a projected old man in the sky turns into Christ, God as Man, God as the essence of Job himself, whom Job has stopped projecting into creation and has recovered as his own real nature. In Blake's mythology there are seven "Eyes," seven historical and social visions or conceptions of God, the sixth and seventh being Jehovah and Jesus. The third, Elohim, is associated with the creation of Adam, or the human form as we know it; the fourth, Shaddai, is a frequent name of God in the Book of Job. Blake may have thought the Book of Job to be or to conceal a very ancient myth, perhaps older than most of the Old Testament. Reminders of this progression of seven Eyes can be seen in the angels of the title page and the shadowy figures behind the appearance of God in the whirlwind in Plate 13. But actually every stage of history has to go through the same struggle of replacing "Jehovah," the projected old man in the sky who is Zeus and Jupiter as well, with Jesus, the divine and human Logos, who is every "Eye" when imaginatively used.

The transformation of Jehovah into Jesus occupies the four plates 14, 15, 16, and 17. Job in his original prosperity is an imaginative child, but his childlike state of innocence turns into experience, and his vision of innocence, like the child's, is driven into the submerged part of his mind, where it becomes a helpless but still defiant part of his "integrity," a bound Orc. Satan's world is a world in which everybody is an object or thing, and the pressure put on Job to make him admit that he is a thing too is very powerful, but not omnipotent. Satan's world, to adapt a phrase of Kierkegaard's, *is* but does not *exist.* Job begins to exist, in this sense, when he remains defiant and calls loudly for some explanation of what has happened to him, paying no attention to the frantic expostulations of his friends and Elihu that such an attitude is blasphemous and will only make matters worse. There is a core of truth in what they say, even in the remark that they considered Job "righteous in his own eyes." The *dieu fainéant* who turned into Satan was a creation of Job's mind, and in a sense Job keeps him in business by resisting him, somewhat as Prometheus in Shelley kept Jupiter in business until he recalled his curse.

So Job's existence is at first negative, the existence of an isolated conscious being. In this position he feels that the Satanic order is not simply indifferent but actively hostile. This attitude becomes positive with God's speech, and Job, though still isolated, begins to feel not separated from everything else but identified, or, as Blake would say, outlined. The turning point comes when he realizes that the Satanic state of experience is not something inevitable or ultimately mysterious but something to be fought, and that his dethroned vision of innocence is something that he can fight it with.

If we look at the series of Old Testament books as Blake did, and as the King James Bible usually presents them, in the Septuagint order with the books of the Apocrypha omitted, we see an order which may be the result of sheer accident, but nonetheless points to a simple and profound analysis of the Old Testament as a whole. The books from Genesis to Esther are concerned with law, history and ritual; the books from Job to Malachi with prophecy, poetry and wisdom. In this order Job would occupy the place of a poetic and prophetic version of Genesis, an account of the fall of man which avoids the moralizing and the breach of contract so dear to theological lawyers, and concentrates on the limiting of imaginative range and the mutilation of the physical body. We noticed earlier that the account of the fall in *Jerusalem* echoes Job more than it does Genesis. When Albion goes in for "imputing sin and righteousness to individuals," including himself, the Zoa Luvah, representing Urizen as well as the bound Orc, takes charge of him, smites him with sore boils, and starts him on the dreary path of misery and persecution symbolized in Blake by the "Druid" symbols of serpent and tree, which we find in the stories of the fall of Adam, the fall of Israel (Numbers 21), and the Crucifixion of Christ. We can see traces of a serpent-wound tree in the background of Plate 2.

The crucial act of renewed vision is the one between Plates 14 and 15, the vision of the Creation and the vision of behemoth and leviathan. Plate 14 is the reappearance of the vision of innocence, the Beulah vision of Plate 1, except that it is coming the other way, out of Job's mind and not from his circumstances. There are three levels in this plate: Job and his friends are on earth; above them is a Demiurge or creator-God controlling the order of nature; and above that is the infinite human universe, in which the morning stars and the sons of God have become the same thing. It is still an imperfect vision, because, although it does distinguish the "good" world that God originally made from the bad world that man fell into later, it has not yet detached itself from the world of experience. God's rhetorical questions about the creation, his insistence that Job was not present when the world was made, have for Blake a very different meaning from a mere attempt to shout Job down with the voice of his own superego. God is really saying: "don't look into Nature to find me: I'm not there; there's nothing there but idols and demons. Don't look for a first cause: the important question is how can you get out of your situation, not how you got into it. You are not a participant in the creation: your consciousness or imagination is something wholly detached from it. And because you are not a participant in creation you can be delivered from it." The next step is to realize that Satan is the enemy of God, that his rule is not inevitable but is to be fought by God's creative power, and that this creative power is man's creative power. This takes us into Plate 15, where there are only two levels, God and Job united on top, and below them the cycle of nature dominated by behemoth and leviathan.

In this plate we can see that, for Blake, Satan does not disappear from the action of the Book of Job after the prologue, nor does Job really fail to learn the truth about the Satanic origin of his calamities. Satan *is* leviathan, looked at from the right point of view as the body of fallen nature, and not a mysterious cause of human suffering but a symptom of it to be attacked. If we had seen Job restored to prosperity, with all his brand new daughters and livestock, we might not have seen any daughters or livestock: we might have seen nothing but a beggar on a dunghill. But the beggar would know something we do not know, and would have seen something that we have not seen, which is how leviathan looks from the outside. Leviathan being Satan revealed instead of Satan mysterious and disguised as God, he represents not only the natural miseries of drought and famine and pestilence and boils, but also the social and political miseries symbolized in the Bible by Egypt and Babylon, and in the Book of Job itself by the Sabean raiders. Ezekiel (29) identifies the leviathan with the Pharaoh of Egypt, and Daniel (4) tells how Nebuchadnezzar of Babylon turned into a variety of behemoth, this latter being a favorite pictorial subject for Blake. The political aspect of the two monsters is brought out in the phrases in the text emphasized by Blake on Plate 15: behemoth is "chief of the ways of God" and leviathan is "King over all the Children of Pride." Their "natural" kernels are the hippopotamus and the crocodile, both Egyptian animals.

At the same time the root of human tyranny, for Blake, is still natural religion, taking the order of nature to be the circumference or horizon of all human effort, the word horizon being reflected in the name "Urizen." All of us are born inside the belly of leviathan, the world of stars and its indefinite space, which is symbolically subterranean, the tomb out of which the Resurrection takes us, and submarine as well, for leviathan is a sea-monster and Noah's flood has never receded. Those delivered from leviathan, like Job and Jonah, normally have to be fished for, hence the prominence of fishing imagery in the Gospels. Similarly in Blake the kingdom of the imagination is Atlantis, underneath the "Sea of Time and Space." After Job has attained the enlightenment of Plate 15, the prophecy of Jesus is fulfilled and Satan falls from heaven in Plate 16, cast out of and separated from the divine nature. The deity in Plate 17 is unmistakably Jesus, as the New Testament quotations at the bottom of the plate make clear: if he looks older, it is because he is the divine essence of Job's own mind, and Job is an old man in Blake, if not necessarily so in the Book of Job itself. The casting out of Satan from God's nature in Plate 16 is repeated in reverse in the sacrifice scene of Plate 18, which is, as said, really a scene of self-sacrifice, and represents Job's casting the demonic principle out of himself.

Job has to be an individual, for Satan's assault on him is part of a struggle between alienation and identity, in which the former carries its conquests up to the very last stronghold of the latter, which is the individual consciousness. Everything Job *has* disappears into the illusory Satanic world of time. He is alienated from his own body by his boils, and from society by the accusing or "Elect" friends, to use the language of Blake's *Milton*, leaving Job himself in the position of the "Reprobate" prophet, the scapegoat driven like Elijah into the wilderness, with only his wife to represent "Redeemed" society. Finally Elihu, pointing to the stars so far above him, alienates him from his earlier view of God, who is now wholly replaced by the accuser. Part of the situation Job is in is one that frequently occurs in tragedy: what are the limits of one's "property," in the Aristotelian sense? That is, how much can a man lose of what he has without losing something of what he is? The implication in God's injunction to Satan, that he could take away whatever Job had but not his life, is that Job's identity must remain untouched: the test is whether he will cling to that identity or throw it away. As he is not being punished for anything but tested, the metaphor of a "trial" or lawsuit, held in a court of God with accusers and defendants, hangs over the entire book. Job keeps trying to identify his prosecutor and to call on his advocate (the word translated "redeemer" in 19:25), and he eventually finds that his accuser is the ghost or "Spectre" of his redeemer.

But a trial is a social metaphor, and Job has to represent, not simply an individual, but mankind as a whole. If we think of God as a trinity of power and wisdom and love, it may seem strange that there is so much about God's power and wisdom in the Book of Job and so little about love of any kind. But the implications of the social dimension of love are there in the text, and Blake makes them the main subject of the final three plates. We are told, in a passage quoted on Plate 18, that Job's captivity was "turned" when he prayed for his friends; the friends are received into the new community in Plate 19, and the family, symbolized by the three daughters, is reestablished in Plate 20. In Plate 1 we see a community of twelve, Job, his wife, his seven sons, and his three daughters, making up a figure of the twelvefold Israel who, in Blake's view of the Exodus, achieved liberation from Egypt only to be enslaved once again by the hypnotizing twelvefold Zodiac of stars over their heads:

> That fiery joy, that Urizen perverted to ten commands,
> What time he led the starry host through the wide
> wilderness. (*America*, plate 8)

In Plate 21 this community of twelve is restored, with the differences from the beginning already noted.

The ambiguity between Job as individual and Job as social being or patriarch is of a kind central to all mythical structures of this descent-and-return shape. The suffering Job must be an individual, but when we think of the restored Job as an individual too, continuous with his previous sufferings, difficulties arise. The origin of the Book of Job appears to have been an ancient folk tale preserved in the prose opening and ending of the book we now have, and in such a folk tale the restoration of Job as an individual can be accepted without question. But for the book we have, restoration of an individual alone could only be an arbitrary act of a deity separate from Job, and a somewhat vulgar act at that, because of its elimination of love. Even in a society as patriarchal as Job's, three new daughters would hardly "make up for" the loss of the previous daughters. We can see the restoring of an individual Job, perhaps, in terms of the analogy of waking up from a dream, where anxiety and humiliation are dealt with simply by abolishing the world in which they exist. But if the restoration of Job is not imaginatively continuous with his misery, what is the point of the poem? If, when Job improves his state of mind or his theology, his misery disappears too, we go back to the point at which the book began, and, in spite of the phrase "twice as much as he had before" (42:10), the book itself becomes meaningless. To say that Job is restored in a different world from the world of his sufferings would be more logically consistent, but it would considerably impoverish the human significance of the story.

The general critical principle involved is that in a descent-and-return mythical structure, as a rule, only the individual descends; only the community returns. Temptation, alienation, despair, decisive choice, death itself, are ordeals that only the individual can carry to their limit. But only a re-created society, like the one that crystallizes in the final scene of a comedy around a hero's marriage, can fully experience the sense of redemption. In Plate 20 Job's arms, outspread over his daughters, show that he with his daughters forms part of a larger human body, so that although the objective order from which his calamities came has been annihilated for Job (the calamities being depicted on the walls "In the shadows of Possibility," as Blake says in *Jerusalem*), Job's renewed state is not a subjective one. His daughters constitute his "Emanation," the total body of what he loves and creates through love. The ambiguity of the phrase "human body," which may be an individual or a social body, is involved in the contrast between the natural body which dies and the spiritual body which rises again. Job has what Paul calls a "vile body," given over to boils, but it is in his "flesh" (19:26) that he sees the God who appears in Plate 17.

At the beginning of the creation we are told that "the earth was without form, and void; and darkness was upon the face of the deep." Darkness and chaos, the latter being symbolized by the sea, have a twofold role in the Bible. They are, essentially, Satan and the leviathan, and hence Satan and the leviathan may be thought of as eternally enemies of God, totally shut out of the divine nature, reduced to annihilation at the Last Judgement. (In traditional Christianity they go on surviving indefinitely in hell, along with most of the human race, but that doctrine was for Blake a political ploy on the part of the Church, and a most contemptible one.) Yet, we are also told, the first act of creation was to separate light from darkness, and the second to separate land from sea. Hence darkness and chaos are also dialectically incorporated into the creation, and therefore Satan and the leviathan could also, in a different context, be regarded as creatures of God, on whom God would look with a by no means unfriendly eye. They are so regarded in the Book of Job, though nowhere else in the Bible.

The question of whether death was also incorporated into the original creation is more difficult. For man, according to Genesis, death came only as a consequence of disobedience. In any case we are now confronted by a nature with death as well as darkness and chaos built into it, and have to realize the influence on our minds of two gods. One, who allowed darkness, chaos and death into the natural order, is really Satan, the death-impulse in us, and the other is Jesus, who escaped from death and is our own essential life. Blake's Laocoon engraving describes the three figures of the sculpture as Jehovah with his two sons Satan and Adam, and around "Jehovah's" head he puts, in addition to the "*Malak Yahweh*" and "Angel of the Divine Presence" already mentioned, the inscription:

> He repented that he had made Adam (of the Female, the Adamah) & it grieved him at his heart.

This last phrase, from Genesis 6:6, is also quoted in the Job illustrations (Plate 5), and the rest of it is from the Hebrew text of Genesis 2:7. The total meaning is that the alleged creation of Adam was really the separating of a subjective consciousness from an objective existence, a dying mind from a dead body. The "lapsed Soul" of the "Introduction" to the *Songs of Experience* is not Adam, but the unity of man *(adam)* with the nature and the rest of life (the female *adamah* or "ground"), which are now united only by death.

The traditional creating God, then, is really a destroying God, the flood being another version of the creation of the order of nature at the beginning of the Bible, including man as he now exists. This "creation" is at the opposite pole from the destruction of the world by fire prophesied in the Book of Revelation at the end. Such a destruction would be an utterly pointless firework display if we did not realize that the traditional creation was itself a destruction, and the traditional destruction in the future the real creation and the manifesting again of what was there before the so-called creation. The Book of Job, for Blake, tells the same story as his own *Jerusalem*, whose theme is:

> Of the Sleep of Ulro! and of the passage through
> Eternal Death! and of the awaking to Eternal Life.

But it also tells the story of the "Bible of Hell," the Bible as Blake read it. The God who saves man is not a God who comes down out of the sky to impose order and authority and obedience, but a God who bursts out of the tomb of death with his face blackened by the soot of hell. This is the drama going on behind the wings of the quiet sequence of visions in the last third of the Job engravings. Blake's vision of the Book of Job was certainly a work of the creative imagination, but what made it possible was a powerful critical analysis of the book, of the whole Bible of which it forms a microcosm, and of the human life which, according to Matthew Arnold, is the theatre in which creation and criticism have become the same thing.

The Rising of the Moon

As I am dealing only with *A Vision* in its totality, having abandoned the project of tracing its development from its sketchy first edition, I am using the latest (1962) edition of it, subtitled 'A Reissue With the Author's Final Revisions', and my page references are to that edition.

I

Literature is one of the products of the constructive or imaginative power in the mind, and is the verbal part of the process of transforming the non-human world into something with a human shape and meaning, the process that we call culture or civilisation. In literature, particularly in poetry, the non-human or natural world is symbolically associated with the human world. The two great principles of association are analogy and identity, which are reflected in the grammatical forms of the simile and metaphor respectively: 'A is like B', and 'A is B'. Identity is found in mythology, which is concerned with gods, that is, beings in human shape identified with various aspects of physical nature. Hence mythology is a congenial language for poets, and even the more conceptual language of theology has to deal with some doctrines, such as the identity of Christ with God and Man, which can be expressed grammatically only in the form of metaphor. Another religious language, typology, is founded on analogy, and appears in Swedenborg's conception of 'correspondence', which he applies to his interpretation of the Bible. Analogy and identity are prominent in the associative cosmology of the Ptolemaic universe, where the seven planets are associated with the seven metals, the four elements with the four humours, and so on. As the sense of the objective validity of these associations waned, they became increasingly confined to occultism, in its various branches. Occult constructs, or constructs that unite occult and mythological or typological concepts, such as we find in Boehme, Swedenborg, and later Blavatsky, have played an important part in the mythopoeic poetry of the last two centuries. It is unnecessary to labour the point that Yeats had absorbed an immense amount of associative apparatus, much of it traditional, from his Rosicrucian and Golden Dawn studies.

These associative constructs, considered apart from whatever assertions they may make about the structure of the external world, become a framework of associations of imagery, in other words, 'metaphors for poetry', which is what Yeats's instructors said they were bringing him. In this context we can understand Valéry's remark that cosmology is one of the oldest of the *literary* arts. Nobody would attempt the serious study of Dante's *Commedia* or *Paradise Lost* without studying their cosmologies, and the fact that no objective validity is now attached to these cosmologies does not affect their importance as structural principles of the poems they are in. Further, every major poet has his own structure of imagery, and we soon become familiar with the way in which certain images are repeated in different contexts through his work. If we push this familiarity into a systematic study, we find ourselves creating out of the poet's total work a single and symmetrical world of images: in short, a cosmology. Yeats himself provides a brilliant and pioneering example of such criticism in his early essay on 'The Philosophy of Shelley's Poetry'. The word 'philosophy' is misleading, as he is not looking for ideas that express meaning but for images that contain it: his reason for using the word is to emphasise the consistency of structure that he finds in Shelley's work.

A further step would lead us to the more schematic elements in poetic thought which are implicit in the whole process of association. Poetic thought is inherently schematic, though some poets, of course, are more obviously schematic than others. Blake is very obviously so: there are several diagrams in his engraved poems reminding us of similar diagrams in *A Vision,* and Crabb Robinson tells us of his enthusiasm for the diagrams that William Law provided for his translation of Boehme. The study of the cosmology of the *Commedia* or *Paradise Lost,* just mentioned, would, if our commentaries provided no diagrams, soon bring us to pencil and paper, and this is even more true of Dante's *Convivio,* which, if closer to more widely accepted speculations in Dante's day, is a work not different in kind from *A Vision.* Yeats, in company with Edwin J. Ellis, made an early study of Blake, laying great stress on the schematic elements in Blake's imagery, and the second volume of their edition of Blake, whatever Ellis may have contributed to it (not much, one gathers from Yeats's letters), represents a kind of trial run for *A Vision.* The influence of Dante is also very strong, though later, and 'Ego Dominus Tuus', one of the central poems of the *Vision* period, takes its title from the *Vita Nuova.*

Analogy and identity produce, not only the two commonest figures of poetic speech, but the two major patterns of poetic imagery. One of these is the cyclical pattern, based on the assimilation of the death and rebirth of life in the human world to the natural cycles of sun, moon, water and the seasons. The other we may call the dialectical rhythm, the movement towards a separation of happiness from misery, the hero from the villain, heaven from hell. The two halves of this separation correspond in imagery to the two phases of the cycle, the images of the desirable world being youth, spring, morning and the like, and of the undesirable world their opposites.

In the traditional Christian pattern of symbolism, as we have it in Dante, there are, at the poles of reality, two eternally separated and opposed worlds, heaven and hell, beatitude and damnation. Heaven is symbolised by the starry spheres, now all that is left of the order of nature as God originally planned it. In between is the present order of nature, which exists on two levels.

One is the level of physical nature and fallen humanity, the ordinary world of experience, Italy in 1300, which pervades the poem though it is not a setting for any part of it. The other is the level of human nature as it was before the Fall, represented by the Garden of Eden, which Dante reaches by climbing the mountain of Purgatory. This mountain is a narrowing cone or gyre in shape, a winding stair *(escalina)*, and as Dante proceeds up it, shedding a deadly sin at each stage, he recovers the freedom of will and the moral innocence that man had before his fall. When he reaches Eden he is told that it is among other things a place of seed, that all forms of life on earth, except human lives, proceed from and return to it.

Dante's order of nature is, then, a cyclical movement. Christian doctrine prevents Dante from ascribing this cyclical movement to human life, but purgatory and rebirth are associated even in him. Yeats saw in the doctrine of purgatory, which in Dante is a second life on the surface of this earth, an accommodating of Eastern and Platonic conceptions of reincarnation to Christianity. Dante's mountain of purgatory, again, is directly underneath the moon, where the vision of *Paradiso* begins, and so it suggests the conception of nature as a cycle under the moon, the mountain forming a gyre narrowing to a point. An opposite gyre, though this is not explicit in Dante, would begin to broaden again for all forms of life that are reborn at that point. For Yeats the 'pern mill' whose smoke made Ben Bulben look like a burning mountain was an early source of an associating of a mountain with fire and with the spinning of double gyres.

In Spenser's *Faerie Queene*, though there are brief glimpses of a heaven and a hell, the main concern is with the two intermediate worlds: the England of Spenser's own day, which, like Dante's Italy, is present only by allegory, and the world of 'Faerie', which is a world of moral realisation, like Dante's purgatory, where the good is separated from the bad. In this world of faerie we find the Gardens of Adonis, a 'Paradise' on a 'Mount' which is also a place of death and rebirth, not said to affect only non-human lives. It is not said either to be directly under the moon, but in the *Mutabilitie Cantos* the 'sublunary' principle of change and decay, Mutability herself, thrusts her way into the moon and demands to be recognised as the ruler of the world above as well. The debate of being and becoming that results confines Mutability to the lower world, and leaves the starry spheres in their place as symbols of heaven. The trial to hear her case is held on top of 'Arlo Hill', like Ben Bulben an Irish mountain.

In Blake the main bent of symbolism is increasingly dialectical, towards the final separation of human redemption from human misery that he depicts in so many pictures of the Last Judgement. His treatment of the cycle is more complicated. Coming as he does after Newton, Blake rejects the traditional association of the starry spheres with the unfallen world. For him the starry heavens are also a projection of man's fallen state, and the unfallen world has to be sought within. The child, taking the world for granted as a place made chiefly for his benefit, lives in a state of innocence recalling the traditional unfallen life in the Garden of Eden. Blake calls this state of innocence Beulah, and associates it with the moon. As the child grows into an adult he moves into the state of experience, and his childlike wish to see the world in a better shape is driven underground into the subconscious. Beulah thus becomes an explosive, volcanic world which breaks into experience periodically in revolution, and its presiding genius is the youthful rebel Orc, as the presiding genius of experience is Urizen, the old man in the sky.

In *The Marriage of Heaven and Hell* the principles of rebellion and of conservatism are associated with 'Devils' and 'Angels' respectively, the 'Devils' being called that because they are regarded with such horror by their opponents. The two principles represent 'Contraries', and without contraries, according to Blake, there is no progression. These contraries have a close relationship to Yeats's conceptions of antithetical and primary, presently to be considered. Human life, both individual and social, tends to run in a cycle from Orc's revolt to Urizen's conservatism and back. A similar cycle is traced in the poem called 'The Mental Traveller', a major and acknowledged influence on Yeats's *Vision*. In this poem the entire cycle is divided into four main phases, but another poem of Blake's, 'My Spectre Around

Me', which again deals with a cycle, assigns seven 'loves' to four phases, making twenty-eight in all.

In his *Descriptive Catalogue,* written as a commentary on some of his paintings, Blake discusses the General Prologue to the *Canterbury Tales.* Considering Chaucer's constant use of astrology, including a tantalising allusion to the twenty-eight phases of the moon in *The Franklin's Tale,* and assuming his interest in combinations of the seven planetary and the four humorous temperaments, one would expect his 'Well nine and twenty in a company' to consist of twenty-eight characters plus Chaucer himself. In actual count there may be one or two more, but more important than the number is Blake's suggestion that 'The characters of Chaucer's Pilgrims are the characters which compose all ages and nations: as one age falls, another rises, different to mortal sight, but to immortals only the same; for we see the same characters repeated again and again'. This sounds very like a statement of Yeats's own theory of personal archetypes, of which more later. There are echoes of the *Descriptive Catalogue* in *A Vision* and elsewhere in Yeats: compare, for example, the discussion of beauty, ugliness and the Dancing Faun in the commentary on Phase Two (pp. 106–7) with Blake's commentary on his picture 'The Ancient Britons'. In Blake's later prophecies human history from Adam to Milton is divided into twenty-eight periods or 'Churches', and the twenty-eight cathedral cities of England, or 'Albion', the hero of *Jerusalem,* play a prominent role in that poem. In Blake's version of the apocalypse, Albion becomes absorbed into the body of Jesus, who is portrayed in the Book of Revelation as surrounded in heaven by twenty-eight beings, the twenty-four 'elders' and the four 'Zoas'.

In Classical literature there are two visions of recurrence and rebirth that particularly impressed Yeats. One is the myth of Er (or 'the man of Ur', as Yeats insists on calling him) in Plato's *Republic;* the other is the journey of Aeneas to the underworld, where it is foretold that 'Another Troy shall rise and set', in Yeats's echo of Virgil's words. Virgil's tendency to see the moon as the symbol of cyclical human life is recorded in his phrase *per amica silentia lunae* (*Aeneid ii,* 255), employed by Yeats as a title.

The cave of the nymphs in Homer's *Odyssey,* which has a southern gate for gods and a northern one for mortals, is the subject of an allegorical commentary by Porphyry, *De Antro Nympharum,* a source of 'Among School Children', and the same symbolism had previously found its way into Blake's *Book of Thel.* The two gates are reflected in the opposed Phases 15 and 1 of Yeats's lunar cycle, the former being a beauty too great for human life and the latter the point of mortality. Many other suggestions came to Yeats from his reading which we have no space to deal with. His debt to the Catholic poets of the later nineteenth century has perhaps not been sufficiently studied: he quotes (p. 250) from one very remarkable prototype of his Easter symbolism, an ode by Francis Thompson.

The well-known introduction to *A Vision* explains how it was dictated to Yeats by invisible spiritual instructors who worked through his wife's gift for automatic writing. Not having any explanation of my own to offer of this account, I propose to accept his at its face value. But it seems obvious that *A Vision* should be approached as a key to the structure of symbolism and imagery in Yeats's own poetry, as what Yeats calls in another connection 'the emergence of the philosophy of my own poetry, the unconscious becoming conscious'. If we did not have *A Vision,* a critic could still do with Yeats what Yeats did with Shelley: extract a poetic cosmology or created world of images from his work. Such a cosmology would have, or at least begin with, the same general outline as *A Vision.* It would lack its detail, but the detail is seldom rewarding either for the light it throws on Yeats or in its own right as part of 'a rule of thumb that somehow explained the world', in Yeats's phrase. That is, no critic could discover from Yeats's poetry that Queen Victoria belongs to Phase 24 of a lunar historical cycle, but then this does not tell us anything of much value about either Yeats or Queen Victoria. On the other hand, the cosmology that one could extract from Yeats's poetry would be more complete than *A Vision,* for the poet in Yeats knew much more about poetic symbolism than his instructors did.

To say this is to define an attitude to his instructors, so far as they may be thought of as instructing us. The great advantage of *A Vision* was that it increased Yeats's awareness of and power to control his own creative process, and so did much to provide the self-renewing vitality, the series of bursts of energy from within, like a jet engine, which is so extraordinary a feature of Yeats's development. It also emphasised certain forward intellectual developments for him, such as the sense of the poetic relevance of history and philosophy, and thus helped to make his later poetry more concrete and precise. One obvious modern parallel to *A Vision* is Poe's *Eureka*, but *Eureka* is neurotic in a way that *A Vision* is not: it hints at vast significance but expresses itself with very little precision, whereas *A Vision* at least says what it has to say. The schematic elaboration of *A Vision* was not very congenial to Yeats's temperament, and would probably never have been undertaken had it not come to him in this involuntary form: one thinks of the condescension with which, in the poem 'The Dawn', he looks down upon

> the withered men that saw
> From their pedantic Babylon
> The careless planets in their courses,
> The stars fade out where the moon comes,
> And took their tablets and did sums. (C.P., 164)

But there were also disadvantages in being 'overwhelmed by miracle'. The traditions about the kind of spirits that Yeats evoked seem to suggest that they are, when separated from the mind of the person who controls them, mischievous, irresponsible, even malignant. This is doubtless why Prospero in *The Tempest* nagged and bullied his spirits unmercifully. Yeats distinguishes such spirits as 'Frustrators', but whether or not the warning 'Remember we will deceive you if we can' came from them, he subjected himself passively to his instructors, in a way that made it impossible for him to detect frustration or irrelevance until pages of it had been written. *A Vision*, as a result, is a fragmentary and often misleading guide to the structure of imagery in Yeats. It is to the students of Yeats what *De Doctrina*

Christiana is to the student of Milton: a nuisance that he can't pretend doesn't exist.

The analogy between human and natural worlds founded on the cycle is a central principle of symbolism, and we have seen that it is traditional to make the moon the focus of it. Structures of the same cyclical and lunar shape may be found in *Finnegans Wake,* with its twenty-eight 'Maggies', in Robert Graves's white goddess mythology, in Pound's *Pisan Cantos.* In Western cyclical symbolism the human emphasis falls on the social and historical rather than the individual. Reincarnation was never accepted in Christianity nor widely held in the West, and so it has been the cycle of nations and empires that for Western poetry is assimilated to the rotation of life and death and rebirth. Yeats's interest in reincarnation gives his cyclical symbolism an individual emphasis as well, but his instructors knew far less about this than they did about the more solidly established historical cycle. One fragment of this part of the construct survives in a letter to Ethel Mannin, and there Yeats says that he only half understands it himself. There remains the dialectical structure of symbolism, the separation of reality into an apocalyptic and a demonic world where all images in each world are identified by metaphor. This symbolism is quite clear in Yeats's poetry, but *A Vision* is not an adequate guide to it. We proceed to deal with the three main aspects of Yeats's symbolism, the historical cycle, the individual cycle, and the apocalyptic imagery, using *A Vision,* for the reasons just given, in a progressively more fragmentary way.

II

There are two great rhythmical movements in all living beings: a movement towards unity and a movement towards individuality. These are opposed and contrasting movements, and are symbolised in Yeats by a double gyre, a movement in one direction which, as it grows more pervasive, develops the counteracting movement within itself, so that the apex of the next gyre appears in the middle of the base of the preceding one and moves back through it. The simplest way to represent the entire double-gyre rotation is by a circle. Because of its traditional association with the moon, this circle has twenty-eight phases, and the twenty-eight-phase cycle exists, Yeats says, in every completed movement, whether it takes a moment or thousands of years to complete itself. But, of course, it is in the larger rhythms of history that the detail is easiest to see. Yeats sees history as forming a series of cycles, each lasting about two thousand years, with each cycle going through twenty-eight parallel phases. The conception is similar in many ways to that of Spengler's *Decline of the West*, and Yeats often remarks on the similarity of his views to Spengler's.

In Spengler, who is most rewarding when he is read as a Romantic and symbolic poet, each historical cycle or 'culture' exhibits the rhythms of growth, maturation and decline characteristic of an organism, though Spengler also uses the metaphor of the four seasons. There were, for instance, a Classical and a Western cycle, each having a 'spring' of feudal economy and heroic aristocracy, a Renaissance 'summer' of city-states, an 'autumn' in Periclean Athens and the eighteenth century, when the cultural possibilities of the cycle were exhausted, and a 'winter', ushered in by Alexander and Napoleon respectively, when a 'culture' changes to a technological 'civilisation' of huge cities, dictatorships and annihilation wars. In between comes a Near Eastern or 'Magian' culture, with its spring at the birth of Christ and its later stages in the period of Mohammedanism, the religion of the crescent moon. In each cycle the period of highest development is the period of greatest individuality in both art and political life, and both the early and the late stages are marked by a strong sense of communal or mass-consciousness.

In Yeats this communal consciousness is part of the drive toward unity. It is the primitive mentality in which all historical cycles begin, and the decadent mentality in which they end, hence it is the 'primary' rhythm of existence. Over against it is an 'antithetical' development of individuality, which reaches its greatest height in the hero. In primitive society the communal consciousness is so strong that there hardly seems to be any real individuality, as we know it, at all. Those who show signs of individual consciousness often have simply a different kind of unity, with animals or with the fairies and other spirits of the invisible world, like the inspired fools who haunt romantic literature (Phase 2). The types from Phase 2 to about Phase 6 are intellectually simple and self-contained: Phase 6 is the phase of Walt Whitman, who never quite distinguished individual from communal well-being. Individuality begins in the unhappy and tormented souls who are aware of a double pull within them around Phase 8. As we cross the quadrant of Phase 8 we begin to move into the antithetical area, beginning with intense and withdrawn figures like Parnell (Phase 10) or Nietzsche (Phase 12). Individuality then advances to heroic proportions, and we have 'sensualists' so complete that they represent a kind of antithesis to sanctity (Phase 13), artists of tempestuous passion, women of fully ripened physical beauty, and heroes of arrogant pride like the heroes of Shakespeare's tragedies.

At the point of highest development represented by Phase 15 the counter-movement back to communal consciousness begins. Artists become less embodiments of passion and more intellectualised (Phase 21), or technicians (Phase 23); heroes come to think of themselves as servants of impersonal force, like Napoleon (Phase 20), or the money-obsessed characters in Balzac; women come to be guardians of a generally accepted morality like Queen Victoria (Phase 24). The 'personality', which is the fully developed individuality, becomes the 'character', a subjective conception implying that something objective to it is greater. Yeats speaks of the antithetical types as subjective too, but their subjectivity creates its own world, whereas primary subjectivity first separates itself from the objective world, then is increasingly drawn to it as a unity destined to absorb all subjects. These two aspects of subjectivity are symbolised in Yeats by two expressions of the eye: the stare, which sees nothing but expresses an inner consciousness, and the glance, the subject looking *at* a reality set over against it. At later primary stages personality becomes more fragmented, this fragmentation being represented by the physical deformity of the hunchback (Phase 26), and the mental deformity of the fool (Phase 28). What Spengler calls the 'second religiousness' comes into society in the forms of spiritualism, theosophy, and various forms of revived occultism, seeking the same kind of kinship with the invisible world, at the other end of the social cycle, that primitive societies show in their myths and folk-tales and so-called superstitions. Yeats often recurs to the similarity between the primitive and the sophisticated conceptions of unseen beings, the legendary rumour in remote cottages and the seances in suburban parlours. The entire cycle describes a progression through the four elements of earth, water, air and fire, each quadrant having a particular relationship to each element.

The conception on which the whole of *A Vision* turns is the contrast of antithetical and primary natures, which is part of a dichotomy that runs through Yeats's writing and thinking. In an early letter he says: 'I have always considered myself a voice of what I believe to be a greater renaissance—the revolt of the soul against the intellect—now beginning in the world', and this involves a preference of the swordsman to the saint, of the aristocratic to the democratic virtues, of the reality of beauty to the reality of truth, of (to use categories from Eliot's 'Burnt Norton') the way of plenitude to the way of vacancy. The contrast is so far-reaching that it may be simplest to set all its aspects out at once in a table, though many of them will not be intelligible until farther on in this essay.

ANTITHETICAL	PRIMARY
individuality	unity
Leda and Swan	Virgin and Dove
Oedipus	Christ
son kills father	son appeases father
incest with mother	redemption of mother and bride
drive toward nature	drive toward God
tragic	comic
master-morality	servant-morality
aristocratic	democratic
discord	concord

quality	quantity
freedom	necessity
fiction	truth
evil	good
art	science
ecstasy	wisdom
kindred	mechanism
particularity	abstraction
lunar	solar
natural	reasonable
war	peace
personality	character
Michael Robartes	Owen Aherne
Oisin	St. Patrick
(Eros)	(Agape)
(Chinese Yang)	(Chinese Yin)
(Nietzsche's Apollo)	(Nietzsche's Dionysus)
(Blake's Orc, 'Devils', Rintrah, 'Science of Wrath')	(Blake's Urizen, 'Angels', Palamabron, 'Science of Pity')

Many of these categories come from page 52 of *A Vision*, that of quality and quantity from page 130. The Apollonian and Dionysiac categories seem curiously placed, but Yeats thinks of Apollo as a creative force and of Dionysus as a transcendent one.

The drive to individuality is a drive toward nature, Yeats says, and has for its goal a complete physical self-fulfilment or 'Unity of Being', which may be attained in the phases close to Phase 15, the phase of the full moon. Phase 15 itself realises this so completely that it cannot be achieved in human life at all. We thus arrive at the difficult conception of a creature which is superhuman because it is completely natural. We are not told much about these Phase 15 beings, beyond a mysterious passage in 'The Phases of the Moon', but, of course, a perfect human harmony could also be symbolised by perfect sexual intercourse, and we are told in that delightful poem 'Solomon and the Witch' that a union of this kind would restore man to the unfallen world. Yeats strongly hints that Christ was a superhuman incarnation, a unique entry of Phase 15 into human life, though an explicit statement on this point would doubtless have annoyed his instructors. He often refers, for instance, to an alleged belief that Christ was the only man exactly six feet high. Why so arbitrary a measure as the foot should have been in the mind of the Trinity from all eternity is not clear, but the meaning is that Christ had the perfect 'Unity of Being' which, Yeats tells us, Dante compares to a perfectly proportioned human body.

The opposite drive toward an objective unity is a drive toward 'God', and has as its goal an absorption in God (Phase 1) which is similarly a superhuman phase of pure 'plasticity'. Hence the real direction of the attempt in the primary phases to subordinate oneself to objective powers is revealed in the religious leader (Phase 25) and most clearly of all in the saint (Phase 27). As far as this twenty-eight-phase cycle of being is concerned, 'God' for Yeats appears to be a character like the button-moulder in *Peer Gynt*, pounding everything to dust with the pestle of the moon, a cosmic spider or vampire who swallows the Many in the One. In short, God occupies the place of Death, which makes Yeats's remark that he tends to write coldly of God something of an understatement.

We have spoken so far of a general social cycle from primitivism to decadence, but there are two more specific ones in Yeats, which correspond to the Classical and Western cycles in Spengler. Draw a circle on a page and mark its four cardinal points 1, 8, 15 and 22. These phases on Yeats's historical calendar (or at least the most important of several he uses) are a thousand years apart. Phase 1 is 2000 B.C.; Phase 8 is 1000 B.C.; Phase 15 is the time of Christ; Phase 22 is A.D. 1000; Phase 1 is therefore our own time as well as 2000 B.C., and Phase 8 is also a thousand years from now. Classical civilisation extends from Phase 8 to 22, 1000 B.C. to A.D. 1000, and Christian civilisation, which is our own, from A.D. 1000 to 3000, Phases 22 to 8. We are half-way through the latter now, at the same point Classical civilisation reached in the time of Christ. Phases 8 and 22 are represented by Troy and Byzantium, one an Asiatic city destroyed by Europeans and the other a European city captured by Asiatics, yet so close together that Byzantium, when it became a centre of Roman power, was thought of as a new Troy. Each civilisation is the opposite or complement of its predecessor. Classical civilisation was essentially antithetical, tragic, heroic and strongly individualised; Christian civilisation is therefore essentially primary, democratic, altruistic and based on a subject-object attitude to reality. Byzantium was the main source of early Irish culture, and its place in Yeats's thought gives a special significance to his allusions to people roughly contemporary with its golden age, such as Charlemagne and Harun Al-Rashid.

Half-way through, a civilisation generates the beginning of its counteracting movement, hence Christ, the presiding genius of the civilisation that began a millennium later, appears in the middle of the Classical cycle. 'The Incarnation', says Yeats, 'invoked modern science and modern efficiency, and individualised emotion.' Thus a religious movement cuts the cycle of civilisations at right-angles, and Christianity as a religion extends from the time of Christ to about our own day. It follows that a similar Messianic figure announcing Classical civilisation must have appeared around 2000 B.C., and that another, announcing a second antithetical civilisation of the future, is to appear somewhere around our own time. Yeats speaks of an antithetical influx setting in 'a considerable time before' (p. 208) the close of its predecessor, perhaps to rationalize his conception of his own function. In 2000 B.C., in the middle of a pre-Classical culture associated vaguely by Yeats with 'Babylonian starlight', the annunciation of the Greek culture pattern was made, in what way we do not know, but surviving in two myths. One is the myth of Leda and the swan, the divine bird impregnating the human woman, the fulfilment of their union being, eventually, the fall of Troy, which began Greek history, properly speaking. The other is the myth of Oedipus, whose parricide and mother-incest set the tragic and heroic tone of an antithetical culture. The complementary myths appear with the birth of Christ, the myth of the dove and the Virgin and the myth of the son appeasing his father's wrath and redeeming his mother and bride. Our own day is the period of the annunciation of a new Oedipus and Leda mythology, heralding the tragic and warlike age of the future and ushering in a religion contrasting with Christianity. The Messiah of our day is an Antichrist, that is, an antithetical Christ, the terrible reborn Babe of Blake's 'Mental Traveller'. As Christ's mother was a virgin, so the new Messiah's mother, in 'The Adoration of the Magi', is a harlot and a devotee of the Black Mass, resembling the Virgin only in being rejected by the society of her time. In *The Herne's Egg* the new Messiah is to be born in Ireland, the Judea of the West, the offspring of a heron and his fanatical priestess. What this Messiah has to announce, of course, is the future age when 'another Troy shall rise and set'.

In Spengler each culture has a 'prime symbol' expressing its inner essence, which is a Doric column for the Classical, a cavern for the Magian, a garden for the Chinese, and so on. For some reason he gives no primary symbol for Western culture, saying only that it is characterised by a drive into the infinite. Yeats, learning from Pound that Frobenius found two major symbols in Africa, a cavern and an altar with sixteen roads leading from it, suggests that Spengler took his Magian cavern from Frobenius, and should have provided us with the altar for the Western symbol. In Yeats the middle 'Magian' cycle is replaced by the conception of a religious cycle cutting the historical one midway, but Yeats resembles Spengler in associating Christ, who was born in a manger and rose from a tomb, with the cavern. Hence 'At or near the central point of our civilisation must come *antithetical* revelation, the turbulent child of the Altar'. Yeats, however, does not use the altar as a symbol for our own time in his poetry, though the cavern appears as an image of the passage from death to rebirth (Phase 1, more or less) in 'The Hour Before Dawn'. The chief images he does use are those of birds and animals. The bird is often the swan, for obvious reasons, but with a whole parliament of fowls in addition. If we take three representative poems on this theme, 'The Second Coming', 'Demon and Beast', and 'On a Picture of a Black Centaur by Edmund Dulac', we find a gyring falcon in the first, a gyring gull and a green-headed duck in the second, and 'horrible green birds' in the third, accompanying the age in which the 'demon' (not daimon, which is a quite different conception) of late phases gives place to the 'beast' of early ones, the 'rough beast' of 'The Second Coming' who modulates into the centaurs of the Dulac poem.

Everybody belongs fundamentally to one of the twenty-six human phases or types, but, of course, a man of any phase can be born at any time in history. If a social cycle has reached, say, Phase 22 (more or less the Victorian period in European culture), those who belong to phases near 22 will be typical of their time, and those of early phases (George Borrow and Carlyle in Phase 7, for example) have a more difficult adjustment to make. But a man may also be typical or atypical of his own phase, and Yeats begins many of his descriptions, very confusingly, by dealing with the 'out of phase' variant of the type. Yeats further tells us that he cannot point to historical examples of several of the phases, partly because many of the more primary ones do not produce types who make any impression on history.

For one reason or another, what Yeats calls in 'The Gift of Harun Al-Rashid'

> Those terrible implacable straight lines
> Drawn through the wandering vegetative dream (*C.P.*, 517)

turn out in practice to be nearly as accommodating as Baconian ciphers in Shakespeare. For instance, Yeats says that each millennium of the two-thousand-year cycle can be considered as a complete twenty-eight-phase wheel in itself, so that we are also near the Phase 1 end of the first millennium of our Christian civilisation, which adds to its chaos. This millennium reached its antithetical height of Phase 15 at the Quattrocento, when 'men attained to personality in great numbers', and when Europe was infused by the spirit of the recently fallen Byzantium. This curtailed millennial version of the rhythm of Western culture, which incidentally is much closer to Spengler, lies behind most of Yeats's references to Michelangelo and to one of his seminal books, Castiglione's *Courtier* (see, for example, 'The People'). In the Renaissance there was also a kind of minor annunciation of the opposite kind of civilisation, and so Yeats has reasons (he tells us in a passage in *On the Boiler* inexplicably omitted from the recent volume *Explorations*) both to 'adore' and to 'detest' the Renaissance.

Again, there are larger rhythms in history, obtained by adding a solar and zodiacal cycle to the lunar one. One of these is the 'Great Year', traditionally formed by the precession of the equinoxes, and which lasts for twenty-six thousand years, a 'year' of twelve 'months' of two thousand odd years each. One of these Great Years ended and began with Christ, who rose from the dead at the 'full moon in March' which marks that point. Caesar was assassinated at another full moon in March a few decades earlier. Yeats points out how contemporaries of Christ, such as Virgil in the Fourth Eclogue and Horace in the *Carmen Saeculare*, felt a peculiar cyclical significance about that time which Christianity itself, anxious to get away from cyclical theories, ignored. The birth of Christ took place at a (primary) conjunction of Mars and Venus, and our new Messiah will be born at the opposite conjunction of Jupiter and Saturn, when the 'mummy wheat' of the buried Classical civilisation will start to sprout.

The emotional focus of *A Vision* is also that of Yeats's life, the sense that his own time is a time of a trembling of the veil of the temple, eventually defined as a myth of a new religious dispensation announcing a new God to replace Christ and accompanied by the traditional signs of the end of the world. Yeats traces his sense of an imminent Armageddon back to such early poems as 'The Hosting of the Sidhe' and 'The Valley of the Black Pig'. A note to the former poem tells us that the sidhe or fairy folk of Ireland dance in gyres or whirlwinds which are called the dance of the daughters of Herodias: the last section of 'Nineteen Hundred and Nineteen' applies this imagery to Yeats's own time. Although our own time is Phase 15 of the Christian era, it can be read in different ways on Yeats's various clocks, and Yeats tends to think of it primarily as a passing through Phase 1, when a great age has finally reached the crescent of the 'fool' and hears the irrational cry ('the scream of Juno's peacock') of a new birth.

Yeats's treatment of the theme of contemporary annunciation exhibits a complete emotional range, from the most raucous nonsense to the most serene wisdom. We may divide his personal reactions to it into a cycle of six phases. First comes the phase of the deplorable if harmless rabble-rouser of *On the Boiler*, shouting for a 'just war', hailing Fascism as the force that will restore all the traditional heroic dignities to society, and prophesying a new 'science' compounded of spiritualism and selective breeding. Some of Yeats's instructors appear to have been incapable of distinguishing a lunar vision from a lunatic one, and this phase in Yeats seems to be part of the backwash from revising *A Vision* around 1937. In an early letter Yeats says: 'Every influence has a shadow, as it were, an unbalanced—the unbalanced is the Kabalistic definition of evil—duplicate of itself.' Fortunately this phase is not allowed to spoil much of his poetry, though it is creeping around the fringes of 'Under Ben Bulben'.

The second phase is that of the traditionalist who stresses the importance of convention and manners, 'where all's accustomed, ceremonious', and sees the preservation of this as preliminary to developing a new aristocracy. Yeats's cabinet of great Irishmen, Swift, Burke, Berkeley and others, are called upon to endorse this attitude, which is also heard in a simpler form in the contented reveries emanating from Coole Park and Stockholm on the values of hereditary privilege. The third phase is that of the neo-pagan, the poet who celebrates a rebirth of physical energy and sexual desire, who insists on the sacredness of bodily functions, who helps Crazy Jane to refute the Bishop on the primacy of the life of the soul, and who asks the unanswerable question:

> If soul may look and body touch,
> Which is the more blest? (*C.P.*, 344)

The fourth phase is that of the teacher, the author of the *Samhain* essays who stands out against a 'primary' mob, assuming the role, in his own literary context, of

> A great man in his pride
> Confronting murderous men. (*C.P.*, 264)

This is the critic who patiently points out to his Irish audience that no true patriotism can be built on the stock response and no true religion on the consecration of it; that the morality of art must always be liberal, and that the sectarian instinct, 'a pretended hatred of vice and a real hatred of intellect', is always part of the mob, whether it expresses itself in politics, religion or art. The fifth phase is the prophet, the troubled visionary of 'The Second Coming' and elsewhere, who sees and records but does not try to rationalise the horror and violence of his own time, who can understand the ferocity of 'The weasel's twist, the weasel's tooth' without confusing it with heroism. Finally, there is the phase of the sage, the poet of 'Lapis Lazuli' who can speak of the 'gaiety that leaps up before danger or difficulty', and who understands that even horror and violence can inspire a kind of exuberance. We notice that all these phases which are directly connected with literature are very precious attributes of Yeats, but that for the others the best we can do is to apply to Yeats what Yeats himself says of Shelley: 'Great as Shelley is, those theories about the coming changes of the world, which he has built up with so much elaborate passion, hurry him from life continually.'

Or, as Yeats also says, 'All art is the disengaging of a soul from place and history'. It has doubtless occurred to more than one reader of *A Vision* that Yeats might more easily have seen his cycle, not as the archetypal forms of human life, but of human imagination: in other words as a perfect circle of literary or mythical types, which is how Blake saw the pilgrims of Chaucer. Many of Yeats's examples are writers who, like Whitman at Phase 6, have made their lives conform to literary patterns, or who, like Shakespeare at Phase 20, are described by the kind of poetry they produced and not personally. The primitives of phases 2 to 7 are much easier to understand as archetypes of pastoral or Romantic conventions in literature; Dostoievsky's Idiot is the only example given of Phase 8; and Nietzsche's Zarathustra fits better into the 'Forerunner' position of Phase 12 than Nietzsche himself. Phase 15 would then become intelligible as the phase of the poet's ideal or male Muse: the Eros of Dante and Chaucer, the 'Ille' of 'Ego Dominus Tuus'; the beautiful youth of Shakespeare's sonnets, and the like. The high antithetical phases would be much more clearly represented by characters in Shakespeare or Irish legend, and the high primary ones by characters in Balzac and Browning, than they are by Galsworthy or Lamarck or 'a certain actress'.

Such a rearrangement would bring out the real relation of the *Vision* cycle of types to Yeats's own characters. The fool and the blind man who remain on the stage at the end of *On Baile's Strand* symbolise the disappearance of the Cuchulain cycle (which is symbolically the Christian cycle, too, as Cuchulain was contemporary with Christ), the blind man representing the dark moonless night of Phase 1. The happy natural fool of *The Hour-Glass* is also a fool of Phase 28, with a Creative Mind from the 'Player on Pan's Pipes' of Phase 2. In *Resurrection* a blind man and a lame man, the two together making up the physical deformity of the 'hunchback', appear beside a saint, and in *The Player Queen* the opposition of Decima and the Queen she supplants is a burlesque illustration of the opposition of Phases 13 and 27, antithetical and primary perfection. The Queen in any case is a much better example of what Yeats appears to mean by sanctity than the historical examples he gives, which are Socrates and Pascal.

III

In the cycle of 'The Mental Traveller' Blake symbolises the subjective and objective aspects of life as male and female. All human beings including women are symbolically male, part of the reborn 'Boy', and nature, or the physical environment that is temporarily transformed into human shape by a culture, is what is symbolically female. Male and female cycles rotate in opposite directions, one growing older as the other grows younger. *A Vision* refers briefly to this symbolism (pp. 213 and 262), but *A Vision* says little about the objective aspect of civilisation. The conception of the individual is much more complicated. Here, as in Blake, there are subjective and objective factors, but there are two of each, making four 'Faculties' in all. An individual may be thought of as acting man (Will) or as seeing, knowing or thinking man (Creative Mind). In so far as he thinks or knows or sees, man operates on a known or seen world, a set of *données* or given facts and truths and events that make up what Yeats calls the Body of Fate. In so far as he acts, he acts in the light of a certain vision of action, which Yeats calls the Mask, and which includes both what he wants to make of himself and what he wants to make of the world around him. In 'antithetical' phases action is motivated by an 'image' springing from the self which complements the Will: in 'primary' phases, where man is more apt to say, with Hic in 'Ego Dominus Tuus', 'I would find myself and not an image', it is motivated by a desire to act on the world as a separated or impersonal thing, and eventually by a desire to be absorbed in that world. Each man is defined by the phase of his Will, and his Mask comes from the phase directly opposite, fourteen phases away. The Body of Fate is similarly opposite the Creative Mind, and Will and Creative Mind are related by the fact that, like male and female principles in Blake, they rotate in opposite directions. The details are too complicated to go into here, but a man of Phase 23 is actually made up of a Will of Phase 23, a Mask of Phase 9, a Creative Mind of Phase 7, and a Body of Fate of Phase 21.

In the Platonic tradition the relation of Creative Mind and Will is differently conceived. There is a superior intelligible world and an inferior physical world. In the latter the body perceives and acts on the image; in the former the soul perceives the form or idea, not as an object, but as something ultimately identical with itself. The soul and the world of forms are imprisoned in the physical world and struggle to break out of it. For Yeats, too, there is another way of looking at the four Faculties we have just dealt with. If we think of man as actor and creator, we see his life as an interplay of action and thought; if we think of him as a creature, we see his life as a physical contact with objects out of which a higher kind of identity is trying to emerge. In this perspective the four 'Faculties' become four 'Principles'. Will and Mask now become two lower Principles, Husk and Passionate Body, the physical subject and the physical object. Creative Mind and Body of Fate become Spirit and Celestial Body, the soul and the world of forms. This introduces a dialectical element into the cycle, a movement out of it into a world of changeless being.

From the beginning Yeats's poetic world comprised a state of experience and a state of innocence, the latter being associated with the Irish fairy world, a 'land of heart's desire' where there was an eternal youth of dancing and revelry. In *The Celtic Twilight* this world is once described as the Paradise still buried under the fallen world, but its associations are usually more specific. Yeats quotes legends indicating that the seasons of this world are the reverse of ours, like the southern hemisphere, and, in the *Autobiographies,* a remark of Madame Blavatsky that we live in a dumb-bell-shaped cosmos, with an antipodal world at our North Pole. This conception is most readily visualised as an hour-glass, the emblem of time and the basis of Yeats's 'double gyre' diagrams, and in the play that is explicitly called *The Hour-Glass* we are told that 'There are two living countries, the one visible and the other invisible; and when it is winter with us it is summer in that country'. The fairy world has occasionally, according to legend and folk tale, caught up human beings, who found, when they returned to their own world, that time moves much faster here than there, and that a few days in fairyland had been many years of human life. As Yeats began to try to fit together what he knew of Irish legend with what he read in Swedenborg or learned at seances, he also began to think of his fairy world as complementary to our own in time as well as climate, and as moving from age to youth. He often refers to Swedenborg as saying that the angels move towards their youth in time, as we move towards age.

Yeats's doctrine of reincarnation eventually annexed this world and transformed it into the world that we enter at death and leave again at birth, which is also a rebirth. It lost most of its cheerfulness in this process and acquired many of the characteristics of a penal régime. Book III of *A Vision,* called 'The Soul in Judgment', is supposed to tell us what his instructors knew about the antipodal world, but Yeats speaks of this section with some disappointment as more fragmentary than he hoped it would be. It uses a good deal of material from the earlier essay 'Swedenborg, Mediums, and the Desolate Places'. The discarnate soul is pulled in the ideal direction of Spirit and celestial Body, and away from Husk and Passionate Body, by a series of spiritual or imaginative repetitions of the major emotional crises of its earthly life, which tend eventually to exhaust them, as the confessional techniques of psychology are supposed to do with neuroses. Yeats calls this the 'dreaming back', the most important of several stages of the return to rebirth. A violent crime may be re-enacted for centuries in the same spot, a fact which accounts for many types of ghost story; brutal masters and submissive slaves may exchange roles in a tenebrous saturnalia. Yeats suggests that our dreams, though they use our own experiences and desires as material, are actually part of the psychic life of the dead moving backwards to rebirth through us. The more fully a life has been lived, the less expiation is needed and the more successful the next life. Another life is, in fact, part of the whole 'dreaming back' operation, so that every life is a movement from birth to death and simultaneously part of a purgatorial movement from death to rebirth. When a Spirit is completely purified and ready for what in Christianity would be heaven, it may seek rebirth as an act of deliberate choice, like the Bodhisattva in Buddhism.

In the Eastern religions the cycle of life, death and rebirth is regarded as an enslavement, from which all genuine spiritual effort tries to liberate itself by reducing the physical world to unreality. The attitude of the Christian saint, even without a belief in reincarnation, is similar. Such a course is, according to some moods of Yeats, opposed to that of the poet and artist, whose function it is to show the reality incarnate in the appearance of the physical world and in the physical emotional life of man. The poet accepts the plenitude of the phenomenal world, and in the cycle of Faculties the most strongly 'antithetical' types, heroes and beautiful women who are driven by the passions of a titanic ego, are the poet's natural subjects. Long before *A Vision* Yeats had written: 'If it be true that God is a circle whose centre is everywhere, the saint goes to the centre, the poet and artist to the ring where everything comes round again.' Hence his emotional preference of the 'antithetical' to the 'primary', of the way of the poet to the way of the saint, leads to a preference for cyclical and rebirth symbolism in contrast to the kind of symbolism that separates reality into an apocalyptic and a demonic world.

The conflict of the abstract vision of the saint and the concrete vision of the poet, one seeking deliverance from the wheel of life and the other ready to accept the return of it, is the theme of many of Yeats's best-known poems. The setting of such poems is some modification of the top of Dante's mountain of purgatory, a winding stair in a tower leading upwards to a point at which one may contemplate both an eternal world above and a cyclical world below. In 'A Dialogue of Self and Soul' the Soul summons to an upward climb into the dark; the Self, preoccupied with the dying-god symbol of the Japanese ceremonial sword wrapped in embroidered silk with flowers of 'heart's purple', looks downward into rebirth and maintains 'I am content to live it all again'. In 'Vacillation', where there is a similar dialogue between Soul and Heart, the opening image is the tree of Attis which stands between eternity and rebirth, and the final contrast is between the saint whose body remains uncorrupted and the poet who deliberately seeks the cycle of corruption in generation symbolised by Samson's riddle of the lion and the honeycomb. In 'Among School Children' there is a similar antithesis between the nun and the mother, the former symbolising the direct ascent to eternity and the latter the cycle of generation. Here the tree, appearing at the end instead of at the beginning, seems a resolving or reconciling image rather than one of 'vacillation', but the contrast remains in the poem's argument.

However much imaginative sympathy we may have with these poems as poems, they indicate a deficiency in *A Vision* as an expression of some of Yeats's more profound insights. Yeats speaks of Emerson and Whitman as 'writers who have begun to seem superficial precisely because they lack the Vision of Evil', but his own lack of a sense of evil borders on the frivolous. Visions of horror and violence certainly haunt his poetry, but in *A Vision* and elsewhere in his later essays, even in much of the poetry itself, they are all rationalised and explained away as part of the necessary blood-bath accompanying the birth of his new and repulsive Messiah. The absence of any sense of a demonic world, a world of evil and tyranny and meanness and torment, such as human desire utterly repudiates and bends every effort to get away from, is connected with, and is perhaps the cause of, the absence in *A Vision* of the kind of dialectical imagery that appears in, say, 'The Two Trees', which in Blake would be the tree of life and the tree of mystery. Occasionally in earlier prose writings we get glimpses of a whole dimension of symbolism that seems to have got strangled in *A Vision.* Yeats says in an early essay: 'To lunar influence belong all thoughts and emotions that were created by the community, by the common people, by nobody knows who, and to the sun all that came from the high disciplined or individual kingly mind.' This imagery is repeated in 'A Dialogue of Self and Soul', but in *A Vision* the sun is 'primary', and has been absorbed into the lunar cycle: the solar and zodiacal symbolism in *A Vision,* already glanced at, only extends the lunar cycle, and adds nothing new in kind.

What we miss in *A Vision,* and in Yeats's speculative prose generally, is the kind of construct that would correspond to such a poem as 'Sailing to Byzantium'. This poem presents an eternal world which contains all the concrete imagery and physical reality associated elsewhere with the cycle of rebirth, which is not a mere plunge into nothingness and darkness by an infatuated soul, and yet is clear of the suggestion that nothing really lasts except what Blake calls the 'same dull round'. Such a poem is apocalyptic, a vision of plenitude which is still not bound to time. *The Shadowy Waters,* also, differs from the later poems of the 'Vacillation' group in that the chief characters go on to finish their quest and the subordinate characters (the sailors) return to the world. The goal of the quest is also described in apocalyptic terms:

> Where the world ends
> The mind is made unchanging, for it finds
> Miracle, ecstasy, the impossible hope,
> The flagstone under all, the fire of fires,
> The roots of the world. (*C.P.,* 477)

For a theoretical construct to match this apocalyptic imagery we have to set aside the main body of *A Vision,* with its conception of unity and individuality as opposed and impossible ideals which only superhuman beings can reach, and look for another construct in which they are at the same point, and that point accessible to human life.

There are two apocalyptic symbols in *A Vision:* one is the 'Record' (p. 193) or consolidated form of all the images of 'ultimate reality', associated by Yeats, I think correctly, with Blake's Golgonooza. The other and more important one is the 'Thirteenth Cone', which is not really a cone but a sphere, and which 'is that cycle which may deliver us from the twelve cycles of time and space'. We are further told, in what ought to be one of the key passages of *A Vision,* that this thirteenth cone confronts every cycle of life, large or small, as 'the reflection or messenger of the final deliverance', and at the very end of the book it is said to exist in every man and to be what is called by man his freedom. There are also 'teaching spirits' of this thirteenth cone who direct and inspire those who are in the cycle, and Yeats calls the thirteenth cone his substitute for God. He speaks of it as 'like some great dancer', recalling the great last line of 'Among School Children' which unites being and becoming, imagination and image.

The temporary mixture of four Faculties that constitutes what is ordinarily thought of as an individual is not final human reality. A poet discovers this, for example, when he realises that the images that great poetry uses are traditional, archetypal, conventional images, and that the emotions he employs to set these images forth are traditional and conventional emotions, representing states of being greater than himself. Thus the poet finds himself drawn out of his Husk into his Spirit, and thereby enters into much larger conceptions of what subject and object are. He is drawn up into a world in which subject and object become the human imagination and the human image, each being archetypes that recur in every individual man and poem. These great traditional states of being which the poet enters into and expresses are akin to the 'giant forms' of Blake's prophecies, Orc, Tharmas, Los and the rest, and, more generally, to the 'gods' of beauty and nature and war who inform so much of literature. Yeats sometimes calls them 'moods', and speaks of them as divine beings whose dreams form our own waking lives. Thus in *The Shadowy Waters* the central characters discover that

> We have fallen in the dreams the Ever-living
> Breathe on the burnished mirror of the world. (*C.P.*, 478)

In *A Vision* the poetic imagination begins in the self of the individual, but moves in the direction of identifying with a greater self called the 'daimon', and the process of purgation between lives has for its eventual goal a similar identification.

Apart from the contrast of self and soul, there is also an abstract vision associated, not with sanctity, but with art itself. This is the vision linked with the name of Pythagoras, whose mathematical genius 'planned' the art of exquisite proportion embodied in Greek sculpture and architecture. The role of art in imposing mathematical proportion on reality is connected by Yeats also with the geometrical diagrams of his own *Vision*, which he compares to the forms of Brancusi sculpture. Here we see how art, no less than sanctity, moves in the direction of a greater identity. In the poem 'To Dorothy Wellesley' it is not the soul that climbs the stair towards darkness, but the poetic power, which ascends in search of identity with the greater forms and figures of existence represented by the 'Proud Furies'. Such identity is no loss of individuality; it is merely a loss of what we might call the ego. In Yeats's terms, it loses character and gains personality. The saint attains a powerful personality by forgetting about his ego; but the poet, too, as Yeats says, 'must die every day he lives, be reborn, as it is said in the Burial Service, an incorruptible self'. For the poet, Yeats also says, 'is never the bundle of accident and incoherence that sits down to breakfast: he has been reborn as an idea'.

'I think', says Yeats, 'that much of the confusion of modern philosophy . . . comes from our renouncing the ancient hierarchy of beings from man up to the One.' The process of entering into a life greater than our ordinary one, which every poet knows, is a process of entering into this hierarchy, and of beginning to ascend the stair of life. The Thirteenth Cone, therefore, is a symbol of the way in which man emancipates himself by becoming part of Man, through a series of greater human forms. Here we move toward an existence in which Phases 1 and 15, unity and individuality, are the same point. It is therefore impossible that the 'One' could be anything but Man, or something identical or identifiable with man. Yeats refers occasionally to the 'One' as a sleeping giant like Blake's Albion or Joyce's Finnegan ('The Mountain Tomb', 'The Old Stone Cross', etc.), but he is even nearer the centre of his own intuitions when he speaks of man as having created death, when he says that there is nothing but life and that nothing exists but a stream of souls, and that man has, out of his own mind, made up the whole story of life and death and still can

> Dream, and so create
> Translunar Paradise. (*C.P.*, 223)

The Thirteenth Cone, then, represents the dialectical element in symbolism, where man is directly confronted by the greater form of himself which challenges him to identify himself with it. This confrontation is the real form of the double gyre. 'The repose of man is the choice of the Daimon, and the repose of the Daimon the choice of man . . . I might have seen this, as it all follows from the words written by the beggar in *The Hour-Glass* upon the walls of Babylon.' He might also have seen that this conception of the double gyre reduces his twenty-eight-phase historical cycle to something largely useless as a commentary on his own poetry, except for the poems deliberately based on it.

Yeats often speaks of entering into these personal archetypes, daimons or moods as a process of literal or symbolic death. 'Wisdom is the property of the dead', he says, and his fascination with the remark in *Axël*, 'As for living, our servants will do that for us', is connected with the same conception. Yeats's own interpretation of the *Axël* passage is indicated in 'The Tables of the Law': 'certain others, and in always increasing numbers, were elected, not to live, but to reveal that hidden substance of God which is colour and music and softness and a sweet odour; and . . . these have no father but the Holy Spirit'. Two of his poems describe the direct passage across from ordinary life to archetype, 'News for the Delphic Oracle' and 'Byzantium'. The latter poem is mainly about images, which are, as often in Yeats, generated in water and borne across water by dolphins into the simplifying and purgatorial world of fire. The former poem applies the same movement to human souls, and makes it clear that nothing of the physical or concrete world is lost, or even sublimated, by the kind of redemption here described.

These two poems, then, deal with the consolidation of imaginations and images, the true subjects and the true objects, into a timeless unity. But, of course, the image is a product of the imagination: in the imaginative world the relation of subject and object is that of creator and creature. In this perspective the whole cycle of nature, of life and death and rebirth which man has dreamed, becomes a single gigantic image, and the process of redemption is to be finally understood as an identification with Man and a detachment from the cyclical image he has created. This ultimate insight in Yeats is the one expressed in his many references (one of which forms the last sentence of *A Vision*) to a passage in the *Odyssey* where Heracles, seen by Odysseus in hell, is said to be present in hell only in his shade, the real Heracles, the man in contrast to the image, being at the banquet of the immortal gods. Here we come to the heart of what Yeats had to say as a poet. The vision of Heracles the man, eternally free from Heracles the shadowy image bound to an endless cycle, is nearer to being a 'key' to Yeats's thought and imagination than anything else in *A Vision.* To use the phraseology of *Per Amica Silentia Lunae,* it is an insight he had acquired, not by eavesdropping on the babble of the *anima mundi,* but from his own fully conscious *anima hominis,* the repository of a deeper wisdom than the ghostly house of rumour ever knew.

Wallace Stevens and the Variation Form

The following abbreviations for works by Wallace Stevens are used in this paper:

CP *The Collected Poems of Wallace Stevens* (New York: Knopf, 1954).

L *Letters of Wallace Stevens,* selected and edited by Holly Stevens (New York: Knopf, 1967).

NA *The Necessary Angel: Essays on Reality and the Imagination* (New York: Knopf, 1951).

OP *Opus Posthumous,* edited by Samuel French Morse (New York: Knopf, 1957).

We cannot read far in Wallace Stevens's poetry without finding examples of a form that reminds us of the variation form in music, in which a theme is presented in a sequence of analogous but differing settings. Thus in "Sea Surface Full of Clouds" the same type of stanza is repeated five times, each with just enough variation to indicate that the same landscape is being seen through five different emotional moods. Another type of variation form appears in "Thirteen Ways of Looking at a Blackbird," where a series of thirteen little imagist poems are related by the common theme of the blackbird, and which, to pursue the musical analogy perhaps further than it will go, gives more the effect of a chaconne or passacaglia. Sometimes the explicit theme is missing and only the variations appear, as in "Like Decorations in a Nigger Cemetery."

We notice also that in the titles of Stevens's poems the image of variation frequently turns up, either literally, as in "Variations on a Summer Day," or metaphorically, as in "Nuances of a Theme by Williams," "Analysis of a Theme," and, perhaps, "Repetitions of a Young Captain." "The Man with the Blue Guitar" also gives us a strong sense of reading through a set of thirty-three variations, or related imaginative presentations, of a single theme. Then again, the long meditative theoretical poems written in a blank tercet form, "Notes toward a Supreme Fiction," "The Auroras of Autumn," "An Ordinary Evening in New Haven," "The Pure Good of Theory," are all divided into sections of the same length. "An Ordinary Evening" has thirty-one sections of six tercets each; the "Supreme Fiction," three parts of ten sections each, thirty sections in all, each of seven tercets; and similarly with the others. This curious formal symmetry, which cannot be an accident, also reminds us of the classical variation form in which each variation has the same periodic structure and harmonic sequence. Even the numbers that often turn up remind us of the thirty Goldberg variations, the thirty-three Diabelli waltz variations, and so on.

The variation form in Stevens is a generic application of the principle that every image in a poem is a variation of the theme or subject of that poem. This principle is the first of three "effects of analogy" mentioned in Stevens's essay of that title. There are two other "effects." One is that "every image is a restatement of the subject of the image in the terms of an attitude" (*NA*, 128). This is practically the same thing as Eliot's objective correlative, and is illustrated in "Sea Surface Full of Clouds," where five different moods are unified by the fact that they all have the same correlative. Stevens also says, "In order to avoid abstractness, in writing, I search out instinctively things that express the abstract and yet are not in themselves abstractions" (*L*, 290). His example is the statue in "Owl's Clover," which he also calls a "variable" symbol (*L*, 311). The implication is that such images are variations on the idea of the poem which is within the poem of words, the true as distinct from the nominal subject or theme (*OP*, 223). We note that the correlative in Stevens may pair with a concept as well as with an emotion, which helps to explain why his commentaries on his own poems in the letters are so often woodenly allegorical.

The third "effect of analogy" is that "every image is an intervention on the part of the image-maker" (*NA*, 128). This principle takes us deep into Stevens's central notion of poetry as the result of a struggle, or balance, or compromise, or tension, between the two forces that he calls imagination and reality. We notice that in the musical theme with variations, the theme is frequently a composition by someone else or comes from a different musical context. Similarly the poet works with imagination, which is what he has, and reality, which is given him. So, from Stevens's point of view, poems could be described as the variations that imagination makes on the theme of reality. In "Sea Surface Full of Clouds" a question is asked in each variation about who or what created the picture in front of us, and the answer, given each time in French, defines a distinctive mood of the imagination.

In a letter Stevens says, "Sometimes I believe most in the imagination for a long time, and then, without reasoning about it, turn to reality and believe in that and that alone. But both of these things project themselves endlessly and I want them to do just that" (*L*, 710). This somewhat helpless remark indicates the strength of the sense of polarity in his poetic world. Stevens often speaks of the intense pressure that the sense of external reality exerts on the modern mind. One of the "Adagia" says, "In the presence of extraordinary actuality, consciousness takes the place of imagination" (*OP*, 165). Consciousness, by itself, is simple awareness of the external world. It sees; it may even select what it sees, but it does not fight back. The consciousness fighting back, with a subjective violence corresponding to the objective violence of external pressure (cf. *NA*, 36), is the consciousness rising to imagination.

The imagination confronts a reality which reflects itself but is not itself. If it is weak, it may either surrender to reality or run away from it. If it surrenders, we have what is usually called realism, which, as Stevens often makes clear, is almost the opposite of what he means by reality. He says, for instance, in connection with the painting of Jack Yeats, that "the purely realistic mind never experiences any passion for reality" (*L*, 597). This maxim would also apply to the "social realism" demanded in Marxist countries, for which Stevens never expresses anything but contempt. The imagination that runs away retreats from the genuinely imaginative world into a merely imaginary one, for, Stevens says, "If poetry is limited to the vaticinations of the imagination, it soon becomes worthless' (*L*, 500). Certain recurring symbols in Stevens represent the kind of facile pseudoconquest of reality which the imagination pretends to make whenever reality is not there: one of them is the moon. Such imaginary triumphs take place in a self-contained world of words which is one of the things that Stevens means by false rhetoric, or "Rodomontade" (*NA*, 61). The world of false rhetoric is a world where the imagination encounters no resistance from anything material, where the loneliness and alienation of the mind, about which Stevens speaks so eloquently, has consoled itself with pure solipsism.

Stevens says that it is a fundamental principle about the imagination that "it does not create except as it transforms" (*L*, 364). It is the function of reality to set free the imagination and not to inhibit it. Reality is at its most inhibiting when it is most externalized, as it is in our own time. In "Two or Three Ideas" Stevens speaks of the way in which the pressure of externality today has created a culture of what he calls "detached styles," and which he characterizes as "the unsuccessful, the ineffective, the arbitrary, the literary, the non-umbilical, that which in its highest degree would still be words" (*OP*, 212). In one prophetic flash, which sums up the essence of the world we have been living through for the past few years, he speaks of this world of false imagination as the product of "irrationality provoked by prayer, whiskey, fasting, opium, or the hope of publicity" (*OP*, 218). It follows that Stevens does not accept the mystique of the unconscious and has nothing of Yeats's or Joyce's feeling for the dream-world as having a peculiarly close relation to the creative process. He always associates creativity with cognition, with consciousness, even with calculation. "Writing poetry is a conscious activity. While poems may very well occur, they had very much better be caused" (*L*, 274).

Stevens associates his word "reality" with the phrase "things as they are," which implies that for him reality has a close relation to the external physical world as we perceive it. The imagination contemplates "things as they are," seeing its own unreality mirrored in them, and its principle of contemplation Stevens calls resemblance or analogy. He also calls it, quite logically, "Narcissism" (*NA*, 80). This word points to the danger of uncontrolled imagination and the ease with which it can assume that there is another reality on the other side of things as they are. Traditional religious poetry, for instance, projects heavens and hells as objective and hidden realities, though it can construct them only out of the material of things as they are. Crispin, the hero of one of Stevens's most elaborate variation poems, soon comes to a point at which he can say, "Here was the veritable ding an sich, at last" (*CP*, 29). But this is a Kantian phrase, and Stevens is not Kantian: reality for him is always phenomenal, something that "seems" as well as is (cf. *CP*, 339), and there is no alternative version of it that the poet should be trying to reach. Hidden realities always turn out to be unreal, and therefore simply mirrors of the imagination itself. Similarly, "poetry will always be a phenomenal thing" (*L*, 300).

Stevens's arguments are poetic and not philosophical, and like many poetic arguments they turn on a verbal trick. The trick in this case consists in using the special-pleading term "reality" for the external physical world, which means that conceptions set over against this "reality" have to be called, or associated with, the unreal. Stevens is not unaware of this by any means, but his use of the word "reality," which becomes almost obsessive in the letters, indicates that, like his spiritual sister Emily Dickinson, he has a Puritanic distrust of all self-transcending mental efforts, especially mysticism. More particularly, he feels that, as the poet's language is the language of sense experience and concrete imagery, any poet who bypasses things as they are, however subtly, is dodging the central difficulty of poetry. Such poets, who look for some shortcut or secret passage through reality to something else, and regard poetry as a kind of verbal magic, have what Stevens calls a "marginal" imagination, and he associates this marginal imagination, which explores itself to find its own analogue in reality, with, among others, Valéry, Eliot, and Mallarmé.

Stevens goes even further in suggesting that the conquest of reality made by the reason is also somewhat facile compared to that of the imagination, because it is possible for reason, in some degree, to live in a self-contained world and shut its gates in the face of reality. One of the products of reason is the theological belief in reality as a creation, a product of the infinite imagination of God. Such a belief is repugnant to Stevens: this would mean that reality is analogous to the imagination. The poet is a Jacob who has to wrestle with the necessary angel of reality, and if reality is itself ultimately a "supreme fiction," or something made out of nothing, then all his agonized efforts and struggles are a put-up job, something fixed or rigged, as so many wrestling matches are. Stevens says:

> The arrangement contains the desire of
> The artist. But one confides in what has no
> Concealed creator. One walks easily
>
> The unpainted shore, accepts the world
> As anything but sculpture.
>
> [CP, 296]

So whatever the imagination may do to reality, reality continues to present something residually external, some donkey's carrot pulling us on, something sticking through everything we construct within it. Even in the moment of death (or what appears to be death, on the last page of the *Collected Poems*), we confront something "outside" giving us the sense of "a new knowledge of reality." Or, as Stevens says in prose, "Poetry has to do with reality in that concrete and individual aspect of it which the mind can never tackle altogether on its own terms, with matter that is foreign and alien in a way in which abstract systems, ideas in which we detect an inherent pattern, a structure that belongs to the ideas themselves, can never be" (*OP*, 236). The imagination is driven by a "rage for order" (*CP*, 130), but it works toward, not the complete ordering of existence, but rather a sense of equipoise or balance between itself and what is not itself.

We soon come to understand that for Stevens there are different levels or degrees of reality (*NA*, 7), arranged in a ladder or mountain or winding stair in which the poet has to undertake what he calls an "ascent through illusion" (*NA*, 81). In his essay "A Collect of Philosophy" Stevens attempts to list a few philosophical conceptions which seem to him to be inherently poetic, meaning by that, presumably, conceptions that particularly appeal to him as a poet. Among these, the theme of anabasis or ascent, the theme of Dante, looms up prominently (*OP*, 193). At the bottom of the ladder is the sense of reality as an undifferentiated external world, or what Stevens calls a *Lumpenwelt* (*NA*, 174). Such a world, Stevens says, is "all one color" (*NA*, 26), a "basic slate" (*CP*, 15), a sinister or scowling "pediment of appearance" (*CP*, 361). As such, it forces the imagination to define itself as its opposite, or nothingness. At this point a construct emerges which is rather similar to the construct of being and nothingness in Sartre. The *Lumpenwelt* is reality on the minimum imaginative basis; the imagination on the same basis is merely the unreal: reality is everything; the imagination is nothing. The imagination never brings anything into the world, Stevens says in an unconscious echo of the burial service (*NA*, 59), though it is not quite so true for him that it can take nothing out. This confrontation of being and nothingness, the starting point of imaginative energy, is the vision of the listener in "The Snow Man," who,

> nothing himself, beholds
> Nothing that is not there and the nothing that is.
> [*CP*, 9]

Traditionally, the world of becoming has always been regarded as the product of being and nothingness. For Stevens there is no reality of being in the traditional sense of something that does not change. Whenever we try to imagine an unchanging ideal, we get involved in the hopeless paradox of Keats's Grecian urn, where the little town on the hidden side of the urn will never be inhabited to all eternity. The woman in "Sunday Morning" asks resentfully, "Why should she give her bounty to the dead?" but soon comes to realize that she cannot have any alternative without change, and therefore death, at the heart of it. Reality is phenomenal and belongs to the world of becoming. In the very late poem "Of Mere Being" (*OP,* 117) the only unchanging thing about being is that it remains external, "at the end of the mind," "beyond the last thought."

Two of the requirements of the "supreme fiction" are that it must change and that it must give pleasure, and it is clear that for Stevens these two things are much the same thing, change being the only real source of pleasure. Over and over Stevens returns to what he calls "the motive for metaphor," the fact that what is change in reality is also pleasure in the imagination. The imagination, the principle of the unreal, breaks up and breaks down the tyranny of what is there by unifying itself with what is not there, and so suggesting the principle of variety in its existence. This is the point of identity on which all art is founded: in the imaginations of Cézanne and Klee, Stevens says, reality is transmuted from substance into subtlety (*NA,* 174). We get the idea of unchanging being from the thereness of the physical world, the fact that it doesn't go away. What does go away, and is to that extent unreal, is what the unreality of the imagination builds on. The imagination, in short, "skims the real for its unreal" (*CP,* 272).

This kind of activity gives us a relatively simple type of variation form, the kind represented by the "Blackbird" poem. Here the variations are what Stevens calls the "casual exfoliations" (*NA,* 86) of an imagination contemplating a real thing. The recipe for this type of variation form is given in the poem "Someone Puts a Pineapple Together," one of "Three Academic Pieces" in *The Necessary Angel:*

> Divest reality
> Of its propriety. Admit the shaft
> Of that third planet to the table and then:

The third planet, he has explained, is the imagination, and there follow a series of twelve numbered variations on the pineapple. It is clear that such a conception of imagination and reality has much to do with the affinity to the pictorial in Stevens, with his fondness for subjects analogous to still life or landscape painting, where the real object and the imaginative variation of it are most dramatically exhibited. Such variation poems are fanciful in Coleridge's sense of the term: Stevens was familiar with Coleridge's distinction, which he acquired through his reading of I. A. Richards (*NA,* 10). They are, so to speak, cyclical poems, where the variations simply surround the theme. As such, they are not the most serious kind of writing. Stevens speaks of the almost total exclusion of "thinking" from such a poem as "Variations on a Summer Day" (*L,* 346) and says also, "I have no doubt that supreme poetry can be produced only on the highest possible level of the cognitive" (*L,* 500). Again one thinks of the musical parallel. The greatest examples of the variation form, such as the last movement of Beethoven's Opus 111, do not merely diversify the theme: they are sequential and progressive forms as well, and we feel at the end that they have, so to speak, exhausted the theme, done what there is to be done with it. We have now to see if we can discover a sequential and progressive aspect to Stevens's variation form also.

We began with a confrontation between imagination and reality, in which the former is a negation, the opposite of reality. Then we found that the imagination can intensify reality by seizing on the "unreal" aspect of it, the aspect that changes and therefore gives pleasure. Stevens says, "A sense of reality keen enough to be in excess of the normal sense of reality creates a reality of its own" (*NA,* 79). As he goes on to say, this is a somewhat circular statement, and one would expect it to lead to some such principle as Blake's "As the Eye, such the Object," the principle that the degree of reality depends on the energy of the imagination. Stevens resists this implication, because of his constant fear that the imagination will simply replace reality and thereby deprive itself of its own material cause. For him the imagination is rather an informing principle of reality, transmuting its uniformity into variety, its "heavy scowl" (*CP*, 362) into lightness and pleasure. Still, it seems clear that we cannot go on indefinitely thinking of the imagination merely as a negation or nothingness.

The fact that the imagination seizes on the changing aspect of reality means that it lives in a continuous present. This means not only that "the imperfect is our paradise" (*CP*, 194), but that the imagination is always beginning. The only reason for finishing anything is that we can then be rid of it and can come around to the point at which we can begin again. The shoddiness of being fixated on the past, of refusing to discard what he calls the "hieratic" (*NA*, 58) meets us everywhere in Stevens. The imagination in the sunlit world of reality is like food in hot weather: whatever is kept spoils. Hence "one of the motives in writing is renewal" (*NA*, 220). This emphasis on constant fresh beginnings is connected, naturally, with the steadfast resistance to anything resembling an echo or an influence from other poets in Stevens, in striking contrast to the absorption of echoes and influences that we find in, for instance, Eliot.

What is true of the past is also true of the future, the desire to use the imagination to make over reality that we find in so many romantics, revolutionaries, and spokesmen of the irrational. Stevens speaks of this desire with a good deal of sympathy and understanding, for instance, in his essay on the irrational in poetry (*OP*, 216), where he links the irrational, once again, with the pressure of external fact on the modern poet and his consequent sense of claustrophobia and desire for freedom. "Owl's Clover" is a carefully considered effort to come to terms with the revolutionary desire for freedom and equality on a vast social scale. But when the imagination is used as part of an attempt to make over reality, it imposes its own unreality on it. The result is that perversion of belief which we see in all religions, including the contemporary atheistic ones. Belief derives from the imaginative unreal: what we really believe in is a fiction, something we have made up ourselves. But all beliefs, when they become institutionalized, tend to ascribe some hidden reality to themselves, a projection of the imagination which can end only in disillusionment or self-hypnotism. The "romantic" of this type (Stevens uses the word romantic in several senses, but this one is pejorative: cf. *L*, 277) is "incapable of abstraction" (*NA*, 139), abstraction being among other things the ability to hold a belief as a "supreme fiction" without projecting it to the other side of reality.

At the same time Stevens holds to an intensely social conception of poetry and its function, though a deeply conservative one. The poet, he says, should try to reach the "centre," and by this he means first of all a social center. The poet expresses among other things "that ultimate good sense which we term civilization" (*NA*, 116). For him reality includes human society as well. As such, the imagination defines the style of a culture or civilization: it is whatever it is that makes everything in Spain look Spanish, and makes every cultural product of Spain a variation on a Spanish theme. Stevens uses the phrase "variations on a theme" in connection with a closely related aspect of culture: the predominance and persistence of a convention, as in medieval or Chinese painting (*NA*, 73).

If we ask what the characteristics of such imaginative penetration of reality are in human life, the words "nobility" and "elegance" come fairly close, though Stevens admits that they are dangerous words. The quality in literature that we recognize as heroic, the power of the imagination to make things look more intensely real, is a quality of illusion in reality that is at the same time a growth in reality. The imagination is thus socially aristocratic, though not necessarily in a class sense. The more power it gains, the more freedom and privilege it enjoys, and the more confident society becomes about its culture. In a time like ours the imagination is more preoccupied in fighting its environment, which presses in on it much harder. In the poem "Mrs. Alfred Uruguay," Mrs. Uruguay herself rides up a mountain in the state of the snow man, looking at her world honestly but reductively, as totally without illusion. She meets going down the mountain a "capable man" who recalls the noble rider of Stevens's earliest prose essay, whose imagination is of the same kind as her own, but is more emancipated, and hence to some extent its fulfillment. It is he who creates

> out of the martyrs' bones,
> The ultimate elegance: the imagined land.
> [*CP*, *250*]

So our confrontation between a negative imagination and a positive reality has reached the point where this negation has informed human civilization and produced a style of living. This process, considered in an individual context, is the theme of the sequential variation form "The Comedian as the Letter C." Crispin, the hero of the poem, begins with the principle: "Nota: Man is the intelligence of his soil," a strictly Cartesian principle in which man is the "sovereign ghost." This first variation is headed "The World without Imagination." The fourth variation brings us to "The Idea of a Colony," which begins:

> Nota: his soil is man's intelligence.
> That's better. That's worth crossing seas to find.
> [*CP*, *36*]

Stevens calls Crispin a "profitless philosopher," says that he never discovers the meaning of life (*L*, 293), that social contact would have been a catastrophe for him *(L, 295)*, that he is an everyday man whose life has not the slightest adventure *(L, 778)*, and symbolizes him by the one letter of the alphabet which has no distinctive sound of its own. Nevertheless, Crispin works very hard to achieve his own kind of reality, and if he is not a poet he is at least a colonizer, someone who achieves a life-style out of a pilgrimage and a settlement in new surroundings. The poem as a whole goes around in an ironic circle, and Crispin ends much where he began, using his imagination as so many people do, to select and exclude rather than create, a realist who rejects reality. Hence the final line of the poem, "So may the relation of each man be clipped." Stevens may also have Crispin partly in mind when he says, "The man who has been brought up in an artificial school becomes intemperately real. The Mallarmiste becomes the proletarian novelist" *(OP, 221).* Still, Crispin represents something of the historical process that produced the culture and the tradition out of which Stevens himself developed, moving from baroque Europe to realistic New England.

We have next to see how a negation can be an informing principle in reality. This brings us to Stevens's conception of the "supreme fiction." The imagination informs reality through fictions or myths (the word "fictive" in Stevens means mythical), which are the elements of a model world. This model world is not "reality," because it does not exist, it is not "there"; but it is an unborn or, perhaps, potential reality which becomes a growth out of reality itself. Stevens quotes Simone Weil, obviously with approval, on the subject of "decreation," a moving from the created to the uncreated, going in the opposite direction from destruction, which moves from the created to nothingness *(NA, 174).* The conception is Stevens's, though the terms are not. The first law of the supreme fiction is that it must be abstract. It is abstract for the same reason that a god is not reducible to his image. The supreme fiction is not a thing, something to be pointed to or contemplated or thought of as achieved. In its totality, the supreme fiction is poetry or the work of the imagination as a whole, but this totality never separates from the perceiving subject or becomes external. Stevens says, "The abstract does not exist, but . . . the fictive abstract is as immanent in the mind of the poet, as the idea of God is immanent in the mind of the theologian" *(L, 434).* This last indicates that God is one of the supreme fictions. God for Stevens, whatever he may be in himself, must be for man an unreality of the imagination, not a reality, and his creative power can manifest itself only in the creations of man. The explicit statement that God and the imagination are one is made by the "interior paramour," an anima-figure working under the direction of the imagination.

According to Stevens, "The wonder and mystery of art, as indeed of religion in the last resort, is the revelation of something 'wholly other' by which the inexpressible loneliness of thinking is broken and enriched" *(OP, 237).* The phrase "wholly other," which is in quotation marks, suggests the existential theology of Karl Barth, as relayed through a poet who calls himself a "dried-up Presbyterian" *(L, 792).* In Barth, of course, the otherness of God and the alienation of man are conditions of man's unregenerate state. God does not remain wholly other for two reasons: first, he has created and redeemed man; and second, he has revealed himself. Let us see what reality in Stevens can do along parallel lines.

When Crispin discovers that the Cartesian principle "Man is the intelligence of his soil" is less true than its reverse, that "his soil is man's intelligence," Stevens is saying that the antithesis of imagination and reality did not begin as such. Man grew out of "reality," and the consciousness which enables him also to draw away from it is a recent development. The human is "alien," but it is also "the non-human making choice of a human self" *(NA, 89).* The imagination is a product of reality, its Adam, so to speak, or exiled son. Just as, in Dante's *Purgatorio,* the poet makes his way back to the Eden which is his own original home, so the imagination contemplates the "rock," the dead inert reality before it, and realizes that it is itself the rock come to life. "I am what is around me" *(CP, 86),* the poet says, and he continually returns to the sense of the "wholly other" as not only the object but the origin of the sense of identity.

The rock is not dead, because it has never died; death is a process, not a condition. It represents rather the unconscious and undifferentiated external world at the bottom of the imaginative ladder, where the sense of thereness is overpowering and the imagination is simply its negation. In the course of time leaves cover the rock: life emerges from the inanimate, breaks up and diversifies the heavy *Lumpenwelt.* Life, then, if Stevens's general argument still applies, is the negation of the inanimate, the unreal at work in the real. The imagination does with "things as they are" what life does with the rock, and the poet's imagination is inseparably attached to the articulating of life in the rest of the world. The "howl" of the doves *(OP, 97),* the "cry" of the leaves

(OP, 96), the sea in "The Idea of Order at Key West," the "Bantams in Pine-Woods," who are praising themselves and not a divine bantam in the rising sun, are all part of the symphony of life in which the poet has his own voice. We speak of a will to live, and similarly "imagination is the will of things" *(CP, 84)*.

The poem "Oak Leaves Are Hands" describes a "Lady Lowzen," who is also the goddess Flora, and who continues to "skim the real for its unreal" in human imagination as formerly in the vegetable world. Lady Lowzen is "chromatic," and the delight of vegetable nature in color supplies Stevens with his chief image for the imagination, which he thinks of as, so to speak, the coloring principle of reality. The basis of nature is metamorphosis, the basis of poetry is metaphor, and metaphor and metamorphosis are for Stevens interchangeable terms. Stevens completes the identification by saying "in metaphor the imagination is life" *(NA, 73)*. In this context the variations which the imagination makes on reality join the Darwinian theme with variations in which every variety is a mutation thrown out toward the environment, the "reality" it has to struggle with, until a successful mutation blends and identifies with that reality.

The limit of poetry, as Stevens himself frequently remarks, has always been the imaginatively conceivable, not what is or "things as they are," and any poet deeply impressed by things as they are is apt to suffer from imaginative claustrophobia. Stevens has relegated God to the imaginative unreal, a fiction the human mind creates. He has made an uncompromising bourgeois rejection of all politically revolutionary values. He dismisses Nietzsche and his doctrine of the self-transcendence of man as being "as perfect a means of getting out of focus as a little bit too much to drink" *(L, 432)*. What is left? How much further can a "harmonious skeptic" *(CP, 122)* carry his rage for order? Even things as they are present themes which the poet cannot avoid and yet can hardly deal with on their terms. For instance, a surprising number of Stevens's poems are about death, and death is one subject where the imagination, like Good Deeds in *Everyman*, may be prevailed on to accompany the poet as his guide, while "reality," in whatever form or disguise, will always mutter some excuse and slope off. When Stevens gets to the point of saying that "Life and Nature are one" *(L, 533)*, he has left very little room for any reality which he has not in some other context called unreal.

In Stevens's cultural situation about the only consistent "position" left is that of a secular humanism. But, he says, the more he sees of humanism the less he likes it, and, more briefly and explicitly, "humanism is not enough" *(L, 489)*. He also says, "Between humanism and something else, it might be possible to create an acceptable fiction" *(L, 449)* and that "there are fictions that are extensions of reality" *(L, 430)*. This last concession means that Stevens is capable, at least in his poetry, of sweeping "reality" out of the way as a superego symbol and of reducing it to its proper role as the material cause of poetry.

In reality, man is a social being, and society is partly an aggregate, a mass of men, often dominated by, and expressing their will through, some kind of hero or leader. The hero in this sense is a fiction which has been, like so many other fictions, misapplied and misunderstood by society. In two poems particularly, "Examination of the Hero in a Time of War" and "Life on a Battleship," Stevens shows us how the dictatorial hero or charismatic leader is a false projection of the imagination, like the heavens and hells that are created by the imagination and are then asserted to be actual places in the world which is there. The genuine form of this fiction is the conception of all men as a single man, where the difference between the individual and the mass has ceased to exist. Or, as Stevens puts it, in commenting on a passage in "Notes toward a Supreme Fiction" which contains the phrase "leaner being" *(CP, 387)*, "The trouble with humanism is that man as God remains man, but there is an extension of man, the leaner being, in fiction, a possibly more than human human, a composite human. The act of recognizing him is the act of this leaner being moving in on us" *(L, 434)*. This "leaner being" is the "central man" or "man of glass" *(CP, 250)* who is all men, and whom Stevens portrays as a titanic being striding the skies *(CP, 212)*. Even Crispin reaches an apotheosis of identity with this being *(OP, 24)*.

In this conception of a "general being or human universe" *(CP,*

378), we are still in the area of fictions, but by now we understand that the poet "gives to life the supreme fictions without which we are unable to conceive of it" *(NA, 31)*. Whatever unreal grows out of reality becomes real, like the graft of art on nature which Polixenes urges on Perdita in *The Winter's Tale*. The human universe is still a fiction and to that extent is not strictly true, but, as Abraham Cowley said of the philosophy of Thomas Hobbes, " 'Tis so like Truth 'twill serve our turn as well." In any case, on this level of fiction we can understand how poetry can be called "a transcendent analogue composed of the particulars of reality" *(NA, 130)*, the word "transcendent" here being used, I think, quite carefully in its philosophical sense as going beyond sense experience but not beyond the mental organization of that experience. Certain sentences in *The Necessary Angel* which Stevens mutters out of the corner of his mouth when he thinks his censor is not listening take on a new and illuminating significance. One such sentence is this one from "Imagination as Value": "The imagination that is satisfied by politics, whatever the nature of the politics, has not the same value as the imagination that seeks to satisfy, say, the universal mind, which, in the case of a poet, would be the imagination that tries to penetrate to basic images, basic emotions, and so to compose a fundamental poetry even older than the ancient world" *(NA, 145)*. This universal mind is the mind that has produced "the essential poem at the centre of things" *(CP, 440)*, which is *the* supreme fiction as such. In this perspective, "reality" becomes the stabilizing principle which enables us, even as we outgrow our gods, to recognize, even in the act of coming around to the beginning again, that the creative faculties are always the same faculties and that "the things created are always the same things" *(OP, 211)*. In all the variations of what might be we can still hear the theme of what is there.

The supreme fiction of the "central," which is the total form of both man and the human imagination, takes us into a very different context of variability, a context less Darwinian than Thomist. It would be easy, but simplistic, to say that ultimately what is real in Stevens is the universal, the universal being the theme of which the individual is the variation. Easy, because one could quote a good many passages from the later poems, at least, in support of it; but simplistic, because the traditional context of the real universal is a kind of essential world that Stevens never at any point accepts. "Logically," says Stevens, "I ought to believe in essential imagination, but that has its difficulties" *(L, 370).* In the early "Peter Quince at the Clavier" we have the line "The body dies; the body's beauty lives." Considering the number of poets, in English literature and elsewhere, who would have drawn a Platonic inference from that statement, it comes as a deliberate and calculated shock for Stevens to say:

> Beauty is momentary in the mind,
> The fitful tracing of a portal,
> But in the flesh it is immortal.

"A Collect of Philosophy" has nothing of medieval realism, though it reflects Stevens's fascination with Plato, but it does express a keen interest in such conceptions as Alexander's "compresence" of mind and existence, and, more particularly, in the great passage in Whitehead's *Science and the Modern World* in which Whitehead rejects the conception of "simple location" in space and announces the doctrine of interpenetration, the doctrine that everything is everywhere at once. Stevens's comment on this passage is, "These words are pretty obviously words from a level where everything is poetic, as if the statement that every location involves an aspect of itself in every other location produced in the imagination a universal iridescence, a dithering of presences and, say, a complex of differences" *(OP, 192).* This last phrase shows that Stevens is still thinking within the metaphor of a theme and variations.

Stevens often refers to Eliot as a poet who represents the exact opposite of everything he stood for himself, and perhaps we are now beginning to understand why. The fifth way of looking at a blackbird, for example, is a way that Eliot constantly refuses to look at it:

> I do not know which to prefer,
> The beauty of inflections

Or the beauty of innuendoes,
The blackbird whistling
Or just after.

"A Collect for Philosophy" assumes in passing that all knowledge is knowledge after the experience of the knowledge *(OP, 190).* For Eliot, the fact that there is a split second between an experience and the awareness of having had the experience is a memento of the Fall of Man. All three dimensions of time for Eliot are categories of unreality: the no longer, the not yet, and the never quite. Our ordinary existence in this time is the fallen shadow of the life we might have lived if there had been no Fall, in which experience and consciousness would be the same thing, and in which the present moment would be a real moment, an eternal now. Eliot's imagination revolves around the figure of Percival in the Grail castle, who, in the words of "The Dry Salvages," "had the experience but missed the meaning," because he was afraid to put the question that would have unified experience and meaning. In this sense we are all Prufrocks, vaguely aware that there is an "overwhelming question" to be asked, and wasting our lives in various devices for not asking it.

Stevens has nothing of Eliot's sense of the phenomenal world as a riddle, to be solved by some kind of conscious experience that annihilates it. When we start climbing the Ash-Wednesday staircase, we have to regard such things as "a slotted window bellied like the fig's fruit" as a distraction. This is because at the top of Eliot's staircase is a total unification and an absorption of reality into the infinite being of God. Like Dante whom he is following, Eliot wants his pilgrimage to pass beyond the categories of time and space and the cycle of nature that revolves within these categories. The slotted window is an image of that cycle, the vegetable cycle of flower and fruit, the cycle of human life that begins with birth from a womb. Stevens does not resemble Yeats any more closely than he resembles Eliot, but, like Yeats, he sides with the "self" in the "Dialogue of Self and Soul." For his Mrs. Uruguay, as for Yeats, the top of the mountain or staircase or whatever has to be climbed is the top of the natural cycle, and the fulfillment of climbing it is in coming down again. In Stevens, the imagination is life, and the only way to kill it is to take it outside nature, into a world where it has swallowed nature and become a total periphery or circumference, instead of remaining "central." So for Stevens, as in a very different way for Joyce in *Finnegans Wake,* the cycle of nature is the only possible image of whatever is beyond the cycle, "the same anew."

There is an elaborate imagery of the seasons of the year in Stevens, where summer represents the expanded and fulfilled imagination, autumn the more restricted and realistic imagination, and winter the reduction to a black-and-white world where reality is "there" and the imagination set over against it is simply unreal. The emotional focus of this imagery comes at the moment in spring when the first blush of color enters the world with "an access of color, a new and unobserved, slight dithering" (*CP, 517:* the last word echoes the comment on Whitehead already quoted), or when a bird's cry "at the earliest ending of winter" signals "a new knowledge of reality" *(CP, 534),* or at Easter. "On Easter," says Stevens, "the great ghost of what we call the next world invades and vivifies this present world, so that Easter seems like a day of two lights, one the sunlight of the bare and physical end of winter, the other the double light" *(OP, 239).* What Easter symbolizes to Stevens is that we are constantly trying to close up our world on the model of our own death, to become an "owl in the sarcophagus." As long as some reality is still outside us we are still alive, and what is still external in that reality is what has a renewing power for us. This vision is the point at which "dazzle yields to a clarity and we observe" *(CP, 341),* when we see the world as total process, extending over both death and life, always new, always just beginning, always full of hope, and possessed by the innocence of an uncreated world which is unreal only because it has never been fixed in death. This is also the point at which the paradox of reality and imagination comes into focus for the poet and he understands that

> We make, although inside an egg,
> Variations on the words spread sail.
>
> [*CP, 490*]

Notes

p. 11, line 20. "fish up." The image comes from the "Conclusion" of T. S. Eliot's *The Use of Poetry and the Use of Criticism* (1933).

p. 24, line 14. "never." Read "seldom," in view of the award to Bertrand Russell. The word "never" is a word that humanists should seldom use.

p. 47, line 29. "Student unrest." In the conference for which I wrote this paper, the specific topic assigned me was the one indicated in the title: the activism inside the university which was aimed directly at the theory of education. Activism in general forms only the wider context of this.

p. 51, line 22. "Alexander Woollcott." *While Rome Burns* (1934), p. 23 (the original reads "life," not "nature").

p. 55, line 23. "myth." The title of *The Great Canadian Novel* (1972) by Harry Boyle, contains an irony that would not be lost on Canadian readers.

p. 82, line 7. "Boileau." *L'Art poetique,* iii, pp. 199–200.

p. 91, line 23. "Juhasz." Quoted from *The Plough and the Pen, Writings from Hungary 1930–1956,* edited by Ilona Duczynska and Karl Polanyi (1963).

p. 120, line 6. "Gurdjieff." P. D. Ouspensky, *In Search of the Miraculous* (1949), p. 248.

p. 123, line 2. "*Beyond Genre.*" Paul Hernadi, *Beyond Genre* (1972): the comment is only on the title, not on the book itself.

p. 131, line 20. "Eskimo chant." Quoted from *Anerca* (1960), edited by Edmund Carpenter.

p. 140, line 22. "Chinese poems." The passage quoted is from *Ch'u Tz'u, The Songs of the South,* translated by David Hawkes (1959); Beacon Press ed. (1962), p. 42.

p. 143, line 4. "Billings." Quoted from Max Eastman, *Enjoyment of Laughter* (1936).

p. 146, line 4. "Ben Jonson." See Edgar Wind, *Pagan Mysteries in the Renaissance* (1958), ch. xiv.

p. 159, line 34. "masque of Shirley's." *The Triumph of Peace,* edited by Clifford Leech, in *A Book of Masques* (1967).

p. 167, line 20. "Enid Welsford." *The Court Masque* (1927).

p. 196, line 21. "German writers." See E. M. Butler, *The Tyranny of Greece over Germany* (1935).

p. 228, line 2. The reference is to Damon's admirable edition of *Blake's Job* (1966).

p. 232, line 19. "*Malak.*" More accurately *mal'ak,* which means angel, not king (*melek*), as in commentaries misled by Blake's omission of the aleph.

p. 243, line 36. "another version." It should have been said more clearly that the first half of the *Laocoon* aphorism refers to the creation of Adam and the second half to Noah's flood; in other words that Blake was thinking of the fall and the flood as two aspects of the same event.

p. 250, line 35. "echo of Virgil's words." The real echo is from the final chorus of Shelley's *Hellas.*

p. 252, line 10. "*Eureka.*" This essay is by some years the earliest writing in the book, and the view taken here of Poe's *Eureka* is not one that I would endorse now.